Praise for

HAVING A MARY HEART
IN A MARTHA WORLD

"Often a book fails to live up to its title, but Joanna Weaver's *Having a Mary Heart in a Martha World* more than lives up to its promise. I found the book easy to read, personal, and well-written with a message much more than surface deep. The book probed, challenged, and encouraged me to live day by day as a Mary in a Martha world, while showing the positive qualities of both Mary and Martha personalities. Readers will be blessed!"

—CAROLE MAYHALL, author of *Come Walk with Me* and *Here I Am Again, Lord*

"Joanna Weaver has a heart that sings. Whenever I'm around her, she makes me smile. Her voice rings out true and clear in *Having a Mary Heart in a Martha World*. This book invites us to join in the chorus of daily communion with Christ, despite the pressures that threaten to silence us. Consider it as sheet music for your soul."

—ROBIN JONES GUNN, best-selling author of The Glenbrooke series and The Christy Miller series

"Balance. That's what it is all about, and Joanna Weaver has found it, described it, and called us to this wonderful, practical work. If you have ever struggled with how you can find one quiet moment while longing for a deep holy communion or if you have been discouraged because neither seems possible, you will be challenged and blessed by *Having a Mary Heart in a Martha World*!"

—JAN SILVIOUS, author of *Foolproofing Your Life*

"With candor, humor, and passion Joanna Weaver invites us to cultivate a 'Mary heart' that delights in time with God and assigns him top priority. Yet she doesn't discard the service-oriented Martha. Instead, she wisely and practically models how to balance the Mary and Martha qualities in us all. I especially appreciate her thoughts on expressing lavish love—to God and to humanity."

—JUDITH COUCHMAN, *Designing a Woman's Life* author and seminar leader

Having a Mary
Heart in a
Martha World

Having a Mary Heart in a Martha World

FINDING INTIMACY WITH GOD
IN THE BUSYNESS of LIFE

JOANNA WEAVER

WATERBROOK
PRESS

HAVING A MARY HEART IN A MARTHA WORLD
PUBLISHED BY WATERBROOK PRESS
2375 Telstar Drive, Suite 160
Colorado Springs, Colorado 80920
A division of Random House, Inc.

ISBN 1-57856-258-9

Published in association with the literary agency of Janet Kobobel Grant, Books & Such, 4788 Carissa Avenue, Santa Rosa, CA 95404

Library of Congress Cataloging-in-Publication Data
Weaver, Joanna.
   Having a Mary heart in a Martha world : finding intimacy with God in the busyness
of life / Joanna Weaver.—1st ed.
      p. cm.
   ISBN 1-57856-258-9
      1. Christian women—Religious life.   I.Title.

BV4527.W43 2000
248.8'43—dc21

                                                           00-022843

Printed in the United States of America
2005

35 34 33 32 31 30 29 28 27 26

To my Mary-hearted mother, Annette Gustafson,
and my Mary-hearted mentor, Teri Myers

The beauty and balanced grace of your lives
continue to challenge and inspire me.
Thank you for making the path to the Master's feet so clear
I couldn't help but follow.

CONTENTS

ACKNOWLEDGMENTS

I've been blessed to have many friends walk with me on this journey called "writing a book." Friends who've read manuscripts, dropped off home-cooked meals, prayed me out of tight spots, and told me to "go for it!" when I felt I couldn't go on. Looking back on the journey, I can't imagine how one could walk it all alone.

Though I can't thank everyone by name, I must thank Erica Faraone and Tricia Goyer for their gifts of perspective and encouragement, as well as the women of my church, FaithBuilders, and One Heart/Blessed Hope for their faithful intercession. Special thanks to my friend, Rosemarie Kowalski, who allowed me to use her story in chapter 4 to illustrate the freedom of grace, capturing the very essence of this book.

To my editor, Anne Buchanan, my heartfelt thanks. Truly "two are better than one." Thank you, Anne, for helping me find the right words to convey the message that has so filled my heart and for all the laughter we've shared along the way.

To the great people at WaterBrook—Carol Bartley and Liz Heaney, to name two—my deepest gratitude as well.

I am especially grateful to my agent and friend, Janet Kobobel Grant. Thank you for all the wonderful things you are.

And finally, to my husband, John, and my two incredible kids, John Michael and Jessica. Your loving support and patience have been precious and costly gifts, treasures I've not taken for granted. John, thank you for believing in me. Kids, thank you for all the chuckles and for letting me share you with the world. You're the best!

But most of all, Lord Jesus, thank you for making it possible for each one of us to know you—really know you!—Marys and Marthas alike. Go beyond these inadequate human words, and by your Spirit, lead each one of us into your presence. Help us discover the joy and the secret of *Having a Mary Heart in a Martha World.*

Soli Deo Gloria. To you alone.

1

A Tale of Two Sisters

As Jesus and his disciples were on their way,
he came to a village where a woman named Martha opened her home to him.
She had a sister called Mary,
who sat at the Lord's feet listening to what he said.

LUKE 10:38-39

Have you ever tried to do it all?

I have, I do, and I probably always will. It's not only in my nature; it's also in my job description—and yours, too. Being a woman requires more stamina, more creativity, and more wisdom than I ever dreamed as a young girl. And that's not just true for today's busy women. It has always been the case.

In 1814, Martha Forman was married to a wealthy Maryland plantation owner. You might expect she spent her days sipping tea, being fitted for lovely gowns, and giving orders to her servants as she chatted with important guests. Instead, Martha worked right beside her servants from four in the morning to eleven o'clock at night. Among her daily activities were the following:

Making thirty to thirty-four pounds of old tallow into candles; cutting out fourteen shirts, jackets or trousers for the slaves (whom she always called "the people" or "our family"); knitting stockings; washing; dyeing and spinning wool; baking mince pies and potato puddings; sowing wheat or reaping it; killing farm animals and salting the meat; planting or picking fruits and vegetables; making jams, jellies, and preserves with her fruit; helping whitewash or paint walls; ironing; preparing for large parties; caring for sick family and slaves.[1]

So, what did you do today? You may not have slaughtered a hog or harvested wheat, but I know you were busy. Whether you were out selling real estate or at home kissing boo-boos (or both), your day passed just as quickly. And your mind and body are probably as tired as poor Martha Forman's as you steal a few moments to spend with this book.

Having a Mary Heart in a Martha World. The thought intrigues you. Deep inside of you there is a hunger, a calling, to know and love God. To truly know Jesus Christ and the fellowship of the Spirit. You're not after more head knowledge—it's heart-to-heart intimacy you long for.

Yet a part of you hangs back. Exhausted, you wonder how to find the strength or time. Nurturing your spiritual life seems like one more duty—one more thing to add to a life that is spilling over with responsibilities.

It's almost as if you're standing on the bottom rung of a ladder that stretches up to heaven. Eager but daunted, you name the rungs with spiritual things you know you should do: study the Bible, pray, fellowship...

"He's up there somewhere," you say, swaying slightly as you peer upward, uncertain how to begin or if you even want to attempt the long, dizzy climb. But to do nothing means you will miss what your heart already knows: There is more to this Christian walk than you've experienced. And you're just hungry enough—just desperate enough—to want it all.

A TALE OF TWO SISTERS

Perhaps no passage of Scripture better describes the conflict we feel as women than the one we find in the gospel of Luke. Just mention the names Mary and Martha around a group of Christian women and you'll get knowing looks and nervous giggles. We've all felt the struggle. We want to worship like Mary, but the Martha inside keeps bossing us around.

Here's a refresher course in case you've forgotten the story. It's found in Luke. It's the tale of two sisters. It's the tale of you and me.

As Jesus and his disciples were on their way, he came to a village where a woman named Martha opened her home to him. She had a sister called Mary, who sat at the Lord's feet listening to what he said. But Martha was distracted by all the preparations that had to be made. She came to him and asked, "Lord, don't you care that my sister has left me to do the work by myself? Tell her to help me!"

"Martha, Martha," the Lord answered, "you are worried and upset about many things, but only one thing is needed. Mary has chosen what is better, and it will not be taken away from her." (10:38-42)

A MARTHA WORLD

When I read the first part of Mary and Martha's story, I must admit I find myself cheering for Martha. I know we tend to sing Mary's praises in Bible studies. But Martha, to be honest, appeals more to my perfectionist tendencies.

What a woman! She opens her home to a band of thirteen hungry men, possibly more. What a hostess! She doesn't whip up an impromptu casserole of Kraft macaroni and cheese and Ballpark franks as I've been known to do on occasion. Not her! She is the original Martha Stewart, the New Testament's Proverbs 31 woman, and Israel's answer to Betty Crocker. Or at least that's the way I imagine her. She's the Queen of the Kitchen—and the rest of the house as well.

And Luke's story starts with Martha in her glory. After all, this is Jesus. She scraps her ordinary everyday menu of soup and bread and pulls out all her cookbooks. This, she decides, will be a banquet fit for a messiah. For *the* Messiah. Martha sends one servant to the field to slaughter a lamb, another to the market to pick up a few of those luscious pomegranates she saw yesterday. Like a military general, she barks commands to her kitchen staff. Soak the lentils! Pound the grain! Knead the dough!

So many things to do and so little time. She must make sure the centerpiece and the napkins match, that the servant pours the wine from the right and not the left. Martha's mind is as busy as a room filled with kindergartners. What would be just right for dessert? A little goat cheese with a tray of fresh fruit? Will Jesus and his followers stay overnight? Someone must change the sheets and fold some towels.

"Where's Mary? Has anyone seen Mary?" she asks a servant scurrying by. If Mary changed the sheets, Martha might have time to fashion an ark from the cheese and carve the fruit into little animals marching two by two. Productions of this magnitude require the skill of a master planner. And Martha's an administrator extraordinaire—a whirling dervish of efficiency, with a touch of Tasmanian she-devil thrown in to motivate the servants.

I happen to be the oldest in my family. Perhaps that's why I understand how frustrated Martha must have felt when she finally found Mary. The entire household is in an uproar, busy making ready to entertain the most famous teacher of their day, the man most likely to become the next king of Israel. I can relate to the anger that boils up inside of Martha at the sight of her lazy sibling sitting at the Master's feet in the living room.

It's simply too much. With everything still left to do, there sits little Mary, being quite contrary, crashing a party meant only for men. But worse, she seems oblivious to all of Martha's gesturing from the hall.

Martha tries clearing her throat. She even resorts to her most effective tool: the "evil eye," famous for stopping grown men in their tracks. But nothing she does has any effect on her baby sister. Mary only has eyes for Jesus.

Pushed to the limit, Martha does something unprecedented. She interrupts the boys' club, certain that Jesus will take her side. After all, a woman's place is in the kitchen. Her sister, Mary, should be helping prepare the meal.

Martha realizes there is a cutting edge to her voice, but Jesus will understand. He, of all people, knows what it's like to carry the weight of the world.

Now of course, you won't find all that in the Bible. Luke tends to downplay the whole story, dedicating only four verses to an event that was destined to change Martha's life forever. And mine as well. And yours, if you will let the simple truth of this passage soak deep into your heart.

Instead of applauding Martha, Jesus gently rebukes her, telling her Mary has chosen "what is better." Or, as another translation puts it, "Mary has chosen the better part" (NRSV).

"The better part?" Martha must have echoed incredulously.

"The better part!" I say to God in the midst of my own whirl of activity. "You mean there's more? I have to do more?"

No, no, comes the answer to my tired heart. Jesus' words in Luke 10 are incredibly freeing to those of us on the performance treadmill of life.

It isn't "more" he requires of us.

In fact, it may be less.

A MARY HEART

The Bible doesn't tell us a lot about Mary and Martha. They are mentioned by name only three times in Scripture: Luke 10:38-42, John 11:1-44, and John 12:1-11. But from these brief accounts, a fascinating picture develops of what life must have been like at the house in Bethany—and what life is often like for us.

They say variety is the spice of life. Perhaps that's why God so often puts people of such different personalities in the same family. (Either that, or he's trying to prepare us for marriage!) Mary was the sunlight to Martha's thunder. She was the caboose to Martha's locomotive. Mary's bent was to meander through life, pausing to smell the roses. Martha was more likely to pick the roses, quickly cut the stems at an angle, and arrange them in a vase with baby's breath and ferns.

That is not to say one is right and one is wrong. We are all different, and that is just as God made us to be. Each gifting and personality has its own strengths and weaknesses, its glories and temptations.

I find it interesting that when Jesus corrected Martha, he didn't say, "Why can't you be more like your sister, Mary?" He knew Martha would never be Mary, and Mary would never be Martha. But when the two were faced with the same choice—to work or to worship—Jesus said, "Mary has chosen the better part."

To me, this implies the Better Part was available to both Mary and Martha. And it's available to each one of us, regardless of our gifting or personality. It's a choice we each can make.

It is true that, personality-wise, the choice may have come easier to Mary than it did to Martha. Mary does seem more mellow by nature, more prone to walk in the dew of the morning than to get caught up in the "dos" of the day.

I'm sure when Jesus dropped by unexpectedly that afternoon, Mary probably began the visit by serving, just as she had many times before. I can see her taking walking staffs and sleeping rolls as the disciples spill into her sister's well-ordered home. Buried beneath cloaks and backpacks, she watches the man who has taken the heart of Israel captive by his words. There is such joy and winsomeness about him, she can't help but be drawn to this man.

Could Jesus be the Messiah the people say he is? Mary wonders. She knows he's a great teacher, but could this actually be the Son of God admiring the tapestry she wove, drawing her out of her shyness and into the circle of his closest friends?

She drops the disciples' belongings in a corner and hurries to pour wine for the thirsty crew. There is an ease about them, a true camaraderie. The men laugh at each other's jokes as they wash down the dust of the road with the liquid she provides. Then they settle on low couches around the room, and Jesus begins to teach.

He speaks as none she ever heard before. There is a magnetism about his words, as though they contain breath and life—breath and life Mary hasn't known she needed until this day. She creeps closer and stands in a dark corner listening to Jesus, her arms wrapped around the empty pitcher.

She's aware of movement around her. Several servants busy themselves washing dirty feet, while another sets the table at the other end of the room for the meal to come. Mary knows there is plenty to do. And yet she is unable to move—except closer.

It isn't customary for a woman to sit with a group of men, but his words welcome her. Despite her natural reticence, she gradually moves forward until she's kneeling at his feet. His teaching envelops her, revealing truth to her hungry heart.

The Bible isn't clear whether or not this was Jesus' first visit to the home in Bethany. Martha's openness with Christ seems to indicate a prior acquaintance, but whatever the case, this day Mary chose to let someone else do the serving so she could do some listening. It isn't every day God visits your house. So she ignores tradition, she breaks social etiquette, and she presses closer. As close to Jesus as possible.

It doesn't matter that she might be misunderstood. She cares little that the disciples look at her strangely. Somewhere in the distance she hears her name, but it is drowned by the call of her Master. The call to come. The call to listen.

And listen she does.

A TALE OF EVERY WOMAN

Against this Bethany backdrop of unexpected guests, I see the struggle I face every day when work and worship collide.

Part of me is Mary. I want to worship extravagantly. I want to sit at his feet.

But part of me is Martha—and there's just so much to do!

So many legitimate needs surround me, compelling me to work. I hear God's tender call to come away, and I respond, "Yes, Lord, I will come." But then the phone rings, or I'm reminded of the check I was supposed to deposit—yesterday. Suddenly all of my good intentions about worship disappear, swallowed up by what Charles Hummel calls "the tyranny of the urgent."

"We live in constant tension between the urgent and the important," Hummel writes. "The problem is that the important task rarely must be done today or even this week. Extra hours of prayer and Bible study can wait. But the urgent tasks call for instant action—endless demands pressure every hour and day."[2]

Does that sound familiar? It does to me. The twenty-four hours allotted to each day rarely stretch far enough to meet all the obligations I face. I have a household to run, a husband to love, children to care for, and a dog to feed. I have church commitments, writing deadlines, lunch engagements to keep. And very little of this is what I would call deadwood. Long ago I tried to cut out what I thought was extraneous. This is my life—and the hours are packed full.

Not long ago, *Today's Christian Woman* magazine sponsored a survey of more than a thousand Christian women. Over 60 percent indicated they work full time outside the home.[3] Add housework and errands to a forty-hour-a-week career, and you have a recipe for weariness. Women who choose to stay at home find their lives just as full. Chasing toddlers, carpooling to soccer, volunteering at school, baby-sitting the neighbor kids—life seems hectic at every level.

So where do we find the time to follow Mary to the feet of Jesus? Where do we find the energy to serve him?

How do we choose the Better Part and still get done what really has to get done?

Jesus is our supreme example. He was never in a hurry. He knew who he was and where he was going. He wasn't held hostage to the world's demands or even its desperate needs. "I only do what the Father tells me to do," Jesus told his disciples.

Someone has said that Jesus went from place of prayer to place of prayer and did miracles in between. How incredible to be so in tune with God that not one action is wasted, not one word falls to the ground!

That is the intimacy that Jesus invites us to share. He invites us to know him, to see him so clearly that when we look upon him, we see the face of God as well.

Just as he welcomed Mary to sit at his feet in the living room, just as he invited Martha to leave the kitchen for a while and share in the Better Part, Jesus bids us to come.

In obedience to his invitation, we find the key to our longings, the secret to living beyond the daily pressures that would otherwise tear us apart. For as we learn what it means to choose the Better Part of intimacy with Christ, we begin to be changed.

This is no cookie-cutter conversion. This is a Savior who accepts us just the way we are—Mary or Martha or a combination of both—but loves us too much to leave us that way. He is the one who can give us a Mary heart in a Martha world.

This transformation is exactly what we see in the continuing stories of Mary and Martha in the Gospels. Martha, as we will discover, doesn't lay aside her personality, give up her hobbies, and burn her cookbooks in order to worship Jesus. She doesn't try to mimic Mary the Little Lamb; she simply obeys. She receives Jesus' rebuke and learns that while there is a time for work, there is also a time for worship. The Martha we see later in the Gospels is no longer frantic and resentful, but full of faith and trust. The kind of faith and trust that come only from spending time at Jesus' feet.

Mary does some changing too. For although her contemplative nature makes her a natural worshiper, it also leaves her vulnerable to despair, as we'll see later in the Gospels. When disaster strikes, Mary's tendency is to be swamped with sorrow and paralyzed with questions. But in the end, when she realizes Jesus' time is short, Mary puts into action what she has learned in worship. She steps forward and seizes the opportunity to serve both beautifully and sacrificially.

That's what I see in the biblical portraits of the two sisters of Bethany. Two completely different women undergo a transformation right before our eyes: a holy makeover. The bold one becomes meek, the mild one courageous. For it is impossible to be in the presence of Jesus and not be changed.

As you read the following chapters, I pray you will allow the Holy Spirit access to all the hidden corners of your life. Whether you tend to be a bit driven, like Martha, or more contemplative, like Mary, God is calling you to intimacy with him through Jesus Christ.

The choice he offered to these two very different sisters—and the transformation they experienced—is exactly what he offers to each of us as well.

First Things First

The Living Room Intimacy Mary enjoyed with Jesus will never come out of the busyness of Martha's Kitchen. Busyness, by itself, breeds distraction. Luke 10:38 shows us a woman with the gift of hospitality. Martha opened her home to Jesus, but that doesn't automatically mean she opened her heart. In her eagerness to serve Jesus, she almost missed the opportunity to *know* Jesus.

Luke tells us that "Martha was distracted by all the preparations that had to be made." Key word: *had*. In Martha's mind, nothing less than the very best would do. She *had* to go all out for Jesus.

We can get caught in the same performance trap, feeling as though we must prove our love for God by doing great things for him. So we rush past the intimacy of the Living Room to get busy for him in the Kitchen—implementing great ministries and wonderful projects, all in an effort to spread the good news. We do all our works in his name. We call him "Lord, Lord." But in the end, will he know us? Will we know him?

The kingdom of God, you see, is a paradox. While the world applauds achievement, God desires companionship. The world clamors, "Do more! Be all that you can be!" But our Father whispers, "Be still and know that I am God."

He isn't looking as much for workers as he is looking for sons and daughters—a people to pour his life into.

Because we are his children, Kitchen Service will be the natural result of Living Room Intimacy with God. Like Jesus, we must be about our Father's business. The closer we draw to the heart of the Father, the more we see his heart for the world. And so we serve, we minister, and we love, knowing that when we do it to "the least of these," we have done it unto Christ.

When we put work *before* worship, we put the cart before the horse. The cart is important; so is the horse. But the horse must come first, or we end up pulling the cart ourselves. Frustrated and weary, we can nearly break under the pressure of service, for there is always something that needs to be done.

When we first spend time in his presence—when we take time to hear his voice—God provides the horsepower we need to pull the heaviest load. He saddles up Grace and invites us to take a ride.

THE CALL

I'll never forget crying in the darkness one night many years ago. My husband was an associate pastor at a large church, and our lives were incredibly busy. Carrying a double portfolio of music and Christian education meant we worked long hours on project after project, and the size of the church meant there were always people in need. I would go to bed at night worried about the people who had slipped through the cracks—the marriages in trouble, the children in crisis. I worried about all the things I didn't accomplish and should have, about all the things I'd accomplished, but not very well.

I remember clinging to my husband that night and sobbing as he tried to comfort me. "What's wrong, honey?" he asked, caressing my hair. But I couldn't explain. I was completely overwhelmed.

The only thing that came out between sobs was a broken plea, "Tell me the good news," I begged him. "I honestly can't remember... Tell me the good news."

Perhaps you have felt the same way. You've known the Lord your whole life, and yet you haven't found the peace and fulfillment you've always longed for. So you've stepped up the pace, hoping that in offering more service, somehow you will merit more love. You volunteer for everything: you sing in the choir, you teach Sunday school, you host Backyard Bible Club, you visit the nursing home weekly. And yet you find yourself staring into the night and wondering if this is all there is.

Or perhaps you've withdrawn from service. You've gone the route I've described above and, frankly, you've had it. You've stopped volunteering, stopped saying yes. No one calls anymore. No one asks anymore. You're out of the loop and glad for it. And yet the peace and quiet holds no peace and quiet. The stillness hasn't led to the closer walk with God you'd hoped for, just a sense of resentment. Your heart feels leaden and cold. You go to church; you go through the motions of worship, then leave and go home the same. And at night, sometimes you wonder, "What is the good news? Can someone tell me? I can't remember."

THE GOOD NEWS

The good news is woven through the New Testament in a grace-filled strand that shines especially bright in the Gospel stories of Mary and Martha. The message is this: Salvation isn't about what I do; it's about what Jesus did.

The Cross did more than pay for my sins; it set me free from the bondage of the "shoulds" and "if onlys" and "what might have beens." And Jesus' words to Martha are the words he wants to speak to your heart and mine: "You are worried and upset about many things, but only one thing is needed."

The "one thing" is not found in doing more.

It's found by sitting at his feet.

Catch that: Mary sat at his feet. She didn't move a muscle. She listened. She didn't come up with clever responses or a doctrinal thesis. Her gift was availability. (In the end, I believe that was Martha's gift as well.)

The only requirement for a deeper friendship with God is showing up with a heart open and ready to receive. Jesus said: "Come to me, all you who are weary and burdened, and I will give you rest. Take my yoke upon you and learn from me, for I am gentle and humble in heart, and you will find rest for your souls" (Matthew 11:28-29).

Jesus invites us to come and rest, to spend time with him in this incredible Living Room Intimacy. Intimacy that allows us to be honest in our complaints, bold in our approach, and lavish in our love. Intimacy that allows us to hear our Father's voice and discern our Father's will. Intimacy that so fills us with his love and his nature that it spills out to our dry, thirsty world in Kitchen Service.

In the Living Room. That's where it all begins. Down at his feet.

An Invitation

Perhaps, like Martha, you never knew you could enter into Living Room Intimacy with God. But that is exactly what Jesus Christ came to do. His death and resurrection made a way for each of us to be reconciled to God. But the gift of salvation he offers is just that—a gift. And a gift must be received.

You can receive this marvelous gift by praying this simple prayer:

Dear Lord Jesus,

I do believe you are the Son of God and that you died on the cross to pay the penalty for my sin.

Please come into my life, forgive my sin, and make me a member of your family. I now turn from going my own way. I want you to be the center of my life.

Thank you for your gift of eternal life and for your Holy Spirit, who has now come to live in me.

I ask this in your name. Amen.[4]

Jesus answered, "I am the way and the truth and the life. No one comes to the Father except through me."

JOHN 14:6

2

"Lord, Don't You Care?"

Martha was distracted by all the preparations that had to be made.
She came to him and asked, "Lord, don't you care that my sister has left me
to do the work by myself? Tell her to help me!"

LUKE 10:40

It had been a busy day. I'd dragged my kids through a morning of errands and grocery shopping, and now it was an hour past lunchtime. We were all hungry and a little bit grumpy, but the day brightened as I pulled the car into our favorite pizza place.

"Pizza, pizza, pizza!" my four-year-old son, Michael, chanted as he bounced up and down in the backseat. Jessica, two, clapped her hands at the thought of the merry-go-round in the kiddy playland. But our joy was cut short when I opened my checkbook and discovered I didn't have enough money in my checking account.

"It just isn't fair!" Michael informed me defiantly from the backseat as we drove toward home and plain old peanut-butter-and-jelly sandwiches. "You promised we could have pizza."

He was right. The pizza bribe had bought good behavior all morning. I sighed as I looked in the rearview mirror. It's difficult explaining to a child that even though you have checks in the checkbook, you may not have enough money in the bank. I have a hard time understanding it myself sometimes.

So we were at a standstill. All my explanations fell on deaf ears. Michael sat scrunched against the car door, arms folded tightly across his chest, a scowl so fierce his eyebrows and angry pout nearly met.

Then from the other side of the backseat, little Jessica piped up, "Life's hard, Miko!"

IT JUST ISN'T FAIR

Life *is* hard and rarely fair. Even when we work diligently and do what is expected, the daily duties of life often seem to provide few rewards. When was the last time you received a standing ovation at the dinner table? "Great tuna casserole, Mom! The best!" Your family applauds, their smiling faces flushed with admiration. Your picky teenager gives you a high-five and calls, "Encore! Encore!"

Or when was the last time your boss and coworkers applauded the fact that you got to work on time, did your job with a smile, and stayed late to finish an assignment? "Great job on the Anderson account," your boss says, poking his head around the door. "Take the next week off with pay! Hey, why not make it two?"

Doesn't happen, does it? The last time I checked, they don't hand out awards for sparkling toilet bowls, and the extra hours and effort we give outside the home often go unnoticed and unrewarded.

Sorry. No pizza for you.

While Martha may have been the first person to ask Jesus the question, "Lord, don't you care?" she definitely wasn't the last. We've all felt the loneliness, the frustration, the left-out-ness and resentment she experienced in the kitchen that Bethany afternoon—doing all that work for others when no one seems to notice and no one seems to care.

We've all echoed my son's complaint. "It just isn't fair!"

In Luke 10:40, we get a clear picture of Martha's struggles. Surprise visitors appear on her doorstep. We don't know how many. If the beginning of Luke 10 is any indication, it could be as many as seventy people descending upon this quiet home. And Martha responds with open arms and a wide smile. But somewhere between the kitchen and the living room, a seed of resentment starts growing. Before long, it sprouts into a question that echoes in women's hearts today: "Lord, don't you care?"

The problem is obvious. Martha is doing all the work while Mary basks in all the glory. It just isn't right. At least Martha doesn't think so, and I know how she feels. A part of me wishes Jesus had said, "So sorry, Martha—terribly insensitive of us. Come on, Mary! Come on, guys, let's all pitch in and give Martha a hand."

After all, that's what Martha wanted. That's what I want when I'm feeling overwhelmed: soft, soothing words and plenty of helpful action. I want everyone to carry his own weight. But most of all, I want life to be fair.

THE SCALES OF JUSTICE

I grew up playing with my mother's decorative scales. Made of ornate brass, the set of balances stood proudly on the piano with several pieces of artificial fruit on either side, dispersed creatively so one side was slightly higher than the other.

Now and then, instead of practicing my piano lesson, I'd adjust the fruit. The exercise was quite educational. One plastic orange equaled two plums. The banana and apple weighed roughly the same, and together they balanced nicely with the grapefruit. If I went about it right, I could take up quite a lot of practice time rearranging fruit on those scales.

Warning Signs of a Martha Overload

You may be prone to the kind of perfectionist overload Martha experienced in Bethany. Carol Travilla, in her book *Caring Without Wearing*, lists five unrealistic expectations that can contribute to servant burnout. Can you see yourself in the following false beliefs?

- There should not be any limits to what I can do.
- I have the capacity to help everyone.
- I am the only person available to help.
- I must never make a mistake.
- I have the ability to change another person.

What you are doing is not good.... You will only wear yourselves out.
The work is too heavy for you; you cannot handle it alone.
EXODUS 18:17-18

Then one day I decided to take my little experiment a step further. After arranging all the plastic fruit in a huge pyramid on one side, I looked around for a counterbalance. Ah. Grandma's glass grapes.

Remember the kind? I loved to look through the big round balls of colored glass wired tightly to a piece of twisted wood. Their purple depths made everything appear wavy and distorted and otherworldly. A perfect distraction for a bored piano student—almost as much fun as playing with the scales.

Almost.

You can guess what happened, of course, when I placed the grapes on the other side of the scale. They dropped like a brick on the mahogany surface of my mother's treasured piano, sending the brass rattling and the plastic fruit flying. Mom came running, and I started playing the "Indian War Song," hoping she'd think it was the pounding bass and not my goofing around that had caused the disturbance.

It didn't work. I deserved everything I got. That time.

But my mother's brass scales are not the only set of balances I've paid undue attention to in my life. I suspect that's true for you, too. Since childhood, we've all had an invisible set that weighs what happens to us against what others experience.

Growing up, for instance, we weighed how our parents treated us by the way they treated our siblings. "Julie has two more Ju-Ju Fruits than I do!" "Daddy, it's my turn to sit in the front seat."

That's just a part of childhood, of course. But many of us have carried the scales into adulthood, unaware, and we waste surprising amounts of time trying to get those scales to balance.

Fair or not fair. Equal or unequal. Just or unjust. We weigh it all. And if we're not careful, our view of the world can become distorted. Every little word can take on a hidden meaning. Each action can turn into a personal attack.

"I do all the work," we mutter to ourselves. "Why do they get all the glory?"

"How dare they treat me like that!"

Like grandma's glass grapes, these "sour grapes" can easily outweigh everything good in our lives, tipping the scale against us. Because when we look for injustice, we usually find it. And when we expect life to always be fair, we inevitably set ourselves up for a big disappointment.

THE THREE DEADLY DS

The story is told of a priest who served a small parish in an obscure countryside. He loved his people, and they loved him, and he was doing God's work quite effectively—so effectively, in fact, that two demons were assigned by Satan to pester him and somehow derail his ministry. They tried every method in their bag of tricks, but to no avail. The placid priest seemed beyond their reach. Finally, they called for a conference with the devil himself.

"We've tried everything," the demons explained, listing their efforts. Satan listened, then offered this advice. "It's quite easy," he hissed. "Bring him news that his brother has been made bishop."

The demons looked at one another. It seemed too simple. They had expected something more diabolical. But it was worth a try. Nothing else had worked.

Several weeks later they returned gleefully. The old priest hadn't taken the happy news of his brother's promotion well at all. The man's former joy had been turned to moping. His encouraging words had been replaced with grumbling and gloom. In a short time, the man's vibrant ministry had been destroyed by the green worm of envy and the black cloud of disappointment—the bitter conclusion that "it just wasn't fair."

Satan's never been terribly creative. The tools he uses today are the same tools he's always used—and no wonder, for they've been quite effective. From the Garden of Eden to Martha's Bethany kitchen to our own everyday world, Satan still plans his attacks around what I call the "Three Deadly Ds of Destruction." They are

- Distraction
- Discouragement
- Doubt

Throughout time, Satan has resorted to these tactics to bring down God's best and brightest. The underlying strategy is fairly simple: Get people's eyes off God and on their circumstances. Make them believe that their "happiness" lies in the "happenings" that surround them. Or send them good news—about somebody else. When they're thoroughly discouraged, tell them God doesn't care. Then sit back and let doubt do its work.

It's really a brilliant strategy, when you think of it. Plant the Deadly Ds deep in human hearts, and sooner or later people will destroy themselves.

Unless, of course, someone intervenes—which is exactly what Jesus came to do.

A Distracted Heart

When Jesus met Martha that day in Bethany, she was "distracted." That's where Satan usually begins. He knows if we're overly worried and bogged down by duties, chances are good our hearts will not hear the Savior's call to come. While distraction may not win the battle for our soul, getting our eyes off of what is important will certainly make us more vulnerable to attack.

The *King James Version* tells us that "Martha was cumbered about much serving." Which is really just another way of saying *distracted*. The *Oxford English Dictionary* defines the word *cumber:* "(1) to overwhelm, overthrow, rout, destroy, (2) to harass, distress, bother, (3) to trouble, confound, perplex." Felt any of those lately? I certainly have.

The original Greek word used in this passage is *perispao*—"to be overoccupied about a thing; to draw away." That sounds eerily familiar to me as well.

Strong's concordance adds another dimension to the word *cumber*, defining it as "to drag all around." Can't you see Martha—all of her responsibilities snapping at her skirt like angry Chihuahuas; all her expectations dragging behind her like balls and chains?

Martha's pursuits were far from trivial. That's important to recognize. In fact, the "preparations" Martha pursued were described by Luke as *diakonia*—the New Testament word for ministry. "But even pure ministry for Jesus can become a weight we drag around," says pastor and author Dutch Sheets. "It's called the 'treadmill anointing,' and it isn't from God."[1]

I've experienced the treadmill anointing in ministry far more than I'd like to admit. Even on those days when I have the best of motives, my heart can be pulled away from doing things "as unto the Lord" and settle for simply getting things done. And when that happens, I can tell you, this Martha isn't very merry.

Neither, of course, was the original Martha. Like the rabbit in *Alice's Adventures in Wonderland*, she had a schedule to keep, but no one seemed to sense the importance of her mission. In fact, they seemed quite oblivious to her need. It wasn't long before the gracious hostess in Martha collapsed and the Queen of Hearts took over, pointing fingers and screaming, "Off with their heads! Off with everyone's head!"

I'm familiar with the Queen of Hearts. She raises her regal head around our house every once in a while. Just let the housework pile up, my schedule run wild, and obligations go unmet, and I have the makings of a royal temper tantrum. The Queen in me stalks the kitchen, slamming cupboards and rattling pans, making wild statements to no one in particular.

Pity the child who crosses the Queen on a rampage. Especially after her highness has made a sweep through the house for laundry, only to find half of it clean and lying on the floor. "Clean socks?" I bellow. "You want clean socks? Try under your bed where you keep the rest of your clothes!"

And by the way, off with your head! I don't say it, but sometimes I feel it.

I'm overwhelmed and distracted. I feel incredibly alone, just like Martha felt. And though you might never know it from my Queen-of-Hearts facade, the weight of discouragement is already tugging at my heart.

A DISCOURAGED HEART

When we're distracted, discouragement is just around the corner. Weariness creeps in as life overpowers us. It causes us to say and do things we would never consider saying or doing otherwise. Discouragement breaks down our perspective and our defenses. Though we may have just completed great things for God, weary discouragement tells us we're useless, hopeless, and abandoned.

Elijah felt that kind of discouragement. Having just won a mighty victory over the prophets of Baal (1 Kings 18), Elijah had been flying high. But when Jezebel took out a contract on Elijah's life, the wicked queen's haughty words brought the mighty prophet back to earth with a thud. Less than a day after holy fire fell from heaven—proving once and for all that God was God—Elijah was running for his life.

Distraction made him fear.

Discouragement made him hide.

"Don't you care?" Elijah asked God as he sat trembling under the broom tree in the desert. "I have had enough, LORD," he whimpered in 1 Kings 19:4. "Take my life." Just let me die.

Have you spent much time under the broom tree of self-pity? I have. It's easy to find a shady spot and feel sorry for ourselves when we're distracted and discouraged. Especially when we run up against unexpected opposition. Especially when it feels like we're running for our lives.

In the dictionary you'll find *self-pity* stuck between *self-perpetuating* and *self-pollinating*. I had to laugh when I saw it, because it's so true. I happen to be an expert on the subject. Being quite the hostess myself, I throw pity parties fairly regularly. Trouble is, no one wants to come. Self-pity is a lonely occupation.

Or perhaps you're more familiar with the broom closet of isolation. Failure seems imminent, and it's easier to hide than face life head-on. So we pull our shredded confidence around trembling shoulders, cover our heads, and beg to be excused from the regular business of life. We're downhearted and downright depressed—and all because of discouragement.

Discouragement can drain us of all hope, of all vision, of all our tomorrows and dreams. It certainly did that for Elijah.

But I love the tender picture of 1 Kings 19:5-7, for it hints at the tenderness available to us in our own discouragement. Remember what happened? God sent an angel to bring food to his downhearted prophet. "Get up and eat," the angel told Elijah, "for the journey is too much for you." Then the angel stood guard as Elijah fell back asleep.

When we're distracted and discouraged, tired and overwhelmed, there is no better place to go than to our Father. He alone has what we need. Don't snivel under a broom tree. Don't hide in a broom closet. Go to the Lord and let him sweep away your discouragement.

As you do, you'll find healing for your hurting heart.

Even when it can't help but doubt.

A DOUBTFUL HEART

Throughout history, Satan has found that trying to make humanity question God's existence is futile. As Paul writes in Romans 1:19-20, God's existence is written upon man's heart. Time and time again, over the course of history, agnosticism and atheism have fallen before the bedrock belief: *God is.* In our lifetime, we've seen a century of atheistic unbelief crumble along with the Soviet Union and the Berlin Wall. Contrary to Communist prediction, belief in God has definitely not died. In fact, the rise of atheistic states in the twentieth century did little except spur the growth of religion.

Five Strategies for Fighting Discouragement

We all dip down now and then into discouragement. The secret is not to stay there. Here are several ways you can beat the downward spiral of the Deadly Ds in your life.

1. *Allow for rest stops.* Discouragement is often our body's way of saying, "Stop! I need rest." Try taking a nap or getting to bed a little earlier. It's amazing how different things will look in the light of morning (Exodus 34:21).

2. *Get a new point of view.* Take a few steps back and ask God to help you see his perspective on your situation. Often what seems to be an impassable mountain in our eyes is only a steppingstone in his (Isaiah 33:17).

3. *Have patience.* It's easy to get discouraged when things don't go the way you planned. But if you've committed your concerns to the Lord, you can be sure he is at work, even when you don't see his hand (Romans 8:28).

4. *Mingle.* Discouragement feeds off isolation. Get out of the house! Go visit some friends. It's amazing how good, old-fashioned fellowship can lift our spirits and chase away the blues (Psalm 133:1).

5. *Set the timer.* Okay. So things aren't so good. I've found it helpful to set the oven timer and allow ten minutes for a good cry. But when the buzzer sounds, I blow my nose, wipe my eyes, and surrender my situation to the Lord so I can move on (Ecclesiastes 3:4).

The LORD himself goes before you and will be with you; he will never leave you nor forsake you. Do not be afraid; do not be discouraged.

DEUTERONOMY 31:8

Since atheism has been less than effective, Satan has returned to another lie in his bag of tricks. If he can't make us doubt God's existence, Satan will do his best to make us doubt God's love. After he has distracted us…after he has discouraged us…Satan's final tactic is disillusionment and doubt.

"You're on your own, baby," he whispers to our loneliness. "See? God doesn't really care, or he would have shown up by now."

Nothing could be further from the truth, of course. And yet, Satan continues to use this deception with great success. Even against God's own children.

I'm ashamed to say my heart has sometimes listened to Satan's siren song. The words of doubt and notes of disillusionment echo the frustration and confusion I feel inside. A countermelody to faith, the mournful tune arises during those times when God neither acts the way I think he should nor loves me the way I want to be loved. Like two songs being played in different keys, the dissonance of what I *feel* clashes with what I *know* and threatens to drown out the anthem of God's eternal love.

LORD, DON'T YOU CARE?

It began one spring as the crocuses pushed their way through hard-crusted soil and the tight buds of trees slowly unfurled toward the sun. All around me the world was waking, but the warmth of the changing season never reached my soul. While I still loved God, he seemed distant and preoccupied with someone other than me. It was, I suppose, my first true spiritual crisis.[2]

Having been raised in a Christian home, I'd eagerly accepted Jesus at the age of four. I loved God with a childlike totality and knew he loved me, though sometimes I wondered why. Yet slowly over the years, mostly without my knowledge, little strands of uncertainty had been spun in my soul, and gradually they had knit themselves together into a dark veil. That spring, after fifteen years of full-time ministry, I began struggling with doubt. Especially in the area of prayer.

God didn't seem to be answering my prayers as he should. "Ask what you will and it shall be given you," he had promised, but I felt as if someone at the pearly gates was marking my prayer mail "return to sender." My friend wasn't healed of terminal cancer, and my mother continued to struggle after open-heart surgery. Even small requests were left unanswered. My van, for instance, still made a frustrating squeal, impervious to the efforts of the mechanics and their lube jobs—and the heater wouldn't work right. Other little things kept going wrong. Nothing major, just enough to keep me worried and, yes, distracted.

The van proved to be the final showdown—my spiritual Alamo. Winter returned to Montana, and I drove down to see my mother, who was battling depression. A year had passed since her surgery, and despite a strict vegetarian diet, her cholesterol level had soared. The medication caused terrible mood swings and chest pains. She was ready to give up.

"I'd rather go be with the Lord," she said. "If the quality of my life is diminished, there's no sense in living."

We cried and prayed together. I wanted to be understanding and supportive, but I felt so frustrated. My mother was ready to end it all because she felt winded after pulling weeds and cleaning house!

"Mom, it isn't what you do that makes you who you are," I told her through my tears. "It's never been that. I love you for you. I need you—please don't give up."

She looked so small and fragile as she leaned in my van to hug me the next evening. I'd come to encourage, to build up, to somehow fix the emotional short circuit that left my normally positive mother negative and hopeless. But the short visit had ended bittersweet with an impasse.

"Did you get the window up?" she asked. A day before, she had lowered my van's power window and there it had stayed, refusing all our creative attempts to close it.

"No, but I'll be okay." I gave her one last hug, glancing at the sky. Snow had begun to fall, and the clouds looked stormy dark.

A gas-station mechanic offered no solutions, so I closed the door on the top of a towel and drove out of town angry. Angry at the window that still wouldn't budge. Angry at my mother, who seemed to be giving up. But most of all, angry at God, who didn't seem to be paying any attention at all.

"Okay, God," I prayed. "You said I have not because I ask not, so here goes. Please Lord, please make the window go up. I've tried everything, You're the only one who can help."

I worked up a reasonable amount of faith and pressed the button on the armrest. Nothing. Wind whipped through the window, tearing the towel from

its place as I joined the traffic on the interstate. Icy snow swirled around the flap-
ping towel and into the cab.

"Lord, you know my heater doesn't work and it's 150 miles home." Tears
spilled over as I groped, trying to zip my coat with one hand. "You say you'll
provide all our needs according to your riches in glory. I just need one little
miracle."

"Please." I paused a moment, as if giving my petition time to make it to
heaven. My eyes closed for a split second as I pressed the little black lever.

Nothing. Frustrated, I pulled over to the shoulder of the road and slammed
on the brakes.

"Fine." I got out of the car and slammed the door. The wind sliced across
the valley floor, burying the highway in a flurry of snow. I removed the towel and
pulled a flimsy bedspread from the backseat. "If you won't take care of me, I
will."

Hostility burned high in my throat, choking me as I spit out the words with
an anger that had built over the long, spiritually frigid summer and fall.

"How can I know you're real if you won't answer one little prayer? I'm desperate, but you're silent. I'm angry, but you don't seem to care."

Earlier that month, I'd driven fifteen miles with the window down in sub-
zero weather. It'd taken hours to feel warm again. I climbed back into the van,
wrapping the bedspread around my shoulders, preparing for a miserable trip.

I finally shut off the faulty heater, as the lukewarm air only aggravated the
cold. We fell into an uneasy silence. My traitorous Friend didn't seem interested
in talking, so I spent the rest of the blizzard alone, struggling beneath the shroud
of angry darkness.

I turned on the Christian radio station and listened as people talked about
God's love. But for the first time in my life, I doubted its reality. Did they ever
question? Did doubt about the Father's sovereignty ever shake their faith? It was
all new to me, this cold, hard cynicism.

The radio's clock glowed 10:59 P.M. when I finally arrived home. I'd driven
slowly most of the trip, staring through the blinding snow for any sign of the
centerline. But somewhere along those fearful, frigid miles I'd lost the anger.

The last remnant of rage melted when I realized, twenty-five miles from home, that I was warm. Truly warm. Though my nose felt chafed by the wind and my cheeks tingled to the touch, the rest of my body was extraordinarily comfortable. Miraculously so.

The Father had heard. The Father had answered. Not in the way I'd asked, and certainly not in the way I'd planned. He hadn't rolled up the window. But he *had* wrapped me in his arms.

I began to cry again. This time the tears weren't those of a demanding child, but those of a chastened daughter.

Trust me, my child. I have your ultimate good in mind.

DOUBTING GOD'S GOODNESS

I wonder how the Father feels when we assume the worst about him rather than the best. Does his heart hurt like mine when we question his love?

"You don't love me," my thirteen-year-old son said with the same pout he'd used that pizza-deprived afternoon many years ago. He was teasing (more or less) and he said it with the hint of a grin, but he still wanted the remark to sting. And it did.

"What do you mean?" I wanted to scream. "I clothe you. I feed you. I make sure you have cleats for football. I have a forever-ugly zipper on my lower belly where the doctor ripped me open so you could live, ungrateful child—and now, I don't love you?"

But none of that counted at the moment. I had told him he couldn't stay up and watch the NFL playoffs on a school night, and suddenly all my love had been erased.

Doubting God's love doesn't require tragedy. It can creep into the everyday just as insidiously, just as dangerously. It happens when our will is crossed, when our needs are ignored, or when we, like Martha, are stuck doing the dirty work while everyone else is having fun.

Now, such doubt in itself is not a sin. It's simply a thought or feeling that springs up almost involuntarily. But when we let it lodge in our heart long enough, wedged tightly like a poppy seed between our teeth, that little doubt can become a big problem. For doubt, left unchecked, can fester into unbelief.

And unbelief, my friend, is not only sin—it's deep trouble. When we no longer believe in God's goodness, when we no longer trust in his care, we end up running away from the very Love we need to live.

Unbelief brought down Judas—he refused to trust God's timing. Unbelief hardened Saul's heart—he closed his eyes to the rightness of God's ways. Unbelief kept the Israelites in the wilderness for forty years because they questioned God's ability to lead them. And it was unbelief way back at the beginning of time that opened a doorway of darkness in a world designed for pure light.

The Garden of Eden must have been wonderful. Just think: no house to clean, no meals to cook, no clothes to iron! Eve had it made. A gorgeous hunk of a husband. Paradise for a living room. God for a playmate. But somehow, in the midst of all these blessings, the marvelous grew mundane, the remarkable ho-hum. And a nagging sense of discontentment sent Eve wandering toward the only thing God had withheld: the Tree of the Knowledge of Good and Evil.

What is it about us women that creates such a desperate need in us to always "know," to always "understand"? We want an itinerary for our life, and when God doesn't immediately produce one, we set out to write our own.

"I need to know," we tell ourselves.

"No," God answers softly, "you need to trust."

But like the original first lady, we push aside his tender voice and head straight for the tree. Not the sacrificial tree of the cross, but the proud, towering beauty called Knowledge. Because, after all, knowledge is power. And power is what we secretly crave.

I believe Eve's eventual sin began with a tiny thought—a small, itching fear she was somehow missing something and that God didn't have her best interest at heart. What could be wrong with something so lovely, so desirable as the forbidden fruit? Perhaps a hidden resentment had worked down into her spirit. Adam got to name the animals while *she* got to pick papayas. Whatever the identity of the tiny irritation, it sent her looking for more.

And Satan was ready and waiting, willing to give her more than she'd ever bargained for. He filled her mind with questions. "Did God really say…?" Satan encouraged Eve to doubt God's word and God's goodness until the continual question marks finally obliterated her trust in God's love.

Humanity has questioned God's love ever since.

ASKING QUESTIONS

"Lord, don't you care?" Like Martha, we have our questions. Like Martha, we have our doubts. I'm so glad God isn't threatened by our doubts and questions, our fears or even our frustration. He wants us to trust his love enough to tell him what we are thinking and feeling. David did that. He is a marvelous example of a heart honest and open before God. The shepherd-boy-turned-king poured out his complaint before the Lord all through the psalms. In Psalm 62:8, he invites us to do the same: "Trust in him at all times, O people; pour out your hearts to him, for God is our refuge."

Our friend Martha was on the right track that day in Bethany. Instead of allowing her doubtful questions to fester, she took her worries and her fears and voiced them to Jesus. While her bristling, abrasive approach is hardly the best model, there are still several important lessons we can learn from her gutsy encounter with Christ.

First, *we can bring our needs to Jesus anytime and anywhere*. "Ask and it will be given to you," Jesus said in Matthew 7:7. In the Greek, the form of the word for *ask* implies "keep on asking." We can't wear our Savior out. He's never too busy to hear our hearts' cries. Martha took full advantage of his availability, even in the midst of her busyness and party preparations.

Second, *Jesus really cares about what concerns us*. "Cast all your anxiety on him," 1 Peter 5:7 tells us, "because he cares for you." Jesus didn't laugh off Martha's concerns. He didn't become angry. Instead, he spoke to her with infinite gentleness and tenderness, recognizing the pain behind her whining words.

Finally, *Jesus loves us enough to confront us when our attitude is wrong*. "Those whom I love," says the Lord, "I rebuke and discipline" (Revelation 3:19). And that is what the Savior did with Martha. He intuitively understood Martha's pain, but that didn't stop him from telling her what she needed to hear.

And Martha, to her credit, listened.

Too often, I think, we hold on to doubt and confusion until our questions explode as accusations. We shake our fists at God, raging from all the hurt. Then human nature makes us want to run and hide, nursing our perceived injustice and licking our wounds.

But Martha didn't do this. She stated her case, yes, but then she stuck around to hear Jesus' ruling. Though she accused him of neglect, she was willing to listen to his response. She was willing to leave the outcome in his hands.

I love the compassion of Jesus in this story. He saw Martha's situation. He understood her complaint. But he loved her too much to give her what she wanted. Instead, Jesus gave her what she needed—an invitation to draw close to him. With open arms, he invited the troubled woman to leave her worries and cares and find refuge in him alone.

Because when you have questions, there is no better place to go than to the One who has the answers.

THE ANSWER TO THE QUESTION

"Lord, don't you care?"

Of course he cares. That's why he came.

If I were God, wanting to touch base with man, I'd drop by for a visit. Maybe a week or two with plenty of advance advertising, hitting the major cities before returning to my comfy celestial throne. Just long enough to get people's attention and straighten things out, then, "Beam me up, Scotty!" I'd be out of there.

Who in their right mind would leave heaven to actually live on earth? Why that would be like a farmer selling his cozy farmhouse so he could live in his pigsty. Like Bill Gates giving up Microsoft's billions so he could run a hot-dog stand for minimum wage. Unthinkable. But that is exactly what Jesus did.

God became one of us so that when we ask, "Lord, don't you care?" we can know without a doubt that he does. Instead of paying a house call or a flashy extraterrestrial visit, he took up residence among us. Through Jesus Christ incarnate, God entered the world through the same doorway we do. Then he stuck around as long as we'd let him, until we sent him, dying, out the same painful exit we will go.

Does he care? You'd better believe it!

You'd *better* believe it. Because until you settle that question once and for all, you will never get past doubt to true belief. You'll forever be faced with a shiny apple and the hiss of temptation to take matters into your own hands.

The fact is, until we stop doubting God's goodness, we can't experience God's love.

Martha spoke her secret fear aloud, and we can too. But, like Martha, we must stick around long enough to hear the sweet reassurance of his answer.

Don't expect any explanations or apologies. After all, God is God. If righteous Job couldn't force God to give an account for his actions, then we shouldn't expect to always understand his mysterious ways.

But rest assured, God will answer. He longs to reveal his love to you. But you won't find it by shaking your fist in his face. You won't find it by barging into his presence and demanding to be treated fairly. You'll find it by sitting at his feet and remembering who he is.

Emmanuel. God *with* us.

He knows the journey is difficult. He knows life is rarely fair. Jesus fought the same frigid winds of distraction, discouragement, and doubt that keep us from knowing God's love. But like the Father, he longs to gather us in his arms. He longs to trade the flimsy blankets of our own self-sufficiency for his all-sufficiency. The Lord Jesus invites us to cast our doubts, our fears and anxiety upon him, to discover how much he really does care.

Trust me, my child, he whispers. *I have your ultimate good in mind.*

3

The Diagnosis

"Martha, Martha," the Lord answered,
"you are worried and upset about many things."

LUKE 10:41

Far out in the Aegean Sea, in the Cycladic chain, lies a Greek island called Naxos. Largely untouched by the march of technology and the information age, Naxos has remained the same for centuries. Olive trees line the island's rocky shores as turquoise waters shimmer in the harbor. Mount Za looms above; its lush meadows and cool streams rush down to meet the sea. The pace of life is unhurried, the people willing to talk to passersby.

One of the first things you notice when you step on this island is the strings of beads worn by many people. Rich and poor. Tall and short. Both the young and the old—but especially the old men, for this is a very old Greek custom. The islanders finger and manipulate the beads around their necks all day long. They say the beads bring comfort, that the process of handling them cuts down on anxiety. They call them *komboloi*—"worry beads."[1]

A quaint custom, we may say. Yet we have worry rituals ourselves. While we may not wear anxiety around our necks, it certainly affects our lives. We bite our fingernails. We pace the floor. We lie awake at night. And all because of worry. Hour after hour, our mental fingers twist around a problem, turning it this way, then that, like a Rubik's Cube. We manipulate and postulate, desperate to solve the puzzle. And yet we seem to find few answers.

The sad fact is, we are an anxious people. We are a nation of worriers.

"I think there's an epidemic of worry," confirms Dr. Edward Hallowell in his book *Worry*. The best-selling author and psychiatrist estimates that one in four of us—about sixty-five million Americans—will meet the criteria for anxiety disorder at some point in our lifetime.[2] Over half of us are what he calls chronic worriers.

But worry is hardly a modern phenomenon. Jesus described precisely the same condition two thousand years ago. He didn't write a book or establish a clinic. He had no medical degree, but he knew the human heart and soul. Out of the vast knowledge known only to a creator concerning the created, Jesus spoke truth to a woman caught in chronic worry.

"Martha, Martha," Jesus observed gently, "you are worried and upset about many things."

THE CURSE OF ANXIETY

Those words must have stopped Martha in her tracks. I know they stop me.

"Now wait a minute, Lord!" Martha must have wanted to say. "I'm just trying to serve you."

But his tender words cut through her excuses and pretense. In one short sentence, Jesus diagnosed the problem that has plagued humankind since the beginning of time. We can trace its roots back to a Garden, a Tree, and the Fall of mankind.

It is the curse of anxiety. The ongoing burden of worry and fear.

It wasn't supposed to happen to us. The Tree of the Knowledge of Good and Evil was off-limits for good reason—our own protection. God had created the man and the woman to enjoy a mutual love relationship with him, the same relationship we were created to enjoy. He would take care of us and provide all of our needs. We, in return, would "enjoy God and worship him forever," as the Westminster Creed so beautifully puts it.

But rather than viewing the boundaries as evidence of God's mercy, Adam and Eve interpreted the command as a power play on God's part—a desire to withhold something good. So they took and they ate. Their eyes were opened. And what they saw was far more than they expected. Instead of receiving godlike power, they were terrified to behold their nakedness and utter helplessness. But instead of running back to God, they hid from him.

Why? Genesis 3:10 tells us they were afraid. But I think it was more than simple fear of God's wrath that sent them diving for cover.

For the very first time, the man and the woman saw themselves apart from God. Like two children lost and alone, they suddenly saw Eden as a frightening place rather than a beautiful paradise. Suddenly, with the knowledge of good and evil, came shadows and dark corners, strange sounds and frightening noises. No longer were God's children innocent and unaware. No longer were they safe under God's protection.

With the bite of the apple came the stark, terrible truth: Adam and Eve were on their own. So like naughty little kids, they ran and hid, trying to buy enough time to figure a way out of this snake-induced mess. Cut off by their own disobedience from the very God they needed, they grew chronically fearful and anxious.

And so it has gone, all the way down to Martha of Bethany. All the way down to you and me.

A BORN WORRIER

I come from a long line of Swedish worriers.

"Käre mej," my Grandma Anna used to say over and over. "Dear me, dear me." Too high, too fast. Too much, too little. With all the potential danger in the world, there seemed to be only one response—worry.

I remember lying in bed at night going over my list of fears. Somehow, as a young teenager, I had determined that the secret for avoiding trouble was to worry about it. In fact, I worried if I forgot to worry about something.

When Mom and Dad went to Hawaii for their fifteenth anniversary, I spent most of the week trying to think of everything that might go wrong. What if the plane crashed? What if a tidal wave wiped out Waikiki? Anything could happen. Rotten pineapples. Bad sushi. Salmonella poisoning from coconut milk left out overnight. I'd be left an orphan, sob. I'd be left to raise my little brother and sister alone. Big, big sobs.

Of course, my parents returned home safe and sound, healthy and tan. But in some twisted way, this merely confirmed my thesis: Worry so it won't happen. And so, little by little, worry became my mode of operation.

What about you? Has worry become a dominating factor in your life?

Dr. Hallowell, who describes himself as a born worrier as well, provides a checklist to help you decide—you'll find it in the sidebar below. If you recognize yourself in these descriptions, chances are you have a problem with worry.

And make no mistake—worry is indeed a problem.

Ten Signs of a Big Worrier

Is worry a problem in your life? Dr. Hallowell says it might be if these worry signs are true about you:

1. You find you spend much more time in useless, nonconstructive worry than other people you know.
2. People around you comment on how much of a worrier you are.
3. You feel that it is bad luck or tempting fate not to worry.
4. Worry interferes with your work—you miss opportunities, fail to make decisions, perform at lower than optimal level.
5. Worry interferes with your close relationships—your spouse and/or friends sometimes complain that your worrying is a drain on their energy and patience.
6. You know that many of your worries are unrealistic or exaggerated, yet you cannot seem to control them.
7. Sometimes you feel overwhelmed by worry and even experience physical symptoms such as rapid heart rate, rapid breathing, shortness of breath, sweating, dizziness, or trembling.
8. You feel a chronic need for reassurance even when everything is fine.
9. You feel an exaggerated fear of certain situations that other people seem to handle with little difficulty.
10. Your parents or grandparents were known as great worriers, or they suffered from an anxiety disorder.[3]

Search me, O God, and know my heart; test me and know my anxious thoughts.
See if there is any offensive way in me, and lead me in the way everlasting.

PSALM 139:23-24

WORTHLESS WORRY

"An anxious heart weighs a man down," Proverbs 12:25 tells us. And yet the heavy burden of anxiety offers no real benefits. Jesus highlighted this basic futility when he reminded us, "Who of you by worrying can add a single hour to his life?" (Matthew 6:27).

It's been said that worry is like a rocking chair—it gives you something to do, but it doesn't get you anywhere. One interesting set of statistics indicates that there is nothing we can do about 70 percent of our worries:

What We Worry About

40% are things that will never happen.
30% are about the past—which can't be changed.
12% are about criticism by others, mostly untrue.
10% are about health, which gets worse with stress.
 8% are about real problems that can be solved.[4]

When it comes down to it, worry is really a waste of time. But it's also more than that. Worry is not only futile. It's actually bad for us.

The physical and emotional damage caused by chronic anxiety is well known and well documented. Years ago Dr. Charles H. Mayo of the Mayo Clinic pointed out that worry affects circulation, the glands, the whole nervous system, and profoundly affects the heart. "I have never known a man who died from overwork," he said, "but many who died from doubt." In the years since then, researchers have established connections between chronic worry and weakened immune systems, cardiovascular disease, neurological imbalances, clinical depression, and other physical and psychological dysfunctions—not to mention specific anxiety-related illnesses such as panic attacks, agoraphobia, and obsessive-compulsive disorders.[5]

All that from worry. No wonder Jesus warned Martha about her anxiety. No wonder the Bible tells us more than 350 times to "fear not."

The truth is, we were simply not wired for worry. We were not fashioned for fear. And if we want to live healthy lives, we have to find a way to leave our chronic anxiety behind.

But beyond our physical well-being, there lies a more pressing spiritual reason not to worry. If anxiety caused God's closest friends, Adam and Eve, to hide from his face, just imagine what worry must do to you and to me.

WHY THE BIBLE TELLS US NOT TO WORRY

When God tells us in the Bible not to worry, it isn't a suggestion. It's a command. Worry and/or anxiety is specifically mentioned twenty-five times in the New Testament alone as something we should avoid.

The words used most often for worry and anxiety in the New Testament come from the same Greek word, *meridzoe,* which means "to be divided, to be pulled in opposite directions, to choke." (Perhaps we wear anxiety around our necks after all.)

In the parable of the sower, Jesus tells us: "The seed that fell among thorns stands for those who hear, but as they go on their way they are *choked by life's worries,* riches and pleasures" (Luke 8:14, emphasis mine). These people have accepted the Word of God, Jesus says, but "they do not mature." Gasping for spiritual breath, worry-bound, thorny-ground Christians may survive, but they never truly thrive.

The Old English word for worry meant "to gnaw." Like a dog with a bone, a worrier chews on his problem all day long. Jesus warned us specifically against this kind of chronic anxiety when he said, "Therefore I tell you, stop being perpetually uneasy (anxious and worried) about your life" (Matthew 6:25, AMP).

Why is the Bible so adamant about our avoiding fear and worry? Because God knows worry short-circuits our relationship with him. It fixes our eyes on our situation rather than on our Savior.

It works a little like a thick London fog—the kind of fog that is legendary. Why, it wouldn't be a Sherlock Holmes story without fog to obscure the villain and allow him to get away. "Thick as pea soup," Londoners describe it. "Can't see your hand in front of your face," they say.

However, while physical fog may seem dense and almost solid, scientists tell us that a fog bank a hundred feet deep and covering seven city blocks is composed of less than one glass of water. Divided into billions of droplets, it hasn't much substance. Yet it has the power to bring an entire city to a standstill.[6]

So it is with anxiety. Our mind disperses the problem into billions of fear droplets, obscuring God's face. Taking our anxiety to the Lord is often the last thing we think of when we are spiritually fogged in. And yet only the "Son" has the power to disperse it. Without him, one fear leads to another, and our lives slow to a painful crawl.

WORRY AS A WAY OF LIFE

In her book *Bring Back the Joy,* Sheila Walsh writes about a group of women she spoke to about fear and the place it occupies in our lives. One woman said, "Fear is what's holding me together. Without it I'd be like a sweater. I'd unravel." The women all laughed, Sheila writes, "but we knew there was some truth to her words. Fear was half the structure of her life, and she was afraid (there's that word again) of what would hold her together if it were gone."[7]

Worry can become a habit, even a way of life—and it's not easy to let go of it. After all, sometimes it actually seems to work.

We may be slightly neurotic, but our kids never get hurt. (We don't allow them to climb on anything higher than the sofa.) Our husband always has clean, freshly ironed undershorts. (In case of an accident, the paramedics will know he has a wife who really cares.) We don't get out much, but our house sparkles. (We'd like to invite someone over, but what if they said no? What if they said *yes?*)

Unfortunately, the belief that worry actually helps us is just an illusion—and a dangerous illusion at that. Worry doesn't prevent bad things from happening. In fact, it may prevent us from leading the full lives God intends us to live. Instead of helping us solve life's problems, anxiety creates new ones, including a tendency to unhealthy introspection. For many of us, our worries can be like Lay's potato chips—you can't stop with just one.

Dr. Hallowell tells of one patient who described her worry like this: "It's like a pattern of frost that shoots across a cold pane of glass. In seconds I am fighting with an enormous net of dangerous, intricate detail. You can't believe how quickly I go from dealing with one worry to having a jumbled mess of them."[8]

My friend Penny agrees. "I can be sitting on the couch, when suddenly one of my thoughts takes on a life of its own." Soon she finds herself crying, downright sobbing. "In a matter of seconds, my children have died, my husband's divorced me, and I'm living on the street!"

Hallowell says it is common for worriers to let their imaginations get the best of them. Rather than relying on facts, they let one worry stack against another until the domino effect sets in—one fear gets the next one moving and so on and so on. This is why truth can be such a powerful antidote to worry. "Get the facts," Hallowell suggests, "because so much of toxic worry is based upon exaggeration or misinformation."[9]

Toxic worry. That's quite a description—but it rings true to me. I've tasted its stomach-churning effects many times.

Unchecked, worry seeps into our thoughts, poisoning our joy, convincing us to give up on solutions before we've even tried them. Like Eeyore the donkey in *Winnie the Pooh*, we can let our lives be consumed by negativity. "What's the use? It will never work." Instead of looking for the best, we assume the worst. And we're not in the least surprised when the worst finds us.

What a terrible way to live! No wonder Jesus commanded us to set our worries aside, to "fear not."

WORRY VERSUS CONCERN

Don't misunderstand. When Jesus told us not to worry, he wasn't asking us to live in denial, a sugarcoated fairy tale. He wasn't telling us there's nothing to be concerned about.

The truth is, we live surrounded by opportunities for fear, anxiety, and worry. Because our world is filled with struggles and real pain, we face legitimate concerns every day. Bad things do happen to good people—and not-so-good people as well. Real problems do occur, usually on a daily basis. People don't act the way they ought to. Relationships falter and sometimes fail. There is potential for pain all around us. And there are certainly things that require concern and action on our part.

Jesus knew this better than anybody. He spent most of his life being harassed and pursued by his enemies. So why did he tell us not to worry? Jesus knew that a life filled with fear has little room left for faith. And without faith, we can neither please God nor draw close to him for the comfort and guidance we need to face the cares and affairs of everyday life.

So what is the difference between healthy concern and toxic worry? Here are a few things I've discovered in my own battle against fear:

Concern	Worry
• Involves a legitimate threat	• Is often unfounded
• Is specific (one thing)	• Is generalized (spreads to many things)
• Addresses the problem	• Obsesses about the problem
• Solves problems	• Creates more problems
• Looks to God for answer	• Looks to self or other people for answers

Pastor and teacher Gary E. Gilley sums up the difference like this: "Worry is allowing problems and distress to come between us and the heart of God. It is the view that God has somehow lost control of the situation and we cannot trust Him. A legitimate concern presses us closer to the heart of God and causes us to lean and trust on Him all the more."[10]

Concern draws us to God. Worry pulls us from him. I think this distinction is especially helpful for those of us who tend to spiritualize worry, convincing ourselves that it's our duty to fret about such things as the state of the world, our finances, or our futures. Oswald Chambers puts it this way in *My Utmost for His Highest:*

Fussing always ends in sin. We imagine that a little anxiety and worry are an indication of how really wise we are; it is much more an indication of how really wicked we are. Fretting springs from a determination to get our own way. Our Lord never worried and He was never anxious, because He was not "out" to realize His own idea; He was "out" to realize God's ideas. Fretting is wicked if you are a child of God…. All our fret and worry is caused by calculating without God.[11]

That's something we all need to remember when it comes to this issue of worry. We face legitimate concerns every day of our lives. But instead of fretting, instead of worrying, we need to focus on discerning what *we* can do (with God's help) and what should be left entirely up to God.

Even more important, we need to keep our focus on who God is and what God can do.

The bills won't pay themselves. But we serve *Jehovah Jireh*—the God who provides. The mole on our arm may indeed need to be checked and may even turn out to be cancerous. But we serve *Jehovah-Rapha*—the God who heals. There is plenty in this world to be concerned about. But we serve *El-Shaddai*—an almighty God.

Jesus warned us, "In this world you will have trouble" (John 16:33). Catch that! He said, "you *will*," not "you might." Troubles come with this earthly territory.

"But take heart!" Jesus says. "I have overcome the world."

If we have Jesus Christ as our Lord and Savior, we are not alone. We are *never* alone. When life comes blustering down the street, threatening to huff and puff and blow our house down, we can rest in ease. Because we live within a mighty fortress. Because we are hidden beneath almighty wings. Because we have a strong older Brother right there beside us. And he's rolling up his sleeves.

That's the reason we *can* leave our worry behind—not because there's nothing to be concerned about, but because we have Someone who can handle them a lot better than we can.

THREE STEPS TO VICTORY

Paul had all kinds of reasons to worry as he sat in a Roman prison awaiting a possible death sentence. But instead of writing the Philippians a sob story, Paul wrote an incredible epistle of joy. And that epistle includes a passage that has been helpful to me as I've tried to learn not to worry.

"Do not be anxious about anything," Paul wrote in Philippians 4:6-7, "but in everything, by prayer and petition, with thanksgiving, present your requests to God. And the peace of God, which transcends all understanding, will guard your hearts and your minds in Christ Jesus."

In this short passage, we find three concise and practical steps to victory over worry.

1. Be *anxious* about *nothing*.
2. Be *prayerful* about *everything*.
3. Be *thankful* for *all things*.

When Paul wrote the words, "Do not be anxious about anything," he literally meant "not even one thing!" Nothing. Not our families nor our finances, not our future nor our past. Not even one thing. That's important for someone like me to hear this because worry is such a treacherous habit. Allow one little worry in, and another is sure to follow, then another. It's better to cut it all off at the source. To be anxious about nothing.

But of course, the only way to carry off that first order is to carry out the second—to "pray about everything." And Paul literally meant "every single thing!" There is nothing too big, nothing too small, that we cannot bring to the heart of our Father. Corrie Ten Boom put it this way: "Any concern too small to be turned into a prayer is too small to be made into a burden."[12]

Realizing that has been enormously helpful to me. One of the ways God brought me out of my worried way of life was just that: prayer. Novel idea, eh? Especially for someone who'd lived most of her life by the axiom: "Why pray when you can worry?"

Here's what I did: Instead of mentally obsessing about my problems, I began consciously turning my worry into prayer.

Instead of worrying, "What if my husband has a wreck while he's on the road," I'd pray, "Dear Jesus, be with John as he drives today…"

Instead of telling myself, "If I don't finish this costume, Jessica will really be disappointed," I'd tell Jesus, "Lord, you know how much this means to Jessica…"

That may sound trite and overly simplistic, but something in this tiny act broke the bondage. Rather than nursing and rehearsing my concerns, I began giving them over to the Lord. And gradually as I did, I found that chronic anxiety had lost its grip on me.

You see, fretting magnifies the *problem,* but prayer magnifies *God.* "The reasons our problems often seem overwhelming is [that] we allow the things of time to loom larger in our gaze than the things of eternity," writes Selwyn Hughes in *Every Day Light.* "The tiniest of coins, when held close to the eyes, can blot out the sun."[13]

Perhaps that's why Paul finishes his prescription for worry with one last piece of crucial advice: "Be thankful for all things!" Look at everything God has done. In the words of the old hymn, "Count your blessings, name them one by one!" If we aren't grateful for what God has done in the past and in the present, we won't have the faith to believe God for things in the future.

Gratitude is important because it has the power to change our attitude. When we are willing to give thanks to God in *all* things, not just some things—to consciously thank him even when we don't feel very grateful—something in us begins to shift. We begin to see life as Christ sees it, full of opportunities rather than obstacles. And when we view life through eyes of faith, fear just has to flee.

THE CHOICE THAT LEADS TO PEACE

So much depends on our perspective. If my God isn't bigger than life, then my life is bigger than God—and that's when anxiety takes over.

"It's an interesting thing, the human mind," say authors Bill and Kathy Peel in their book *Discover Your Destiny.* "It can only focus on a couple of things at a time. When we're preoccupied with a problem and focus on our own inadequacy to handle it, there's really no room to add God to the picture. The ability to think rationally returns only when we refocus on God's adequacy."[14]

And when we do that, Paul says, "The peace of God, which transcends all understanding, will guard your hearts and your minds in Christ Jesus" (Philippians 4:7). When we decide to pray instead of worry—when we choose to have a grateful heart in not-so-great circumstances—then the peace of God comes and takes us into "protective custody." It stands guard at the door of our heart, transcending, surpassing, and confounding our own human understanding, bringing us peace.

Relieved of duty, we can take off our worry beads and pick up our shield of faith. And then we can stand back and watch God move.

Speaking of worry beads, the use of *komboloi* had declined significantly in Greece over the past three or four decades as young Greeks tried to adopt more modern ways. But now, it seems, these ancient stress reducers are making a big comeback. Even in cosmopolitan Athens, they're everywhere. You can pick up plastic worry beads cheaply at newsstands or fork out as much as a thousand dollars at a jewelry store for something more ornate. Executives in Armani suits flick their fingers over ivory beads and smooth black stones. Old men click wooden ones. Hip young Greeks twirl their strings of beads, comparing styles and price tags. It's a tradition that still brings a form of comfort.

I wonder how many of them know where the *komboloi* originated? I wonder if they would trade in their clicking and clacking for the original purpose these strings represented? *Komboloi,* you see, were first used in other cultures for the sole purpose of counting prayers. Bead by bead, prayer by prayer, the *komboloi* were an outward expression of a godward heart.

It is the same choice we are offered today. Will we pray? Or will we worry? We really can't do both.

THE BATTLEFIELD OF THE MIND

"Finally, brothers, whatever is true, whatever is noble, whatever is right, whatever is pure, whatever is lovely, whatever is admirable—if anything is excellent or praiseworthy—think about such things" (Philippians 4:8). Paul closes his advice on worry with a checklist of things to think about. Will our thoughts center on things *true* or false? *Noble* or nasty? *Right* or wrong? *Pure* or putrid? *Lovely* or lewd? *Admirable* or abominable? *Excellent* and *praiseworthy?* Or sordid and contemptible?

"Garbage in, garbage out." We've all heard the saying. What we put in our minds affects our hearts. And out of the abundance of our hearts, our mouths speak. Our minds churn. Our lust burns. And lives overturn.

We cannot underestimate the effect of what we think about. The war of worry, as well as the trial of temptation, is won and lost on the battlefield of our minds.

The young woman's gray eyes darted nervously behind wire-rimmed glasses as she looked around the crowded library. For a moment, I thought she might turn and leave. Instead, she stepped up to the librarian's desk and waited her turn.

"Do you have any books on fear and worry?" she asked the man behind the desk, her voice soft and low. I recognized the pain that laced her every word. I, too, had lived in her anxious world.

But God had done so much in my life in the area of anxiety. I had been a fixer, trying to make everyone happy, trying to make everything okay, while somehow impressing God with all my works. Like Martha, I had been continually upset and worried about many things. I had wanted to grow in Christ, but every time I came up against an obstacle, I had balked in fear. Rather than leaping over the roadblock "through Christ who strengthens me," I'd skid to a stop. Then I'd back up for a good look and try to figure a way around it on my own.

Now, as I stood there in the library, I wondered if I would have a chance to share what God had done for me. The young woman came toward me, her arms stacked with books on overcoming fear. *Should I stop her, Lord?* my heart whispered. But she and the librarian were still talking, so I waited.

"By the way," I heard the young woman ask, "do you have the latest Stephen King novel?"

A NEW MIND

I'm embarrassed to admit I didn't talk to the young woman. The moment to speak seemed lost in irony and awkwardness. I wandered back to my work, feeling my advice would have been unwelcome at that point.

It's been my experience that God won't usually take away our "friends," those things we look to for comfort—even if those friends aren't good for us. We must be willing to release them ourselves. And until we do, the battle for the mind will rage on.

So many of us, even Christians, complain about our struggle against sin, but then we secretly supply Satan with all the ammunition he needs. We *know* we shouldn't be reading that book. We *know* the telephone conversation we had yesterday was less than glorifying to the Lord. We *know* the unforgiveness we've harbored for so long is hardening into rage. But still we cling to it—and then we wonder why we have such a hard time making positive changes in our lives.

We must be willing to take an active role in the battle against anxiety. For too long I'd allowed Satan total access to my thought life, and by doing so, I'd given him free rein.

But as I began to "take captive every thought to make it obedient to Christ" (2 Corinthians 10:5), anxiety began to lose its hold. Instead of being led astray by fear, I took a second look at each thought as it came. Many were incognito, disguised to look like ordinary emotions. But instead of entertaining them, I handcuffed the intruding thoughts that triggered fear and took them to Jesus. Together we interrogated them, asking two questions:

- *Where did you come from?* (What is the source of this fear? Is it real or imagined?)
- *Where are you going?* (Will this thought draw me to God or into fear? Can I do anything about this problem, or should I turn it over to God?)

For so long, I had let thoughts come and go without realizing that if Satan controls my thought life, he controls me. Before that time, I'd carelessly let my emotions lead me down the treacherous paths of self-reliance rather than trusting in God. I'd allowed my worry to lead me by the poisoned waters of doubt. My fears had made me lie down in green pastures of self-pity.

But no longer. A note in the margin of the old British *Revised Version* translates Isaiah 26:3, "Thou wilt keep him in perfect peace whose *imagination* is stayed on Thee."[15]

The Word leapt to life for me the day I read that particular translation. It was the diagnosis I'd needed to hear. My imagination had controlled my life for so long that it had grown into a giant sheepdog, loping unrestrained across the meadows of my mind. My emotions trailed behind my imagination like frolicking puppies, never certain where they were being led, but quite happy to go along for the ride.

"Here, Imagination! Here, boy." Sometimes I said it out loud. So strong was the pull to fear that it took a living word picture to pull me back to center. Back to faith. I'd point to the ground beside me and instruct both my imagination and any stray emotions to "Stay."

Crazy? Yes, maybe. But it worked for me. Nothing could be crazier than the anxious way I had lived before.

I began to search the Scriptures for verses on fear and worry and the mind. When I found a verse that fit, I memorized it. Then, when the temptation to fear came, I could answer it with the Word of God: "For God hath not given us the spirit of fear; but of power, and of love, and of a sound mind" (2 Timothy 1:7, KJV).

Like King David in Psalm 1:2, I began to meditate on God's Word day and night. The word for *meditate* has been likened to a cow chewing on its cud. Instead of gnawing on my problem, I trained my mind to chew on the promises of God. And as the Holy Spirit and I brought back the Word to remembrance, something exciting happened. Anxiety fled in the face of truth, and peace—the kind of peace that quieted the disciples' raging storm—came to take its place.

The kind of peace only Jesus can give. *Peace, be still.*

PERFECT PEACE

"Perfect love casteth out fear," 1 John 4:18 (KJV) tells us. I love the way J. B. Phillips translates this verse: "Love contains no fear—indeed fully developed love expels every particle of fear, for fear always contains some of the torture of feeling guilty. This means that the man who lives in fear has not yet had his love perfected."

That particular verse is helpful to me because it speaks to the root of my worry habit. I was anxious for the same reason the first man and woman became anxious: I was not secure in God's love.

Oh, I knew that I was saved and that if I died, I'd go to heaven. But somewhere along the way, I had twisted God's love into something I had to earn. If I could just be good enough, then God had to love me. But of course I stumbled again and again. Each time it took me weeks to work up enough spiritual brownie points to feel like I was back on God's good side.

No wonder I worried. No wonder I was afraid. I was constantly sewing fig leaves, trying to cover up my inadequacy.

When Jesus said, "Martha, Martha…" so gently that frantic day in Bethany, he was speaking to you and me as well. Lovingly, if we'll listen, he whispers his diagnosis concerning the state of our souls: "You're worried," he points out. "You're anxious. It isn't just about this meal; it's about everything."

And with the diagnosis comes a choice.

Come find love, Jesus invites us. Come find a love so perfect that it covers all your faults and pronounces you "not guilty." Come find a love that chases fear out the door! Come find everything you've ever longed for. Come find peace for your soul.

"Joanna, Joanna…," the Lord speaks to my life today. Listen closely. You'll hear him calling your name as well. "Do not let your hearts be troubled," he's saying. "Trust in God; trust also in me" (John 14:1).

He's urging us all to lay aside our worry beads, to give up fiddling with things we can never hope to fix and to seek his face instead.

He's calling us to the Great Exchange—the one where we can never lose. As we trade the "many things" that make us anxious, he gives us the "one thing" that calms our hearts. Himself.

For he is the Prince of Peace.

Top Ten Ways to Tame Your Worry Habit

10. *Separate toxic worry from genuine concern.* Determine if you can do anything about your situation. If so, sketch a plan to handle it (Proverbs 16:3).

9. *Don't worry alone.* Share your concerns with a friend or a counselor. You may receive helpful advice. Talking your fears out with someone often reveals solutions that were invisible before (Proverbs 27:9).

8. *Take care of your physical body.* Regular exercise and adequate rest can defuse a lot of worry. When our bodies are healthy, our minds can handle stress better and react more appropriately (1 Corinthians 6:19-20).

7. *Do what is right.* A guilty conscience can cause more anxiety than a world of problems. Do your best to live above reproach. Take care of mistakes quickly by confessing and seeking forgiveness (Acts 24:16).

6. *Look on the bright side.* Consciously focus on what is good around you. Don't let yourself speak negatively, even about yourself (Ephesians 4:29).

5. *Control your imagination.* Be realistic about the problems you face. Try to live in the "here and now" not in the "what might be" (Isaiah 35:3-4).

4. *Prepare for the unexpected.* Put aside a cash reserve and take sensible measures so you'll be ready if difficulties arise (Proverbs 21:20).

3. *Trust God.* Keep reminding yourself to put God in your equation. Then, when fear knocks, you can send faith to answer the door (Psalm 112:7).

2. *Meditate on God's promises.* Scripture has the power to transform our minds. Look for scriptures that deal with your particular areas of anxiety. Answer life's difficulties with God's Word (2 Peter 1:4).

1. And the number one way to tame a worry habit? *Pray!* Joseph M. Scriven's hymn says it all: "O what peace we often forfeit, / O what needless pain we bear, / All because we do not carry / everything to God in prayer"[16] (Colossians 4:2).

I sought the LORD, and he answered me; he delivered me from all my fears. Those who look to him are radiant; their faces are never covered with shame.

PSALM 34:4-5

4

The Cure

You are worried and upset about many things, but only one thing is needed.

LUKE 10:41-42

The story is told of a man who met God in a lovely valley one day.[1]

"How are you this morning?" God asked the fellow.

"I'm fine, thank you," the man replied. "Is there anything I can do for you today?"

"Yes, there is," God said. "I have a wagon with three stones in it, and I need someone to pull it up the hill for me. Are you willing?"

"Yes, I'd love to do something for you. Those stones don't look very heavy, and the wagon's in good shape. I'd be happy to do that. Where would you like me to take it?"

God gave the man specific instructions, sketching a map in the dust at the side of the road. "Go through the woods and up the road that winds up the side of the hill. Once you get to the top, just leave the wagon there. Thank you for your willingness to help me today."

"No problem!" the man replied and set off cheerfully. The wagon pulled a bit behind him, but the burden was an easy one. He began to whistle as he walked quickly through the forest. The sun peeked through the trees and warmed his back. What a joy to be able to help the Lord, he thought, enjoying the beautiful day.

Just around the third bend, he walked into a small village. People smiled and

---

[1.] Adapted from a story by Rosemarie Kowalski. Used by permission.

greeted him. Then, at the last house, a man stopped him and asked, "How are you this morning? What a nice wagon you have. Where are you off to?"

"Well, God gave me a job this morning. I'm delivering these three stones to the top of the hill."

"My goodness! Can you believe it? I was just praying this morning about how I was going to get this rock I have up to the top of the mountain," the man told him with great excitement. "You don't suppose you could take it up there for me? It would be such an answer to prayer."

The man with the wagon smiled and said, "Of course. I don't suppose God would mind. Just put it behind the other three stones." Then he set off with three stones and a rock rolling behind him.

The wagon seemed a bit heavier. He could feel the jolt of each bump, and the wagon seemed to pull to one side a bit. The man stopped to adjust the load as he sang a hymn of praise, pleased to be helping out a brother as he served God. Then he set off again and soon reached another small village at the side of the road. A good friend lived there and offered him a glass of cider.

"You're going to the top of the hill?" his oldest friend asked.

"Yes! I am so excited. Can you imagine, God gave me something to do!"

"Hey!" said his friend. "I need this bag of pebbles taken up. I've been so worried that it might not get taken care of since I haven't any time to do it myself. But you could fit it in right between the three stones here in the middle." With that, he placed his burden in the wagon.

"Shouldn't be a problem," the man said. "I think I can handle it." He finished the cider, then stood up and brushed his hands on his overalls before gripping the handle of the wagon. He waved good-bye and began to pull the wagon back onto the road.

The wagon was definitely tugging on his arm now, but it wasn't uncomfortable. As he started up the incline, he began to feel the weight of the three stones, the rock, and the pebbles. Still, it felt good to help a friend. Surely God would be proud of how energetic and helpful he'd been.

One little stop followed another, and the wagon grew fuller and fuller. The sun was hot above the man pulling it, and his shoulders ached with the strain. The songs of praise and thanksgiving that had filled his heart had long since left his lips as resentment began to build inside. Surely this wasn't what he had signed up for that morning. God had given him a burden heavier than he could bear.

The wagon felt huge and awkward as it lumbered and swayed over the ruts in the road. Frustrated, the man was beginning to have visions of giving up and letting the wagon roll backward. God was playing a cruel game with him. The wagon lurched, and the load of obligations collided with the back of his legs, leaving bruises. "This is it!" he fumed. "God can't expect me to haul this all the way up the mountain."

"Oh God," he wailed. "This is too hard for me! I thought you were behind this trip, but I am overcome by the heaviness of it. You'll have to get someone else to do it. I'm just not strong enough."

As he prayed, God came to his side. "Sounds like you're having a hard time. What's the problem?"

"You gave me a job that is too hard for me," the man sobbed. "I'm just not up to it!" God walked over to where the wagon was braced with a stone. "What is this?" He held up the bag of pebbles.

"That belongs to John, my good friend. He didn't have time to bring it up himself. I thought I would help."

"And this?" God tumbled two pieces of shale over the side of the wagon as the man tried to explain.

God continued to unload the wagon, removing both light and heavy items. They dropped to the ground, the dust swirling up around them. The man who had hoped to help God grew silent. "If you will be content to let others take their own burdens," God told him, "I will help you with your task."

"But I promised I would help! I can't leave these things lying here."

"Let others shoulder their own belongings," God said gently. "I know you were trying to help, but when you are weighted down with all these cares, you cannot do what I have asked of you."

The man jumped to his feet, suddenly realizing the freedom God was offering. "You mean I only have to take the three stones after all?" he asked.

"That is what I asked you to do." God smiled. "My yoke is easy, and my burden is light. I will never ask you to carry more than you can bear."

"I can do that!" said the man, grinning from ear to ear. He grabbed the wagon handle and set off once again, leaving the rest of the burdens beside the road. The wagon still lurched and jolted lightly, but he hardly noticed.

A new song filled his lips, and he noticed a fragrant breeze wafting over the path. With great joy he reached the top of the hill. It had been a wonderful day, for he had done what the Lord had asked.

AN OVERLOADED WAGON

I've felt like the man hauling rocks—overburdened, overworked, and over-whelmed. What started as a joy became drudgery, and I felt like giving up.

Nothing is harder to bear than a burden we're not called to carry. While God does ask us to bear one another's burdens, he has not asked us to step in and do what people are not willing to do themselves. And while there are many needs, God has not asked us to meet every one.

In fact, we, like Martha, may be surprised by how little God actually requires.

The Jews, eager to please God, were big on rules and regulations. God had given the law, and because they loved him, they were determined to live it out to the fullest. If a little law was good, then surely more law was even better. At least that was the opinion of the Pharisees, one of the two religious sects who most influenced the common people of Jesus' day.

In their desire to be a perfect nation, the Pharisees took the basic precepts God had laid out to Moses and began creating ways to apply them to everyday life. Eventually they created the *Mishnah,* a collection of over six hundred rules and regulations designed to help Jews live out the Law to the last jot and tittle. The mandates ranged from the sublime to the ridiculous. Especially those sur-rounding the Sabbath.

God's law required a weekly day of rest, a ceasing from labor and a laying down of burdens. From the appearance of the first evening star on Friday night until the setting sun on Saturday, Jews were required to cease all work—and the rules about what constituted work were quite exacting. The Pharisees interpreted this to mean that a man who carried a needle in his cloak on the Sabbath was sewing. If he dragged a chair across a sandy floor, he was plowing. If he carried his mattress, he was bearing a burden. If he plucked corn and rubbed it in his hands, he was reaping. In all of these things, he was considered to be breaking the Law.[2]

The Pharisees even argued that it was wrong to eat an egg laid on a Sabbath because the *hen* had been working. The "official" Sabbath burden that one could legally carry was the weight of one dried fig.[3]

But instead of drawing the nation of Israel closer to God, the pharisaic law became a stumbling block. It was impossible to keep every petty particular of what Jesus called "heavy loads" (Matthew 23:2-4).

It is in this legalistic setting that we find Martha. The Jewish religion was patriarchal by nature. Only men were allowed to sit on the Sanhedrin ruling council. Only men were allowed in the synagogue; the women sat outside. Only men were allowed to wear scripture-filled phylacteries upon their foreheads or left arms to remind them to obey God's Law. The outward trappings of godly devotion were largely a male domain.

Women who wanted to show their love for God were encouraged to do it through good works—but that was about their only option. They were allowed to enter the Women's Court of the Temple to worship, but no farther. In the wilderness, they had only been allowed as far as the tabernacle door. Even Solomon, in his description of the perfect woman, mentioned little of her spiritual walk with God—only the duties she fulfilled.

And Jewish women had duties by the dozens. Even keeping the Sabbath meant a lot of work for the women of Jesus' day. Though the Sabbath was mandated as a day of rest for women as well as men, the day *before* the Sabbath was filled with frantic preparation. There were three kosher meals to prepare, lamps to be filled with olive oil, and jugs to be filled to the brim with water for ceremonial washing. The house had to be cleaned, and the whole family needed freshly laundered tunics to wear the next day.[4]

And that was for an "ordinary" Sabbath. Feast days and special events required extra preparations.

The day Jesus visited Martha and Mary was probably busier than usual. The Feast of the Tabernacles was near, and the house was filled with cooking and activity. This pilgrimage feast was held early in the fall and was one of three feasts every adult male Jew within a fifteen-mile radius was required to come to Jerusalem to celebrate.

The Feast of Tabernacles lasted seven days, followed by a special Sabbath. Held just after harvest, it was a time of great celebration and joy. The people left their homes to live in booths or small tents in memory of their time in the wilderness. William Barclay, in his commentary on John, describes it like this:

> The law laid it down that the booths must not be permanent structures but built specially for the occasion. Their walls were made of branches and fronds, and had to be such that they would give protection from the weather but not shut out the sun. The roof had to be thatched, but the thatching had to be wide enough for the stars to be seen at night. The historical significance of all this was to remind the people in unforgettable fashion that once they had been homeless wanderers in the desert without a roof over their heads.[5]

Bethany sat at the eastern edge of the Mount of Olives, just two miles away from Jerusalem. At the time of Jesus' visit, the town's gentle slopes were probably filled with pilgrims' booths. In order to make room for worshipers during the great feasts, the boundaries of Jerusalem were usually extended to include Bethany.

So when Martha invited Jesus and his disciples to stay at her home on their way to Jerusalem, they accepted her kind hospitality. Martha continued with her expected tasks—making everything comfortable so everyone else could worship.

The thought of joining Jesus never occurred to her because it simply wasn't allowed. But she loved Jesus. I think she knew she was entertaining the Messiah. And so Martha showed her devotion by giving the gift she knew best. The gift of service.

But even welcome wagons can grow heavy, as Martha quickly discovered. Especially when they're laden with the extra weight of our human agendas and expectations.

DUMPING ROCKS

Jesus came to earth and immediately tipped the Jewish wagonload of rules and regulations. He hit the religious leadership right where it hurt—smack dab in the middle of their spiritual pride. "Woe to you, because you load people down with burdens they can hardly carry, and you yourselves will not lift one finger to help them" (Luke 11:46).

To those helpless under the weight of Law, Christ became a Burden Bearer: "Come unto me, all ye that labour and are heavy laden, and I will give you rest" (Matthew 11:28, KJV). But to those who put faith in their religious accomplishments, he added yet another load: "One thing you lack," Jesus told the rich young ruler. "Go, sell everything you have and give to the poor.... Then come, follow me" (Mark 10:21). Jesus knew that sooner or later, the legalistic load would grow too heavy to bear alone and the religious would cry out for relief. And he would be there.

Jesus stripped away all the "traditions of men," the layers of dos and don'ts that had obscured the face of God. "This is who God is," he declared to the world. "Look and see! He loves you. He sent me so you could have life and fellowship with him. It isn't outward appearance that concerns the Father. It's your inner person."

That's what Jesus told Martha that busy afternoon. "You're worried and upset about many things, but only one thing is needed." And what was that one thing? Not cooking or cleaning or doing good works, but knowing God. Listening to him. Leaving the Kitchen long enough to experience the intimate fellowship of the Living Room.

"Only one thing is needed." With those words, Christ swept away centuries of chauvinism and bias, tradition and ritual. Women were no longer to be on the outside looking in when it came to spiritual matters. Just as surely as Christ's death would bridge the gap between God and humankind, so Jesus' words this day removed the gender barrier that separated women from their Maker.

Scripture doesn't tell us Martha's response to Jesus' astounding statement. But I can see Jesus offering his hand, welcoming her to join Mary down at his feet.

What did Martha do then, I wonder? Perhaps she sputtered excuses: the dinner, her apron, her hair. Perhaps she just withdrew, chastened. Or perhaps—as she stood there looking into her Master's eyes—Martha simply sank to her knees and began to listen.

The point is, we just don't know. While negative responses to Jesus' invitations in the Bible are usually mentioned—the rich man left downcast, and the keepers of the Law left angry—this particular story is left unfinished. Perhaps it is to leave us room to determine our own response.

What will we do when told we've missed out on the best God has for us? Will we bow our knees, or will we run back to what is familiar? Will we sputter excuses or humble our hearts?

It's hard to ignore the love of Jesus. The sweet wooing of the Holy Spirit calms our fears and shatters our defenses. Based on her subsequent encounters with Jesus, which we will discuss in later chapters, I believe that's exactly what happened to Martha. I believe she followed her Master's leading. She bent her knees and found his feet. She let God dump her wagon, so loaded with care, then allowed him to fill it with his presence.

Only then, as Martha let go of her lengthy list of to-dos and began doing the one thing that was needed, did she begin to give God what he really wants.

Dumping Rocks

When my friend Tricia started feeling overwhelmed by her too-busy life, she and her husband, John, decided to dump some rocks from their overloaded wagons. Here's the simple process they followed. Maybe you'll find it helpful too.

1. They made a list of all the activities they were involved in (children, work, church, etc.).
2. They prayed over and prioritized the activities as to importance, assigning each one a number from one to four.
3. Then they eliminated all the fours.

While this process may sound overly simplistic, it really helped John and Tricia lighten their load. "It was hard to see things we enjoyed go out the door!" Tricia says. "But the freedom and the peace we've gained have been more than worth it."

Now this is what the LORD Almighty says:
"Give careful thought to your ways."

HAGGAI 1:5

GIVING THE GIFT GOD DESIRES

My husband and I had been married less than a year when my birthday rolled around. He was so secretive about his plans to celebrate, I was certain this birthday would be something wonderful. And it was. I came home to find candlelight and roses, the table set with our new china, and a homemade birthday cake on the counter. John had gone over to see Mrs. Chapman, our next-door neighbor, and she'd shown him how to make it—from scratch!

I was terribly impressed. But what intrigued me most was the huge box in the center of the table. What could it be? Lingerie? A new dress? Chocolate? John seemed just as excited as I, insisting that I open his gift before we sat down to dinner.

"I hope you like it," John said, his eyes as bright as a little boy's. "You said you needed it."

"Needed it." That should have been my first clue. But being young and naive when it came to men, I assumed the gift would be even more wonderful than I'd first believed. It just had to be that expensive food processor I'd been admiring downtown.

I carefully removed the bow and began peeling the tape off one end. "Open it!" John urged. "Just rip it open!" We laughed as I tore the beautiful wrapping off in big strips. Neither of us could wait for my reaction.

And there it was, beneath Hallmark's most expensive foil—my birthday gift in all its glory. The love of my life had given me not one, but two (because he is a generous man!) Rubbermaid organizers. One to hang my iron and ironing board on. The other to organize my mop and broom.

I was speechless to say the least. John was so excited, he insisted on hanging them right away. "You said you needed them," he chattered as he searched for a screwdriver.

"I did, didn't I?" I replied weakly, following him to the laundry room.

Fortunately, we were still newlyweds. I managed to bite my lip before offering a thank-you kiss, and for several years John thought he had made gift-giving history. Boy, did he.

So often we give God the gift we think he needs rather than take time to find out what he desires.

We make promises and New Year's resolutions to be more heavenly minded. This year we'll read the Bible through. This year we'll join a prayer group—or start a new one ourselves. This year we'll try that forty-day fast everyone's talking about.

We make goals to be more loving and less selfish. We look for opportunities to serve. We visit a shut-in on Monday, man the crisis pregnancy line on Tuesday, volunteer at school on Wednesday, work at the food bank on Thursday, type the church bulletin on Friday, play with our kids on Saturday, and go to church on Sunday. And everything we do is important. All of it is good.

The problem is, contrary to popular belief, we can't do it all. We're not even supposed to try.

Paul explained just that in Romans 12. He said that the body of Christ has many members, and each of them has a different gifting—which means each has a different job to do. The fact that 20 percent of the church does 80 percent of the work is not at all what God intended.

Jesus' words to Martha are words to those of us who are overextended in service as well: "Only one thing is needed." We must take time to sit at Jesus' feet, to worship him, to get to know him better. When we put that first thing first, then he delights to reveal his will and our part in fulfilling it.

Sometimes I think I struggle to discern God's will because I'm surrounded by the obvious. Someone obviously needs to care for the toddlers during church service. Someone obviously needs to visit Kathleen, who's bedridden with a difficult pregnancy. Someone obviously needs to cut out blocks for missionary quilts—and tell my neighbor about Jesus. I'm surrounded by legitimate needs, and I want to do them all. And so I try. But midway through a blustery day of service, I find myself cross and frustrated, not at all aglow with the saintly aura I'd expected when I'd set out that morning.

That's exactly what happened a few years ago when our church in Oregon scheduled a missions banquet. Someone—*obviously*—needed to head it up, so I cheerfully volunteered, certain I was doing God a favor. I was bursting with creativity and energy for the project. "Oh Lord," I told him, "you are going to love what I have planned for you!" Then I set off, certain he was walking beside me.

Unfortunately, everything about the event was a struggle. There were interpersonal rumblings and my own amount of grumbling. But after it was through,

I felt quite satisfied. The banquet was beautiful, the food delicious, and the decorating exquisite. People were touched by the missionary message, and money was raised for crucial needs.

I remember sighing with pride, "Wasn't that wonderful, God?" But I heard

The Practical Power of "One Thing"

The one thing that Jesus said was needed in Martha's life was fellowship with him—and that's true for us, too. But the principle of "one thing" can also have smaller, practical implications that can help when life feels overwhelming. Here are some ways to practice one-thing thinking when your wagon feels overloaded.

1. *Invite Jesus to rule and reign.* Each morning before you get out of bed, invite the Lord to come take the throne of your life, to be your "one thing." Present your day to him and ask him for wisdom and guidance.

2. *Ask God to reveal the next step.* As you go through your day, keep asking the Lord, "What is the one thing I need to do next?" Don't let the big picture overwhelm you. Just take the next step as he reveals it—wash one dish, make one phone call, put on your jogging clothes. Then take the next step…and the next.

3. *Have faith that what needs to get done will get done.* Since you have dedicated your day to the Lord, trust that he'll show you the one thing or many things that must be done. Do what you can do in the time allotted. Then trust that what wasn't accomplished was either unnecessary or is being taken care of by God.

4. *Be open to the Spirit's leading.* You may find your day interrupted by divine appointments. Instead of resisting the interruptions, flow with the one thing as God brings it across your path. You'll be amazed at the joy and freedom that comes from surrendering your agenda and cooperating with his.

Commit to the LORD whatever you do,
and your plans will succeed.

PROVERBS 16:3

no reply in my spirit. It was as if I'd turned to speak to the Lord, only to find him missing.

"God," I cried in my heart, "where are you?"

His voice answered in the distance, "Over here, Joanna." There he stood, patiently waiting on the path where I'd first told him of my glorious plan.

"I thought you were in this, Lord," I said as I walked back to where he was. "I thought you'd be pleased."

He gently took my hand, then wiped away my tears. "It was good. Perhaps it was even important. But it wasn't my plan for you."

I realized then that, while there are many things that need to be done, things I'm capable of doing and want to do, I am not always the one to do them. Even if I have a burden for a certain need or project, my interest or concern is not a surefire sign that I need to be in charge. God may only be calling me to pray that the right person will rise up to accomplish it. What's more, I may be stealing someone else's blessing when I assume I must do it all.

How I wish I would have learned earlier in ministry to wait upon the Lord. Much of my energy and joy has been swallowed up by jobs and obligations that were not my own. I still tend to rush in, presuming to know his will rather than waiting to hear what he desires.

It is a costly mistake, for often, when the Holy Spirit does ask something of me, I'm either knee deep in another project or too exhausted from my latest exercise in futility to do what God wants of me.

WHAT DOES GOD DESIRE?

Which brings us back to the crucial question—what is it God desires?

If we could just get a handle on what God expects, the overachiever in us surmises, then it would be easy to please him. But that was the downfall of the Pharisees. They had reduced their relationship with God to a series of dos and don'ts, entirely missing the purpose for which God had set them apart. They put on religious work clothes, not realizing God wasn't looking for maids and valets—he was looking for a people to call his own.

Now that's not to say that service for God is unimportant. The Bible tells us, "Whatever your hand finds to do, do it with all your might" (Ecclesiastes 9:10).

"Faith by itself, if it is not accompanied by action, is dead," according to James 2:17. As we will see in chapter 6, serving God and others really is important. Hard work is often part of what we are called to do.

But service was never supposed to be our first priority. Work is not our first order of business—even working for the Lord. In fact, our own efforts are so far down the line when it comes to what God wants that they didn't even register in Jesus' conversation with Martha.

Only *one* thing is needed—and it was happening, not in the Kitchen, but right there in the Living Room.

Notice, however, Jesus didn't rebuke Martha because she was fixing supper, thus instituting the eleventh commandment: "Thou shalt not cook"—although that would be a handy excuse when I don't feel like fixing dinner. Jesus wasn't concerned about Martha's external abilities at all. It was her internal disabilities that he probed—the dark corners of pride and prejudice, the spiritual handicap of busyness that left her unable to enjoy the intimacy of his presence.

After all, intimacy can be threatening. Getting close to Jesus means we can no longer hide our inadequacies. His light illuminates everything that is wrong and ugly about our lives. Unconsciously, therefore, we may flee God's presence rather than pursue it. And Satan spurs on our retreat by telling us we're not good enough to earn God's favor. He tells us that when we get our act together—that's when we can enter the Living Room.

But the truth is, we can't get our spiritual act together unless we go to the Living Room *first*.

It's not always easy to get there. Intimacy with God may require leaving our comfort zones. Some people feel uneasy in the presence of God. They dismiss the act of worship as too emotional, preferring the intellectual pursuit of Bible study or doctrine. Or they simply have trouble being still, because that's their personality. But regardless of our temperament, regardless of our emotional preference, we are all called to intimacy with God. The one thing Martha needed is the one thing we need as well.

If you struggle to stay at his feet, ask the Lord to reveal what is hindering you. There is no need to lay aside your intellect or your personality when you enter the Living Room. Just come as you are.

As a child of God.

Children, after all, love intimacy. "Hug me, Mommy!" With arms stretched upward, they beg, "Daddy, hold me!" From infancy, when frightened or ill, the first place our children long to be is as close to our heart as they can get. They cuddle in, pressing themselves into our arms.

That is the intimacy our Father desires to share with us. Not because we've earned it, but because he hungers for it. And so do we, whether we're aware of it or not.

LONGING FOR FELLOWSHIP

I didn't realize how much I longed for God until that dark night I cried out to hear the good news. Although I had served him since I was a child, there was a devastating emptiness about my relationship with my heavenly Father. I had worked and worked to please him, yet I couldn't feel his love.

The Galatians knew that same kind of emptiness. They had accepted Christ as Savior and thrived under Paul's teaching and care. But when Paul left Galatia, the Judaizers moved in, telling them they still had a long way to go before they could enjoy true closeness to God. These were Jewish Christians who believed that the ceremonial practices of the Old Testament—including circumcision—were still binding upon the New Testament church. Paul, they said, had inappropriately removed legal requirements from the gospel in order to make it more appealing to the Gentiles.

Just as the scribes and Pharisees added rules and regulations to the Law, so the Judaizers attempted to mix a new form of legalism in with the gospel of grace. They wanted an outward manifestation of what could only be an inward work.

That's why Paul sent a wake-up letter to his beloved church in Galatia. He called the Judaizers' gospel slavery, and he added, "You foolish Galatians! Who has bewitched you?... After beginning with the Spirit, are you now trying to attain your goal by human effort?" (Galatians 3:1,3).

If we aren't careful, we can fall prey to the same kind of lies the Galatians fell for—lies that tell us that we must perform in order to earn God's love. We can add so many requirements to our faith that the "one thing" is swallowed by the "many," and the "best" is obliterated by the "good."

The thing we must understand is that God did not choose us to "use" us.

We are not spiritual Oompa-Loompas in some cosmic chocolate factory, working night and day to churn out a smoother, better-tasting Christianity.

We were not created to fill some egotistical need God has for praise—the angels forever encircle his throne with worship.

We are not some celestial science project; laboratory mice let loose in a maze to see how they interact.

No, the Bible makes it clear that God created us because he longs to have fellowship with us. Our Father longs to pour his very life into us, to give us an inheritance and a share in his divine nature.

What does God desire? It is actually very simple.

He wants you. All of you.

ONE THING IS NEEDED

When Jesus told Martha that only one thing was needed in her life, the context of the verse clearly points to a spiritual call. The Better Part that Mary discovered was to be found not on the table, but at his feet.

However, the Greek phrase for "only one thing is needed" may also refer to food portions. Perhaps in a subtle turn of word, Jesus was issuing two invitations:

- First, to know him—to put worship before work
- But also, not to overdo—even in our efforts on his behalf

Instead of partaking from a sideboard of fancy entrées, Jews usually ate out of a large common bowl placed in the middle of the table. Guests would break off pieces of bread and dip them in the soup or broth. Jesus may have gently reminded Martha that her overdone effort in preparing multiple dishes was keeping her so busy in the kitchen that she was missing out on the real "food," the real "life" of the party.

"Her fault was not that she served," Charles Spurgeon writes of Martha in his devotional classic *Morning and Evening*. "The condition of a servant well becomes every Christian. Her fault was that she grew 'cumbered with much serving,' so that she forgot him and only remembered the service."[6]

How easy it is to confuse duty with devotion; the common with communion. That was Martha's downfall, and it can be mine as well. For in her effort to set a table worthy of the Son of God, she nearly missed the real banquet. And I, too, can get so overwhelmed that my worship becomes work rather than delight, and devotion becomes just another duty.

If I am not careful, the spiritual disciplines of prayer, Bible study, and praise can become little more than items to be checked off my to-do list or rocks I'm tempted to dump off my wagon because they slow me down. And so I need to hear Jesus' cure for *all* my worry and distress.

"Only one thing is needed"—and that is found in true fellowship with him.

For he, after all, is the Bread of Life, the Living Water, the only "dish" we need. He wants to change our hearts and empower our lives. He wants us to find the great freedom of Luke 10:42.

I cannot do everything, but I can do "one thing."

I cannot meet every need, but I can respond in obedience to the need the Spirit lays on my heart.

I cannot carry every load, but I can carry the load God has for me.

For his yoke, indeed, is easy, and his burden is truly light.

5

Living Room Intimacy

Here I am! I stand at the door and knock.
If anyone hears my voice and opens the door,
I will come in and eat with him, and he with me.

REVELATION 3:20

Simeon was probably like most boys his age in A.D. 403. The thirteen-year-old spent much of his time caring for his father's flocks on the hillsides of Cilicia.

But one day, while listening to a sermon on the Beatitudes, Simeon's heart was stirred and changed. He left his home and family and began a lifelong pursuit of God that took him from a monastery to the Syrian desert to three decades of sitting upon a pole.

Yes. A pole.

Simeon the Stylite began a spiritual fad that would last more than a thousand years. He was the very first "pillar hermit."

Spiritual zeal has always taken a variety of forms, but the first thousand years of Christianity saw more than its share of the bizarre. As the church grew during the first centuries, so did worldliness. In reaction, many Christians withdrew to a life of poverty, chastity, and separation. Hungry for holiness, monks gathered in communities, often competing with one another in their quest for self-denial.

Simeon, I'd say, won the contest hands down.

"Simeon moved to the Syrian desert and lived with an iron chain on his feet before having himself buried up to the neck for several months," writes Robert J. Morgan in his book *On This Day....* "When crowds flocked to view his acts of perceived holiness, Simeon determined to escape the distractions by living atop a pillar. His first column was six feet high, but soon he built higher ones until his permanent abode towered sixty feet above ground."[1]

There he lived for thirty years, exposed to every element, tied to his perch with a rope to keep from falling while he slept. By ladder, his followers brought him food each day and removed his waste. Thousands came to gawk at this strange man on the pillar. Hundreds listened daily as Simeon preached on the importance of prayer, selflessness, and justice.

But the question that occurs to me, as I'm sure it occurred to some of those who came to listen, is this: Did Simeon's life on a pillar really bring him any closer to God?

THE BURDEN OF SPIRITUALITY

Intimacy with God. What does it mean to you—and how do you achieve it? Does it require sitting on a pillar like Simeon or being buried up to your neck in sand? Is it some mystical level of consciousness attainable only by the deeply devout?

Some religions say that it is. According to Hinduism, a religion based on the karma of good works, one lifetime isn't enough for the soul to achieve spiritual enlightenment. Hindu mathematicians calculate it takes 6.8 million rotations through reincarnation for the good and evil in us to finally balance out so that we can receive the ultimate spiritual level of nirvana.[2]

In the Far East, during religious festivals, men often have hooks inserted under the skin of their backs. These hooks are then tied to wagonloads of rocks, which the men drag through the streets, hoping to obtain forgiveness for their sins. In certain areas of Mexico, the devout crawl miles on their knees in pilgrimage.

All over the world, people go to unimaginable lengths to find God—which is sad when you consider the unimaginable lengths God has already gone to find *us*.

We don't need millions of lifetimes in order to be pure enough to see God. We don't need to stick hooks in our backs or tear the flesh off our knees in order to earn God's favor.

All we really need is Jesus. For he is all the evidence we need. The Father actually *wants* us close and is willing to do whatever is necessary to make sure it happens.

It's hard to imagine the Creator of the universe wanting to know us. We feel so unworthy. That's why many of us persist in thinking that we must earn our way to heaven, that only the superspiritual—only the Simeons of this world—can really know God. Burdened with the weight of our own spirituality, we struggle beneath a load of self-imposed obligations: "I have to do this…" or "I can't really know God until I do that…" We can spend so much of our lives getting ready to know God or backing away out of fear of displeasing God that we never get around to enjoying the Living Room Intimacy Jesus came to provide.

And yet intimacy with God was indeed the very point of Jesus' coming and of his dying. "You who once were far away have been brought near through the blood of Christ," Paul writes in Ephesians 2:13. For when Jesus died, his cross bridged the great chasm of sin that separated us from God. With his last breath, Jesus blew aside the curtain that had kept sinful humans from touching a holy God. Now we could come into God's very presence, clean and approved, not by our works, but by his grace. Jesus "destroyed the barrier, the dividing wall of hostility" (verse 14) that had separated humanity from God.

When we couldn't reach up to heaven, heaven came down to us and welcomed us into the Living Room through the doorway of Jesus Christ.

That is the good news of the gospel.

The way has been made. The price has been paid. All we need to do is come.

THE PRICE HAS BEEN PAID

The story is told of a young man who left the Old Country and sailed to America to make a new life in the New World. Before he left, his father pressed some money in his hand. It wasn't much, but it was all he had. He hoped it would tide the boy over until he found a job. His mother handed him a box of food for the journey, then they kissed and hugged and tearfully said good-bye.

On the boat, the young man gave his ticket to the porter and found his way to the tiny cabin he'd share with several others during the month-long voyage to New York. That evening at mealtime, the young man went topside and unwrapped a sandwich his mother had made. He ate silently as he watched the other passengers file into a large room crowded with tables. He listened to their chatty laughter and watched as waiters brought plates filled with hot, steaming food. But he just smiled, enjoying his mother's fresh homemade bread and the crisp apple his brother had picked that morning. *Bless my family,* he prayed.

The days went by slowly, and the young man's box of food quickly dwindled. But meals such as they offered in the dining room were certain to cost a lot. He'd need that money later.

He ate alone in his cabin now. The smell from the dining hall made his stomach wrench with hunger. He allowed himself a few crackers and some cheese each day, whispering a prayer of thanks before scraping the mold off the hard lump. A shriveled apple and the tepid rainwater he'd collected in a can completed his meager meal.

Three days out of New York, the last of the food was gone except for a wormy apple. The young man could take no more. Pale and weak, he asked the porter in broken English, "How much?" The porter looked confused. "Food," the young man said as he held out some coins and pointed to the dining room. "How much?"

Finally the ship steward understood. He smiled and shook his head. "It costs nothing," he said, closing the immigrant's hand back around his money. "You are free to eat! The cost of food was included in the price of passage."

This story means a lot to me. For years I lived like a pauper instead of a princess. I'd settled for stale cheese and shriveled apples instead of enjoying the rich table God had prepared for me. I kept waiting for the day I'd be worthy to sit at his table, never realizing that the cost of such fellowship was included in the price Christ paid for my passage.

The price has been paid. Please hear this simple truth. If you have accepted Jesus Christ as your Savior, the price has been paid for you.

And that means there is nothing keeping any of us away from Living Room Intimacy. The "dividing wall of hostility" has been torn down, at least on God's side. But there may need to be a bit of demolition work on your end, because the enemy of our souls keeps quite busy building barriers to block spiritual intimacy.

BARRIERS TO INTIMACY

Before salvation, Satan tells us we're just fine. We don't need a savior.

But after we're saved, the Accuser points his bony finger at us and tells us we're no good. We don't deserve a savior.

He's lying, of course. Jesus says so in John 8:44. Satan is "the father of lies." In fact, lying is what he does best—it's "his native language." The word for *lie* in the Greek is *pseudos,* which means falsehood or "an attempt to deceive." We attach the prefix *pseudo* in the English language to convey the thought of a counterfeit, a false look-alike.

And that's exactly what we get when we listen to Satan's lies and settle for less than God's best: pseudo-Christianity, pseudo-grace. Satan usually doesn't try to make us swallow a blatant lie—he's too smart for that. Instead, he just doctors the truth for his own purpose, which is to keep us as far away from God as possible.

"Look at what you've done," he w*hiss*pers. "How could God ever forgive you?" He twists the truth of sin into a bludgeon of guilt and shame and beats us with it. "You're no good, you're no good, you're no good…baby, you're no good."

If we let him, he's gonna sing it again. Because every time we listen to his lying lyrics, we take another step backward, away from the Living Room. Away from the closeness our hearts yearn for.

Now you may not struggle with the lies I've described above. Perhaps you've never experienced the lonely alienation of such doubt and guilt. In fact, your basic relationship and standing with God may be secure and unshakable. But beware! Satan can use other circumstances just as effectively to keep you from drawing close to God.

Take busyness, for example.

Anne Wilson Schaef tells about a flier advertising new twelve-step meetings forming in the San Francisco Bay area. The meetings were especially for workaholics. At the bottom of the flier was this blurb: "If you are too busy to attend these meetings, we'll understand."[3]

I wonder if God understands when we're too busy to attend to his presence in our lives. Or too tired. Or too embarrassed to admit we've done something he would disapprove of.

Make no mistake. Satan enjoys using our hectic schedules, stressed bodies, and emotional upsets in his efforts to put up barriers to our intimacy with God. That's why we need to take a close look at any thought, feeling, or activity that diminishes our appetite for intimacy with God.

SPIRITUAL SNICKERS BARS

Teri Myers was my pastor's wife when my family lived in Grants Pass, Oregon. She was, and still is, a dear friend and a spiritual mentor, a true picture of a Mary heart in a Martha world. As I've watched her walk with God over the years, I've grown more eager for a deeper walk of my own. But Teri's the first to admit that it isn't always easy to stay close to the Lord.

She tells the story of having company over for dinner one night. She'd worked hard all day on a beautiful meal—four courses and a fancy dessert. It was going to be wonderful. But somewhere around the middle of the afternoon, Teri realized she was hungry.

"I'd been so busy cooking and cleaning," she says, "I had completely missed lunch." But it was only four o'clock and the guests weren't due until six. "I always kept a hidden stash of Snickers bars," she says with a grin. So she grabbed a couple of candy bars and sat down to rest, enjoying her clean living room and beautifully set table.

"It did the trick! My stomach wasn't growling anymore. I was able to take my shower, do my hair, and get dressed with plenty of time to spare."

It wasn't until Teri sat down to dinner that she discovered the problem. "There I was with that wonderful dinner I'd worked all day to prepare, but my appetite was gone!" The midafternoon snack had taken the edge off her hunger. She ended up picking at her plate as she watched everyone else dig in, enjoying their meal.

"The Lord spoke to me at that moment," Teri says. "He showed me that we often fill our lives with spiritual Snickers bars—things like friends, books, and shopping. They may be good things, completely innocent things—but not when they take the edge off our hunger for God."

Teri's illustration has stayed with me for years because it applies so aptly to

my own life. I constantly fight the tendency to fill the God-shaped hole he created in me with fluffy stuff. I don't like loneliness, so I fill the space with phone
calls and social events and trips to the mall—but loneliness, as my friend Jeanne
Mayo puts it, can be "God's call to fellowship with him." I don't like quietness,
so I fill up the silence with sitcoms and talk shows, Christian music and CNN—
but it was in the quiet of the night that Samuel heard God's voice.

We were designed to be close to God. Just as our bodies hunger and thirst
for food and drink, our spirits hunger and thirst for his presence. But just as it's
possible to bloat our bodies with empty calories, we can find ways to pacify our
spiritual cravings without really getting the nourishment we need. We can fill up
with spiritual Snickers bars while all the time our spirits are withering for want of
real food.

If you're having a little trouble feeling close to God—or even wanting to
draw close—you might want to consider what activities you are using to fill the
empty places of your life. What's taking the edge off of your hunger for him?

Then again, it could be that you just need to start "eating" the good things
of the Lord to find out how spiritually hungry you really are. You see, spiritual
hunger and thirst don't work the same way as our physical needs. When our
physical body feels hunger pains, we eat and our hunger is satisfied. But spiritually speaking, it isn't until we "eat" that we realize how famished we are. As we
feast at God's table, something strange happens. We get hungrier. Thirstier. We
want more! We have to have more.

"Our souls are elastic," Kent Hughes writes in his book *Liberating Ministry
from the Success Syndrome.* "There are no limits to possible capacity. We can
always open ourselves to hold more and more of his fullness. The walls can
always stretch further; the roof can always rise higher; the floor can always hold
more. The more we receive of his fullness, the more we can receive!"[4]

Once you've tasted the Living Room Intimacy Jesus offers, you'll find nothing else will satisfy. For even Snickers bars taste flat in comparison to the sweet-
ness of the Lord's presence. When you've sampled the best of the best, you'll be
willing to skip the junk food this world offers in order to have a real sit-down
meal with the Savior.

"Taste," as the psalmist says, "and see that the LORD is good!" (Psalm 34:8).

MAKING ROOM FOR THE SAVIOR

Few things have whetted my hunger for God like the discipleship course I took back in 1987. While other people may struggle with worldly temptations, my struggle has always been in the area of spiritual disciplines. My devotional life has been haphazard at best. Because I hadn't developed the habit of a quiet time as a child, when the busyness of adulthood came, I found it difficult to find time alone with the Lord.

Some of you may be aghast at such a thought. Your devotional life runs like clockwork. You find it impossible to make it through the day without time alone with God.

If that is true for you, may I tell you how blessed you are? It has taken me nearly twenty years to come to this discipline, and even then, it has been a gift of grace, not an accomplishment of my own making.

Until I took the Navigator's 2:7 Course, I didn't even know what I was missing. There are many wonderful discipleship programs available, and I don't highlight this one for any reason except that it happened to be the one our church used. It gave me the discipleship tools I needed and some necessary accountability as well.

The class was wonderful. My spirit began to grow and thrive as the soil of my heart was tilled deep and fed by the Word of God. But then my Martha-like perfectionist tendencies kicked in, causing me to approach my devotional time as another duty to perform. I loved the feeling I got as I checked off chapters in my Bible reading and conquered another memory verse. To be honest, much of my motivation came from my competitive nature. I wanted to be the star pupil, one of those disgusting teacher's pets.

Robert Boyd Munger's article "My Heart Christ's Home" changed all that. Through the simple analogy he suggested, I discovered what it meant to have a Mary heart toward God. Suddenly my eyes were open to what true devotion is.

It is not a duty. It is a delight.

It is not an exercise in piety. It is a privilege.

And it is not so much a visit as it is a homecoming.

"Without question one of the most remarkable Christian doctrines is that

Jesus Christ Himself through the presence of the Holy Spirit will actually enter a heart, settle down and be at home there," Munger says. "[Jesus] came into the darkness of my heart and turned on the light. He built a fire in the cold hearth and banished the chill. He started music where there had been stillness and He filled the emptiness with His own loving, wonderful fellowship."

Munger goes on to tell how he showed Christ around the house of his heart, inviting him to "settle down here and be perfectly at home," welcoming him room by room. Together they visited the library of his mind—"a very small room with very thick walls." They peered into the dining room of his appetites and desires. They spent a little time in the workshop where his talents and skills were kept, and the rumpus room of "certain associations and friendships, activities and amusements." They even poked their heads into the hall closet filled with dead, rotting things he had managed to hoard.

As Munger described each room, they reflected my heart as well. But it was his depiction of the drawing room that would forever change the way I viewed my time with the Lord.

> We walked next into the drawing room. This room was rather intimate and comfortable. I liked it. It had a fireplace, overstuffed chairs, a bookcase, sofa, and a quiet atmosphere.
>
> He also seemed pleased with it. He said, "This is indeed a delightful room. Let us come here often. It is secluded and quiet and we can have fellowship together."
>
> Well, naturally, as a young Christian I was thrilled. I could not think of anything I would rather do than have a few minutes apart with Christ in intimate comradeship.
>
> He promised, "I will be here every morning early. Meet with Me here and we will start the day together." So, morning after morning, I would come downstairs to the drawing room and He would take a book of the Bible...open it and then we would read together. He would tell me of its riches and unfold to me its truths.... They were wonderful hours together. In fact, we called the drawing room the "withdrawing room." It was a period when we had our quiet time together.

But little by little, under the pressure of many responsibilities, this time began to be shortened.... I began to miss a day now and then.... I would miss it two days in a row and often more.

I remember one morning when I was in a hurry.... As I passed the drawing room, the door was ajar. Looking in I saw a fire in the fireplace and the Lord sitting there.... "Blessed Master, forgive me. Have You been here all these mornings?"

"Yes," He said, "I told you I would be here every morning to meet with you." Then I was even more ashamed. He had been faithful in spite of my faithlessness. I asked His forgiveness and He readily forgave me....

He said, "The trouble with you is this: You have been thinking of the quiet time, of the Bible study and prayer time, as a factor in your own spiritual progress, but you have forgotten that this hour means something to Me also."[5]

What an amazing thought—that Christ wants to spend quality time with me. That he looks forward to our time together and misses me when I don't show up. Once that message started sinking into my heart, I started looking at my devotional time in a whole new way—not as a ritual, but as a relationship.

And a relationship doesn't just happen. It has to be nurtured, protected, and loved.

THE COMFORTS OF HOME

The place Mary found at Jesus' feet is the same place available to you and me. It's a place where we can be comfortable, where we can kick off our shoes and let down our hair. It's a place of transparency and vulnerability; a place where we are completely known yet completely loved. It is truly a place called home.

If we love him and obey his teachings, Jesus says in John 14:23, God will actually come and live with us. "My Father will love him," he said of those who follow him, "and we will come to him and *make our home* with him" (emphasis mine).

And it goes both ways. Jesus not only wants to be at home in us; he also

Creating a With-Drawing Room

There is something special about a sacred space consecrated to God—a prayer closet set aside especially for your quiet times. But if you don't have a lot of extra room at home, consider the following ideas for creating a prayer closet wherever you are:

- *Emilie Barnes,* a writer and speaker who has inspired thousands of Christian women toward beautiful living, keeps a special prayer basket on hand to help with her devotions. In it she keeps (1) her Bible, (2) a daily devotional or other inspirational reading, (3) a small box of tissues "for the days I cry in joy or pain," (4) a pen for journaling or writing notes, and (5) a few pretty cards in case she feels moved to write a note to someone she's praying for. For Emilie, seeing the basket is both an invitation and a reminder to spend time with the Lord. And because it's portable, she can take it anywhere.[6]

- *Robin Jones Gunn,* a popular Christian novelist, began lighting a candle to set apart her prayer times after a friend made her feel especially welcome by lighting a candle for their visit. "Sometimes the house is still dark and quiet when I sit down and light the candle for my quiet time. Other times life is in full swing around me, but my corner becomes a quiet place of intimate conversation. When my family sees the candle lit, they know to leave mom alone for however long I sit there, opening my heart to the Lord and listening to Him. I've noticed that after I blow out the candle and enter the frenzy of the rest of the day, a sweet fragrance lingers in my house and in my soul."[7]

- For years, *Gwen Shamblin,* a Christian weight-loss advisor, has wakened in the middle of the night to spend her quiet time. To "preplan for these rendezvous with God," she keeps a heating pad tucked under the couch cushion, with a blanket and her Bible on top. "I get all snuggled up, then open my Bible and converse with God. They are times I look forward to."[8]

When you pray, go into your room, close the door
and pray to your Father, who is unseen.
Then your Father, who sees what is done in secret, will reward you.

MATTHEW 6:6

wants us to make our home in him. "God wants to be your dwelling place," Max Lucado writes in *The Great House of God.*

> He has no interest in being a weekend getaway or a Sunday bungalow or a summer cottage. Don't consider using God as a vacation cabin or an eventual retirement home. He wants you under his roof now and always. He wants to be your mailing address, your point of reference; he wants to be your home.[9]

What a beautiful, gracious offer from the Lord of hosts. It's hard to imagine saying no to the opportunity to live in God and rest in him. But we can—and so often we do. Isaiah 28 gives a vivid picture of what happens when we refuse. "This is the resting place, let the weary rest," God told the Israelites through his prophet Isaiah (28:12). "This is the place of repose," he said, inviting them to be at home with him.

But the Israelites would not listen, according to Isaiah. Instead of making God their dwelling place, they insisted on a more independent living arrangement. And what happened then is the very picture of what happens to us when we refuse the Father's offer of at-home intimacy. Isaiah says in verse 13:

> So then, the word of the LORD to them will become:
> Do and do, do and do,
> rule on rule, rule on rule;
> a little here, a little there.

Matthew Henry, writing about these verses, says that the Israelites "would not heed...they went on in a road of external performances.... The prophet's preaching was continually sounding in their ears, but that was all; it made no impression upon them; they had the letter of the precept, but no experience of the power and spirit of it; *it was continually beating upon them, but it beat nothing into them*"[10] (emphasis mine).

Sound familiar, Martha? It does to me. When we refuse God's offer of grace-filled rest in the Living Room, the only alternative is the tyranny of works—

which, as we have seen, doesn't work! We will be driven to do more and more—more service projects, more committee chairmanships, more spiritual extra-curricular activities—trying to win God's approval. And still we will fail, because what the Father really wants is for us to find our identity—our "mailing address" as Lucado puts it—in him and him alone.

HOW TO LIVE TOGETHER

Jesus came to show us the way to the Father's house. Instead of making a once-a-year visit to the Holy of Holies, we're invited to dwell there. To make our home in God's throne room—or, if you prefer, his Living Room.

But practically speaking, how is that possible? Jesus gives us a hint in John's gospel.

"Remain in me," Jesus says in John 15:4, "and I will remain in you."

The *King James* translation of that verse makes the relationship even clearer. "Abide in me," Jesus says. And *abide* means to live or dwell.

Dwell in me, he promises. And I will dwell in you.

Then, to give us an even better idea of what being at home with God really means, Jesus uses a word picture so simple a child can grasp it, though it may take a lifetime to implement.

"See this vine?" I can hear Jesus ask, holding one up for inspection. "See this branch? See where they are connected? Well, that's the way it is with you and me."

"I am the vine" was what he actually said. "You are the branches. If a man remains in me and I in him, he will bear much fruit; apart from me you can do nothing" (John 15:5).

All our "do and do," our "rules on rules," will never accomplish what Jesus can when we let him have his way in our life. But in order for that to happen we must be *connected* to him. It's not enough simply to be associated. To be acquainted. We have to be spiritually grafted on—to draw our life from him, to be so closely attached that we would wither and die if we were cut off.

I missed that point for a long time. I had spent so much of my life concentrating on the "fruit" of my own personal holiness, that I missed out on the connection, the sweet intimacy of being attached to the Vine. And as a result, what I tried to do was as ludicrous as an apple tree branch trying to produce apples by its own effort.

"Be good, be good. Do good, do good," the broken branch chants as it lies on the orchard grass.

"That apple should be popping out anytime," says the helpless, lifeless stick.

But that isn't how it works. It's the tree, not the branch, that determines the fruit. The tree is the life source. The branch has no power of its own. But once it gets connected, once that sap gets flowing and those leaves start growing, that insignificant little twig will find itself loaded with fruit. And it didn't have to do anything—except abide.

STAYING CLOSE

My relationship with God works the same way. My sole responsibility is keeping my connection to Jesus Christ solid and secure. How is that done? It's really not that complicated. As trite as it may sound, the formula for intimacy with God remains the same today as it has always been:

PRAYER + the WORD + TIME = INTIMACY with GOD

We'll talk further in chapter 7 about developing a quiet time, but for now let's take a moment to look at these necessary components of a close relationship with God.

First of all, what is *prayer?* There are entire books written on the subject, but when it comes down to this essential first factor, prayer is simply talking to God. Prayer is my heart crying out to the Lord for guidance and wisdom, for my own needs as well as the needs of others. As I focus my heart on him, prayer allows me to express my love through praise, to declare my absolute dependence on him alone. Then, as I wait before the Lord, he reveals his heart to me.

One of the most precious ways God expresses his love for us is through his Word, the Bible, which is the second essential factor in intimacy. The Hebrew word for *Bible* is *mikra*, which means "the calling out of God."[11]

Isn't that wonderful? We don't have to wonder what God thinks, what he feels about certain topics, because to a large extent he has already told us through Scripture. Better yet, we don't have to wonder whether he loves us or not. According to my dictionary, the Old English word for *gospel* is *godspell*. God spells out his love for the whole world to see. It's right there in his Word.

"Fear not, for I have redeemed you," the Lord tells us in Isaiah 43:1,4. "I have summoned you by name.... You are precious and honored in my sight...because I love you." We are a chosen people. Made holy. Deeply and dearly loved by God. How do I know that? I hear God's voice telling me, "calling out" to me, every time I open his Word.

Time is an essential factor in Living Room Intimacy for a purely practical reason. If I don't take time to pray, there will be no real communication in our relationship. If I don't take time to read God's Word, I won't hear his loving call.

Finding God's Will

Have you ever wondered how other people have learned to discern God's will? George Mueller, a nineteenth-century English pastor who was known for his life of prayer and his close walk with God, once shared this simple method for determining God's will through prayer and the Word:

1. "I seek at the beginning to get my heart into such a state that it has no will of its own in regard to a given matter....

2. "Having done this, I do not leave the result to feeling or simple impression. If so, I make myself liable to great delusions.

3. "I seek the Will of the Spirit of God through, or in connection with, the Word of God.... If the Holy Ghost guides us at all, He will do it according to the Scriptures and never contrary to them.

4. "Next I take into account providential circumstances. These often plainly indicate God's Will in connection with His Word and Spirit.

5. "I ask God in prayer to reveal His Will to me aright.

6. "Thus, (1) through prayer to God, (2) the study of the Word, and (3) reflection, I come to a deliberate judgment according to the best of my ability and knowledge, and if my mind is thus at peace, and continues so after two or three more petitions, I proceed accordingly."[12]

Whether you turn to the right or to the left, your ears will hear a voice behind you, saying, "This is the way; walk in it."

ISAIAH 30:21

And if I don't make time to be alone with Jesus, our relationship will suffer, because time is integral to any relationship.

I love the way Kent Hughes describes the intimate impact of spending time with God. "Think of it this way," Hughes writes. "Our lives are like photographic plates, and prayer is like a time exposure to God. As we expose ourselves to God for a half hour, an hour, perhaps two hours a day, his image is imprinted more and more upon us. More and more we absorb the image of his character, his love, his wisdom, his way of dealing with life and people."[13]

That's what I want. That's what I need. And that's what I receive when I spend time in God's Word and in prayer. I get more of Jesus and, in the process, a little less of me.

MAINTAINING INTIMACY

God longs to make his home in us. And he longs for us to make our home in him. Think of it. Christ "in us" (1 John 4:13). Our lives "hidden with Christ in God" (Colossians 3:3). What an incredible, intimate entangling of humanity and divinity!

There is only one thing that can stop such Living Room Intimacy, and that is our own sin. For though there is nothing we can do to attain our salvation, there is much to be done to maintain our connection to the Vine. Because sin interrupts the life-flow we need to grow, we must do all we can to maintain a pure heart before God.

Here's something I'm learning to do on a regular basis—something I've found that makes a big difference in the level of intimacy I enjoy with Christ.

I call it "spiritual housekeeping."

We tend to suffer from dropsy around our house. You know the affliction? We come in the door and drop whatever we have on the floor. On the next trip, we drop some more. This makes for a quite messy house and a very frustrated housekeeper. Which is me.

But spiritually speaking, I tend to do the same thing. I'll drop an unkind word here, spill a negative attitude there, let a resentment lie where it fell in a corner. It isn't long before the clutter of sin is knee high and my heart is paralyzed, not knowing where to start cleaning up the mess and feeling far away from God.

Not a great way to live, I'm sure you'll agree—either in a house or in a heart. But I'm learning. I'm getting better.

Now, instead of letting sin pile up, I try to do my housekeeping every day. My goal is obedience—avoiding sin by following God's commands. But when I mess up, I try to choose repentance. I tell God I'm sorry and look for ways to make amends for any damage I've caused. I consciously give the Lord those things I just can't fix and resolve to do better, depending on God to make it possible.

Conscious repentance leads to unconscious holiness. That phrase, gleaned from the writings of Oswald Chambers, has done incredible things in my walk with God. It has lifted me from the orchard floor and grafted me to the tree.

Before, I'd tried to produce the fruit of holiness on my own, with little result except failure and self-condemnation. But when I realized that holiness was a work of the Spirit in my life, that my responsibility was to live connected to the Vine, I was able to abandon my own fruitless trying and focus on staying close to the One who gives me life.

Intimacy with God? It's pretty simple, really.

It's not a pillar we sit on; it's a house we live in.

It's not a list of dos and don'ts; it's a branch staying connected to the Vine.

It's not striving to know God, but realizing that our Father longs to know us. And it's free for the taking—at least for you and me.

But we must never forget—it cost Jesus his very life.

6

Kitchen Service

Whatever your hand finds to do, do it with all your might.

ECCLESIASTES 9:10

"I know who you are."

The Chinese president's eyes were calm and unflustered as he spoke in careful English. His comment interrupted the flow of conversation that had carried the room for most of the afternoon.

Don Argue looked at the man, uncertain what he meant.

The year was 1998. As president of the National Association of Evangelicals, Dr. Argue had been invited to meet with the president of the People's Republic of China, Jiang Zemin, to discuss China's stance on religious freedom. Tens of thousands of Christians were being persecuted for their faith, with thousands more in prison or already executed. Dr. Argue had earlier presented the logic of allowing Christians to practice their faith. "They will be your best workers," he had told the president. "They are honest and trustworthy." But the conversation had moved on from there, swallowed up in political posturing and diplomatic niceties.

"I know who you are," President Jiang now repeated, his voice low as he bent toward Dr. Argue. With the help of an interpreter he shared this story: "When I was a youth, I was very sick and in a hospital. One of your people, a Christian nurse, cared for me. Even at the end of a long and busy day, she would not leave until all of our needs were met."

President Jiang smiled and nodded.

"I know who you are."[1]

TEMPLATES OF CHRISTIANITY

Of all the identifying marks of a Christian, Jesus said love would be the thing that gives us away. "By this all men will know that you are my disciples," he said, "if you love one another" (John 13:35). *Agape* is to be our signature—the unconditional, never-ending love of God flowing through and out of our lives. A feel-good *phileo* kind of love isn't enough. We need a love that loves "in spite of" and "because of." In spite of rejection, hardship, or persecution, we love. Because of the great compassion God lavished upon us, we share it with our world—both in words and in sacrificial service.

We've been filled with great treasure for one purpose: to be spilled.

Christ illustrated this *agape* love to his disciples by washing their feet. "As I have loved you, so you must love one another," Jesus told the group of men in John 13:34, their freshly laundered toes a gentle witness to his words.

What Jesus did must have shocked the disciples. The *Midrash* taught that no Hebrew, even a slave, could be commanded to wash feet. The streets and roads of Palestine were rugged back then, unsurfaced and unclean. William Barclay says, "In dry weather they were inches deep in dust and in wet they were liquid mud."[2] Add the fact that most people wore sandals, a simple flap of leather fastened to the foot by a few straps, and foot washing was a dirty job, to say the least.

Though disciples, by tradition, attended to their favorite rabbi's many needs, they never considered such a filthy task. Nor was it expected. It simply wasn't done.

So when Jesus bent his knee to serve his followers, it was a graphic display of humility. Their Teacher became the lowest of the low. Then he invited—no, commanded—them to do the same. "It is noteworthy that only once did Jesus say that he was leaving his disciples an example, and that was when he washed their feet," says J. Oswald Sanders.[3]

Kitchen Service, you see, isn't optional for Christians. We're supposed to spend a good part of our time following our Lord's example. We're supposed to serve others and show love to them—and, in the process, to represent Jesus to the world around us. Unfortunately, as the world well knows, it's easy for Christians to forget what we're here for. It's easy to fall into the hypocrisy of talking one way and living another way—or to get so involved with our religious activities that we neglect to reach out to those around us.

Mahatma Gandhi once said, "If Christians lived according to their faith, there would be no more Hindus left in India."[4] This great leader of the Indian nation was fascinated at the thought of knowing Christ. But when he met Christians, he felt let down. Unfortunately, the world is filled with people who feel the same. They are intrigued by the claims of Christ, but they shrink back because of disappointment with his offspring.

"Don't look at people," we might protest. "Look at Jesus." But while that may be true, the sobering truth remains: Whether we like it or not, we're the only Jesus some will ever see. Dwight L. Moody put it this way: "Of one hundred men, one will read the Bible; the ninety-nine will read the Christian."[5]

The apostle Paul understood the responsibility of representing Christ to others. More than nine times in the New Testament, Paul wrote something to the effect of "Follow me as I follow Christ." Here are a few:

- "I urge you to imitate me" (1 Corinthians 4:16).
- "Whatever you have learned or received or heard from me, or seen in me—put it into practice" (Philippians 4:9).
- "Follow my example, as I follow the example of Christ" (1 Corinthians 11:1).

In verses such as these, Paul was not only encouraging people to replicate *his* life, but to live life in such a way that they themselves became templates of Christianity. Paul says in 1 Thessalonians 1:6-7: "You became imitators of us and of the Lord.... And so *you* became a model to all the believers" (emphasis mine).

There were no Gideon Bibles in the New Testament church. There were no Bibles at all, except for the Hebrew scriptures. The only evidence of this new and living way came in the form of the walking, breathing, living epistles that filled the young church's meeting rooms and spilled out into the street.

"You are a letter from Christ...," Paul reminded the Christians at Corinth, "written not with ink but with the Spirit of the living God, not on tablets of stones but on tablets of human hearts" (2 Corinthians 3:3).

You are a letter that is known and read by everyone, Paul said.

The same is true of us today. We are God's love letter to the world. We were set apart for a purpose—to communicate his glory to a lost and dying world.

FRUITFUL LIVING

I once heard of a man who loved experimenting in his garden. He was always coming up with a hybrid this and a hybrid that. His crowning achievement was a tree he'd pieced together. Part plum, part apricot, part peach, and part prune—it was the craziest mixed-up tree you ever saw. But that tree had a major problem.

Oh, it was alive. It grew fine. The leaves were there. Every once in a while in the spring he would even get a blossom. But it never did bear any fruit.

John the Baptist noticed the same problem in the lives of many of his Jewish followers. He didn't mince words in warning them about the lack of fruit in their lives. He didn't mix pears and kumquats either.

You identify a tree by the fruit it produces, John said—and a tree that doesn't produce is worth nothing at all. "Therefore bear fruits worthy of repentance, and do not begin to say to yourselves, 'We have Abraham as our father.' For I say to you that God is able to raise up children to Abraham from these stones" (Luke 3:8, NKJV).

John was chastising the Jews for believing their DNA—their "root stock" was enough to please God. It wasn't enough to be sons of Abraham, he said. They also needed to live like chosen people—to bear fruit worthy of their lineage. If they wouldn't do it, God was prepared to find people who would. "The ax is already at the root of the trees, and every tree that does not produce good fruit will be cut down and thrown into the fire" (Luke 3:9).

In the same respect, it isn't enough to call ourselves Christians. We must *live* like Christians. "Not everyone who says to me, 'Lord, Lord,' will enter the kingdom of heaven," Jesus once said, speaking of the barren lives of many, "but only he who does the will of my Father who is in heaven" (Matthew 7:21).

Apple trees bear apples. Plum trees bear plums. If we call ourselves Christians, then our lives should be unmistakably and obviously Christlike.

FRUIT HAPPENS

Throughout the Word of God, the analogy of fruit is used. All four Gospels include Christ's picture of the Vine and the branches. Out of the twenty-seven

books in the New Testament, fifteen mention the kinds of fruit we are to have in
our lives, including:

- *The fruit of our lips:* "Let us continually offer to God a sacrifice of
  praise—the fruit of lips that confess his name" (Hebrews 13:15).
- *The fruit of our deeds:* "That you may live a life worthy of the Lord and
  may please him in every way: bearing fruit in every good work, growing
  in the knowledge of God" (Colossians 1:10).
- *The fruit of our attitudes:* "But the fruit of the Spirit is love, joy, peace,
  patience, kindness, goodness, faithfulness, gentleness and self-control"
  (Galatians 5:22-23).

So how can I make sure my life is producing this kind of fruit?

It's not really that difficult. You see, fruit isn't something you can sit down
and manufacture in your life. Fruit *happens.* You get connected to the Vine and
pretty soon you've got zucchini—tons and tons of zucchini.

So much zucchini you just have to share!

As we "abide" in the intimate relationship with Christ that we talked about
in chapter 5, something incredible happens. We begin loving as we never loved
before. Our lives change, and we become examples worth imitating.

We begin producing fruit. Juicy, lusciously lovely, lip-smacking-delicious
fruit. Fruit in our lives that tells the world who we are and what our God is like.
Even when we're stuck doing dishes in the Kitchen.

JOY IN THE KITCHEN

Nicholas Herman was born in the Lorraine region of France in the middle of the
seventeenth century. Largely uneducated, he worked briefly as a footman, then a
soldier. At the age of eighteen, Nicholas experienced a spiritual awakening, and
from that moment on his life had one goal: "to walk as in God's presence."

In 1666, Nicholas joined a Carmelite monastery in Paris. There he served as
a lay brother until he died at eighty years of age, "full of love and years and honored by all who knew him."

Perhaps you'd recognize Nicholas by his Carmelite name: Brother Lawrence.
A group of letters he wrote during his lifetime were collected into a book called
The Practice of the Presence of God. Though Brother Lawrence never meant his

correspondence to be published, this tiny book has sold millions, challenging centuries of Christians to a closer walk with God.

It is a picture of a life devoted to God—a truly fruitful life. A picture of a Mary heart in a Martha world.

More particularly, Brother Lawrence's influential book beautifully illustrates how the fruit-making process is supposed to operate in our lives. In uncomplicated but striking detail he shows that it's not just what we do for Christ that matters, but how we go about it. He didn't learn the secret of fruitfulness sitting high upon a pole like Simeon the Stylite. He learned it in a kitchen. Yeah. A kitchen.

When Brother Lawrence joined the monastery, he had fully expected to spend his days in prayer and meditation. Instead, he was assigned to cooking and cleanup, a position for which he admitted a "great aversion."

Yet once Brother Lawrence decided to "do everything there for the love of God, and with prayer...for his grace to do his work well," he found his own Kitchen Service a joy and an avenue to a closer walk with God. He wrote:

> The time of business does not with me differ from the time of prayer,
> and in the noise and clatter of my kitchen, while several persons are at
> the same time calling for different things, I possess God in as great tran-
> quillity as if I were upon my knees at the blessed sacrament.[6]

What a goal! To be so in tune with the presence of God that washing dishes becomes an act of worship. That the moments of our lives, no matter how mundane, become aflame with the divine.

When Jesus rebuked Martha, remember, he wasn't rebuking her act. He was rebuking her attitude. "He blamed Martha, not for her attentive service of love," author Charles Grierson says, "but for allowing that service to irritate, agitate, and absorb her."[7]

Service without spirituality is exhausting and hopeless. But in the same respect, spirituality without service is barren and selfish. We need to unite the two and do it all "as unto the Lord."

When we do that, something wonderful happens to our work in the Kitchen. Sinks turn into sanctuaries. Mops swab holy ground. And daily chores

that used to bore us or wear us down become opportunities to express our gratitude—selfless avenues for his grace.

SERVING LIKE JESUS

Our sanctification, as Brother Lawrence once said, "does not depend upon
changing our works, but in doing that for God's sake which we commonly do for
our own."[8]

For three and a half years, Jesus of Nazareth did just that. He ministered out
of everyday life. Instead of renting a coliseum or building a synagogue, then

God's Kitchen Patrol

Do you want to be in service for the Lord but aren't sure what to do? Maybe the following tips will spark an idea in your own heart for ways you can serve God as you
serve his children. Once you get started, you'll find the opportunities are endless.

- *Join God's Secret Service.* Find ways to serve anonymously—send an
  encouraging note, leave a plate of cookies on a doorstep, sponsor a kid to
  camp, pay someone's electric bill.
- *Give a cup of cold water in his name.* Volunteer for drink crew at the
  Special Olympics. Hand out Popsicles in the park on hot days. Sponsor a
  refreshment stand for thirsty travelers at a nearby rest stop.
- *Look for your "angel unaware."* God often puts a needy person in our lives
  he wants us to serve. Instead of resisting, accept that person as a "divine
  assignment" and love him or her as unto the Lord.
- *Comfort with the comfort you've received.* Often we serve best in an area
  where we've experienced pain. If you're a cancer survivor, you can offer
  hope and support to someone newly diagnosed. If you've been bereaved,
  you have words the grieving need to hear.

Whatever your hand finds to do, do it with all your might.

ECCLESIASTES 9:10

waiting for people to come to him, Jesus went to them. He took time to meet the needs of people. Our Savior stopped midstride to heal the woman with a bleeding disorder. He cleared his afternoon and made room on his lap for little kids. Jesus confronted religious hypocrites and comforted lost souls—each one as the opportunity arose.

And it is exactly this kind of spontaneous ministry that God entrusts to you and me. "He seems to do nothing of Himself which He can possibly delegate to His creatures," C. S. Lewis writes. "He commands us to do slowly and blunderingly what He could do perfectly and in the twinkling of an eye."[9]

To trembling, inadequate saints like you and me, God gives the ministry of reconciliation—bringing humanity back home to God. A mighty task, yes. But it's not impossible when we take it one day at a time and follow the example that Jesus set—the example Brother Lawrence himself imitated.

I see three simple principles of ministry in the life of Christ that can show us how to live our lives in fruitful Kitchen Service.

- Jesus ministered as he *went on his way.*
- Jesus ministered as he *went out of his way.*
- Jesus ministered in *all kinds of ways.*

ON OUR WAY

First of all, Jesus was available. He ministered as he was needed—*as he went on his way.* He delivered the demon-possessed man as he passed through the Gadarenes (Matthew 8:28-34). On the walk to Capernaum, he used the time to teach his disciples (Mark 9:33-37). While he was returning from Decapolis, he took advantage of opportunities to heal the sick and raise the dead (Luke 8:40-56).

Even the incident that forms the centerpiece of this book—the story of Mary and Martha told in Luke 10:38-42—took place while Jesus was "on the way." Instead of pressing on to Jerusalem, where he was headed, Jesus apparently made an unscheduled stop in Bethany when, as verse 38 tells us, "a woman named Martha opened her home to him."

This is a God who comes to us. When we open our lives, he enters our hearts and dwells within us. Then he invites us to join him on his journey—for that's what serving God is all about. God doesn't come to sign our guest book. He comes to make us his own.

"Jesus watched to see where the Father was at work and joined Him,"[10] Henry Blackaby reminds us in *Experiencing God*. Jesus did nothing of his own initiative, according to John 5:19. Instead the Son did "only what he [saw] his Father doing."

That is the secret of holy Kitchen Service. Instead of expecting God to acquiesce to our plans, dreams, and schemes—or frantically trying to impress him with our efforts on his behalf—we simply need to "watch to see where God is working and join Him!"[11]

When we do that, Kitchen Service becomes a delight rather than a distraction. It becomes a natural outflow of our relationship with God rather than one more duty to keep us from what we really want to do. When we minister *on the way*, every day can become an adventure!

I'll never forget driving home one winter from a youth pastor's retreat. Driving across eastern Montana, we encountered a detour that took us off the rural highway and onto a snow-packed dirt road. Mile after mile we drove, the only car on the vast Montana plain, with only a barbed-wire fence to outline the way.

"I think we're lost," I said.

"We're not lost," John said. "Go back to sleep."

So being the obedient wife I am, I did. I don't know how much farther we went, but I awoke when the car finally slowed and turned into a driveway—the only driveway, I learned later, that John had seen in the last fifty miles.

I rubbed my eyes and sat up in time to see a small, pink-and-white-oxidized single-wide trailer leaning slightly into the wind. I looked over at John as he pulled the car to a stop.

"We're lost," he admitted.

But we weren't lost at all.

The old man who came out to greet us looked a bit disappointed when John crawled out of the car. It was his birthday, you see. And he'd hoped against hope that the car he'd heard in the driveway was his son coming to visit from Minnesota.

But he seemed to cheer up as we stayed and chatted for a while, giving him as a birthday present a small, stuffed animal I'd bought on the trip. There was a tear in his eye but a smile on his face when he shook John's hand and pointed the way back to the main road.

I've found that when we're willing to serve like Jesus did—while we're *on the way*—divine appointments like that start popping up everywhere. And if we'll take the time to stop and listen, we may find our destination, even when we thought we were lost.

GOING OUT OF OUR WAY

In the book *Love Adds a Little Chocolate,* Linda Andersen writes:

> Duty can pack an adequate sack lunch, but love may decide to enclose a little love note inside…. Obligation sends the children to bed on time, but love tucks the covers in around their necks and passes out kisses and hugs (even to teenagers!)…. Duty gets offended quickly if it isn't appreciated, but love learns to laugh a lot and to work for the sheer joy of doing it. Obligation can pour a glass of milk, but quite often, love adds a little chocolate.[12]

That description of love is a beautiful description of the way Jesus led his life. Again and again, he went beyond the call of duty and acted out of love. He *went out of his way* to minister—and I believe he wants us to do the same.

Jesus must have been exhausted that long-ago evening we see sketched in Matthew 14. All day long, the crowds had pressed in with their needs. I have a feeling Jesus didn't mind that. He could still see the sparkling eyes of the little lame girl as she took her first step. He could still hear the joyful cries of the crowd as she grabbed his hand and began to dance. He could still feel the squeeze of the old knotted hand as an elderly man thanked him for making him see. It was the very thing he had come to do—"to heal the brokenhearted, to proclaim liberty to the captives" (Isaiah 61:1, NKJV).

But who would heal Jesus' broken heart? His cousin John had been executed just days before, and Jesus grieved. The sparkling city of Tiberius glowed that evening across Galilee. Torches lit the early dusk, illuminating King Herod's palace. Within its walls was a platter, Jesus had been told. A platter holding his dear friend's head.

Now, as the evening came on, Jesus wanted to be alone. He needed to be alone. Only the Father could comfort this overwhelming sadness and soothe this bone-weary exhaustion.

"There he is!" Voices echoed across the water as a long stream of people made their way around the lake. The disciples groaned. They had seen the pain in their Master's eyes. They, too, were weary from the demands of the day. Surely they deserved a little rest.

"Let's send them away," one of the disciples suggested to Jesus.

But Jesus said no.

Instead of sending the people away, Jesus "had compassion on them and healed their sick" (Matthew 14:14). He moved past his own neediness and loved them. He did what he could do to help them. And then, if that wasn't enough, he provided dinner for the hungry crowd. Fish and chips for five thousand.

The word Matthew uses for *compassion* in this passage is *splagchnizomai*. It means that Jesus didn't respond to the people out of duty; he ministered to them because he felt their distress. So deep, so profound was his compassion, his *splagchnizomai*, Jesus literally felt it in his gut. He laid aside his hurt so he could pick up their pain. He laid aside his wishes so he could become their one Desire. He laid aside his agenda so he could meet all of their needs.

And that is the essence of ministry that goes out of its way. It puts self aside and reaches out in true compassion.

"True love hurts," Mother Teresa once said. "It always has to hurt." And elsewhere she has written pointedly, "If you really love one another, you will not be able to avoid making sacrifices."[13] For many years, this tiny nun and her followers went out of their way to minister to the dying—first in Calcutta, India, and later around the world. Their ministry went far beyond simply holding hands and praying. They physically carried broken bodies in off the streets. They sponged out foul-smelling wounds. They got down on their knees to mop up accidents. They tenderly spooned warm food into toothless mouths.

Now that Mother Teresa is gone from this earth, her Missionaries of Charity still continue the work she began—work that again and again goes out of its way to love and serve.

Why do they do it?

If you ask them, their answer is clear and confident: "We do it because Jesus did."

And so must we.

SERVING IN ALL KINDS OF WAYS

When Brother Lawrence gave himself to service for God, he didn't get to choose his job. If you were to go to Calcutta and volunteer with the Missionaries of Charity, you wouldn't get to pick and choose either. Everyone starts at the same place—at the most humble point of service. But when you're truly a servant, a job title and a position are completely secondary. You're willing to do whatever needs to be done.

Jesus didn't have a luxurious corner office on Jerusalem's east side with a brass doorplate that said "Messiah." He didn't have a multiacre campus to base his ministry. He just ministered as he went along. On his way. As he went out of his way. *In all kinds of ways.*

I think this is an important thing to note when we speak of Kitchen Service—especially in this age of motivational "giftedness" studies. The last two decades have brought a surge of books, seminars, and other educational opportunities designed to help us become aware of our natural and spiritual gifts. These offerings, ranging from the classic *Discovering Your Spiritual Gifts* to the *Wagner-Modified Houts Spiritual Gifts Questionnaire,*[14] have helped Christians by the thousands become aware of the special gifts God has placed within them for building up the church.

The purpose of such offerings was to equip the saints for the work of the ministry. And the principle was sound: Working from our God-given gifts releases ministry potential in greater measure and helps the various members of the body work harmoniously.

I'm afraid, however, that instead of mobilizing the body of Christ, this emphasis on gifts may have provided many of us with a handy excuse. Now when churches call for workers, we have a spiritual reason why we can't help.

"It just isn't my gift," we can say piously, pointing to the twelfth chapters of Romans and 1 Corinthians.

"Sure would like to help, Pastor, but I don't do babies."

"I don't do junior highers."

"I don't do rest homes."

"I'm an exhorter, you know—I don't do toilets!"

When the verbal smoke screen finally clears, a question still remains: What exactly *do* we do?

I don't want to minimize the importance of understanding our strengths and our weaknesses. There is much to be learned about the ministry gifts God gives to the church and our part in the body of Christ as outlined in Romans 12. Besides, as we've discussed before, a need is not necessarily a call—and no one is called to do *everything*. That is why we always must start in the Living Room, spending time waiting before the Lord and asking him what he'd have us do.

But as far as I can tell, the biblical description of gifts and the reminders to serve wisely were never intended as excuses to pick the kind of service that feels comfortable and convenient and ignore all the others!

After all, the same chapter of Romans that lists spiritual gifts also makes it clear that we are *all* called to serve regardless of our specific gifts. We may or may not have the *gift* of servant hospitality (Romans 12:7), but we are *all* called to "practice" hospitality (verse 13). We may or may not have the *gift* of giving (verse 8), but we are *all* called to "share with God's people who are in need" (verse 13).

"Rather than picking and choosing ministry opportunities based solely on our talents and interests," Jack Hoey writes in *Discipleship Journal*, "we are directed, 'Always give yourselves fully to the work of the Lord.'"[15]

That's what our Savior did. He ministered everywhere he went in all kinds of ways. He stopped to chat with a lonely woman. He told stories to children and cooked fish for his disciples. He had dinner with publicans and sinners, even calling one down from his hiding place in a tree so they could share a little *koinonia* fellowship.

Instead of guarding his life, Jesus gave it away—and he beckons his followers to do the same. When we surrender ourselves to be used by God, we don't always get to pick the time, the method, or the place of ministry. In fact, sometimes, we may find ourselves doing nothing at all—except praying and waiting for God's leading.

"He also serves who only stands and waits," the great English poet John

Milton once wrote.[16] Frustrated by the limitations of becoming blind, Milton had struggled with feelings of worthlessness—feelings that God couldn't use him. But as the poet discovered, the key is not in our activity, but in our receptivity to God's voice—and in our willingness to be used in whatever ways he brings to our attention.

When we bring to him our willingness to serve, he'll always, eventually, point us toward something we can do for him. And that task will always have something to do with love.

PASSION, COMPASSION, AND POWER

A true passion for God will naturally result in compassion for people. We can't love the Father without also being willing to love his kids—even when they're less than lovable.

In his beautiful book *Love Beyond Reason,* John Ortberg tells the story of his sister's rag doll, Pandy. "She had lost a good deal of her hair, one of her arms was missing, and, generally speaking, she'd had the stuffing knocked out of her." But she was his sister's favorite doll.

Checking Your Motives

Kitchen Service is a vital part of any Christian life, but we must never forget that *why* we serve is as important as *how* we serve—the motives of our heart really make a difference. Jan Johnson, author of *Living a Purpose-Full Life,* suggests a series of helpful questions that can help us "do the work of Christ with the heart of Christ."

- Am I serving to impress anyone?
- Am I serving to receive external rewards?
- Is my service affected by moods and whims [my own as well as others']?
- Am I using this service to feel good about myself?
- Am I using my service to muffle God's voice demanding I change?[17]

The LORD does not look at the things man looks at.
Man looks at the outward appearance, but the LORD looks at the heart.

1 SAMUEL 16:7

So when Pandy turned up missing on the way home from family vacation, Ortberg's dad turned the car around and drove all the way back to Canada to find her. "We were a devoted family," Ortberg writes. "Not a particularly bright family, perhaps, but devoted." They found Pandy at the hotel, wrapped in sheets and down in the laundry, "about to be washed to death."

What made Pandy so valuable to that family? It wasn't her beauty. It was the fact Ortberg's little sister loved her so much. "If you loved [my sister], you just naturally loved Pandy too."

And so it is with our heavenly Father. As his children, we are flawed and wounded, broken and often bent. "We are all of us rag dolls," Ortberg says. "But we are God's rag dolls." And Jesus made it clear that serving him also involves serving the ones he loves.

"'Love me, love my rag dolls,' God says," writes Ortberg. "It's a package deal."[18]

I think that's why, in Acts 3, Peter and John couldn't just walk by the lame man sitting at the temple gate called Beautiful. When they looked at the crumpled rag doll of a man they didn't see a cripple, they saw a child of God. So they loved him. They wanted to help. Their passion for God spread out naturally into compassion for one in need. But instead of offering the man money, they gave him something far more valuable—something we all need to remember when we offer compassionate service.

"Silver and gold have I none," Peter said. Then, with all the passion and power of the Holy Spirit within him, Peter continued, "but such as I have give I thee: In the name of Jesus Christ of Nazareth rise up and walk" (Acts 3:6, KJV).

Compassion, you see, is just the beginning of what we have to offer the people Jesus loves. After all, the world is filled with charitable works, people, and foundations that give money and time and do incredible things on behalf of the poor. And I know such compassion pleases the heart of God—even when it comes from non-Christians.

But it wasn't Peter's charity the lame man needed that day. He needed something not found in pockets or purses or even in other people's sympathy. That man needed healing. He needed the power of God to transform his life.

And power was exactly what he got. By the empowerment of the Spirit, Peter took the man by the right hand and helped him up. "Instantly the man's feet and ankles became strong. He jumped to his feet and began to walk...walking and jumping, and praising God!" (3:7-8).

WHAT WE HAVE TO OFFER

And that, more than anything, is what the world needs from us today. They've heard the TV sermons; they've seen our church buildings and read our ads. What they're hungry for is the manifest glory of God. Something bigger than they are. Something bigger than we are. They want to see God.

It's always been that way. Paul referred to the same reality when he wrote in 1 Corinthians 2:4-5, "My message and my preaching were not with wise and persuasive words, but with a demonstration of the Spirit's power." Why was that important? "So that your faith might not rest on men's wisdom, but on God's power."

The world has had enough of man's wisdom. If a little extra know-how was all your neighbor needed, she'd find the answers to all life's questions on *Oprah*. If all your brother-in-law needed was advice, he could get it from coworkers or on the Internet, but what he can't get there is what he needs—a new life. If human wisdom were enough to solve the world's problems, we'd have already gotten rid of war, famine, and disease. And we'd have no need of God.

Obviously, that hasn't happened. The world is still embroiled in strife, still wasting away from physical and spiritual emptiness, still hurting and dying. Still desperate for the kind of healing only God can offer.

It might be a good idea, then, for each of us to stop ourselves periodically in the midst of serving and ask, "What am I relying on? Whom am I pointing people to?"

Because if our Kitchen Service doesn't point people to Jesus, we risk becoming surrogate messiahs. If we, not God, end up being their source of hope, we are setting them up for profound disappointment and ourselves for profound burnout—because we, in ourselves, are simply not up to the task of saving the world. In ourselves, like Peter and John at the gate called Beautiful, we have nothing to offer. But in Christ, we are given the power to give people what they most desperately need.

Only God, you see, can make rag dolls whole. Only God can put Humpty Dumpty together again. Our job is just to be his rag-doll emissaries, formed in his likeness, filled with his love, and endued with his power. And gifted with the privilege of sharing a loving Father with our orphan world.

STICKING OUT ALL OVER

The story is told of a young boy who approached an evangelist after a revival tent meeting. "Excuse me, sir?" the little boy said politely. "You said everyone should ask Jesus into their hearts, right?"

"That's right, son." The evangelist squatted down so he could look the boy in the eye. "Did you ask him in?"

"Well, I'd like to," the boy said, shuffling dirt with the toe of his shoe before returning his gaze to the evangelist. "But I got to figurin'…I'm so little and Jesus is so big—he's just gonna stick out all over!"

"That's the point, son," the evangelist said with a smile. "That's the point."

I don't know about you, but I want Jesus to be so evident in my life that people don't just consider me a nice moral person, full of good works. I want my relationship with God to be so real and vital, so like that of the apostles Peter and John, that people can't help but sit up and take notice.

Wouldn't it be wonderful to have words said of us like those Acts 4:13 records? "When they saw the courage of Peter and John and realized that they were unschooled, ordinary men, they were astonished and they took note that these men had been with Jesus."

I think that's what President Jiang Zemin was saying when he told Don Argue the story at the beginning of this chapter. He'd "taken note" of the difference in an obscure Christian's life. It remained etched upon his memory.

Unfortunately, unlike Paul Harvey, I have no "rest of the story" for this particular tale. Chinese Christians are still being persecuted for their faith every day. Chinese officials give no appearance of softening their stance.

But who knows? It may be the tender compassion of one woman—a Christian nurse who, while she was *on her way, went out of her way, in all kinds of ways*—that ultimately changes the heart of a president and his country.

One thing is certain. The cause of Christ is alive and well in China because of Christians like her. Christians who dared to love. Christians who dared to serve. Christians who dared to let Jesus stick out all over.

Instead of fighting the government during the last forty years of communist rule, "Chinese Christians devoted themselves to worship and evangelism, the original mission of the church," Philip Yancey writes in *What's So Amazing About Grace?* "They concentrated on changing lives, not changing laws." And something incredible has been happening in those forty years.

"There were 750,000 Christians when I left China," one elderly missionary, an expert on China, told Yancey. And now?

"You hear all sorts of numbers," the man says. "But I think a safe figure would be 35 million."[19]

One life truly can make a difference. Your life plus my life makes two.

Let's get connected to the Vine so that we start bearing fruit. Let's start living in such a way that Jesus sticks out all over. Let's start loving in such a way people can point at our lives and say, "I know who you are!"

Or better yet, "I know *whose* you are"—because they see our Lord and his love in us.

7

The Better Part

There is need of only one thing. Mary has chosen the better part,
which will not be taken away from her.

LUKE 10:42, NRSV

Sometimes a picture is worth a thousand words.

My thirty-something birthday had dawned bright and busy. Tucked into a pile of bills and credit-card applications I found a card sent from my friend Janet McHenry. The message inside wished me a "hoopy birthday," and that made me smile, but the picture on the front was what really grabbed my attention. It illustrated everything I'd been feeling that dreary, getting-older day.

"That's me," I said to my husband, poking at the black-and-white glossy.

Taken back in the early 1950s, the photo showed a young woman in Greta Garbo shorts with eight or nine Hula-Hoops swinging madly around her waist. "How does she do that?" I wanted to know.

It had been a frustrating day of too many responsibilities and not enough of me to go around. One by one, I named the Hula-Hoops I had been trying to keep in motion: wife, mother, pastor's wife, friend, writer, piano instructor, cook, cleaning lady, and the big one—Little League mother. If we weren't racing to baseball games, we were rushing to church; if I wasn't folding laundry, I was stealing a few moments to write.

"That's me!" I laughed. I made exaggerated motions with my hips, trying to keep my invisible hoops afloat. My eyes darted from the photo to my husband's concerned face then back again. "That's me!"

After a few cups of chamomile tea and some chocolate-chip sedatives—I mean, cookies—I calmed down and read my friend's letter while my husband ran our kids to yet another ball game. Chatty and full of humor, Janet shared her hectic schedule and the things the Lord had been teaching her.

I finished the letter, then closed the card and looked once more at the girl on the front. There were so many hoops, but she appeared calm. Her upper body seemed to be perfectly still, her arms outstretched slightly, as the hoops raced around her waist in synchronized chaos.

Her face captured me. Looking straight into the camera, she smiled peacefully as though she hadn't a care in the world.

Then it dawned on me—I saw her secret. "She found a rhythm," I whispered to myself. "She established her center, then let everything move around that."

That's exactly what I *wasn't* doing in my life. All the things I'd been trying to accomplish were important, but I had lost my center. Busy being busy, I'd forgotten to tend to my inner self, the spiritual me. Like a wheel without an axle, I'd careened through life, bouncing off one duty and onto another.

If there was an adequate pause, I'd spend some time with the Lord. But lately, more often than not, my busy days had slipped by without a quiet time. And my life was revealing what my spirit had missed.

"Teach me, Lord. Show me the rhythm of life," I found myself praying.

"Be my center."

HULA-HOOPS AND HOLINESS

Life is filled with Hula-Hoops. We all have responsibilities, important things that need our attention. If we're not careful, however, our hearts and our minds can be consumed with the task of keeping them in the air. Rather than centering ourselves in Christ and letting the other elements of our lives take their rightful place around that center, we end up shifting our attention from one important to-do item to another, frantically trying to keep them all in motion.

It's easy to forget that while there is a time to work, there is also a time to worship—and it's the worship, the time we spend with God, that provides the serene center to a busy, complex life.

Mary of Bethany didn't fall for that. She knew the difference between work and worship. Martha didn't. That is why she nearly missed the Better Part.

I can almost see Martha as she greeted Jesus on his way through Bethany. I don't suppose the Hula-Hoops were actually visible as she came out to meet him, but I wouldn't be surprised if there was a slight movement around Martha's hips. "Come in! Come in!" she probably said. "Mi casa, su casa! Now, if you'll excuse me, I need to check the soup."

I, too, have been guilty of giving my Lord a breathless hello and a quick hug. I've welcomed him into my life and gotten him situated, but then moved on like Martha, gyrating frantically as I pursued other duties.

Mary didn't do that. She dropped her Hula-Hoops and sat at his feet. Who has time for recess games when you're in the presence of the wisest Teacher who ever lived?

Now it's been argued that Mary probably didn't have any hoops (the lazy thing!) "That's why *she* had *time* to sit at his feet," we Marthas like to emphasize. But we have no proof of that, and I believe Scripture is vague for a purpose.

Stereotypes keep us from embracing truth. The story of Mary and Martha was never meant to be a psychological profile or a role play in which we choose the character with whom we most identify. This is the story of two different responses to one singular occasion. In it, we should find not our personality type, but the kind of heart Christ longs for us to have.

A heart centered in him alone.

KEEPING A FOCUS

As I read the birthday card in my hand that day, I couldn't help but marvel at the work God had done in my friend. A mother of four and married to a farmer-lawyer, Janet had a full-time job teaching high school English and wrote books and articles in moments found here and there. Her life was busy. Hula-Hoops galore.

A year earlier, Janet had sent out an SOS to the e-mail fellowship we both belong to. A number of painful crises, including an unjust lawsuit, had slammed into her family's lives without warning. "Pray for me," she wrote. "I'm going under."

Melancholy in personality, yet driven to excel, Janet found herself swamped by despair. She couldn't fix her situation. She couldn't change it. But in the middle of it all, God was calling her to himself.

"I'm getting up an hour early and prayer walking," she had written us several months later. Each morning before work, Janet donned her sweats and spent an hour walking around her small California town, praying for people and situations as they came to mind. "I can't believe the change getting alone with God is making in my life," she wrote in the birthday card. "I actually caught myself singing the other day!"[1]

Hudson Taylor once said, "We will all have trials. The question is not when the pressure will come, but where the pressure will lie. Will it come between us and the Lord? Or will it press us ever closer to His breast?"[2] Rather than let her circumstances drag her away from God, Janet chose to let them draw her closer.

My friend was experiencing the truth Selwyn Hughes writes about: "Life works better when we know how to glance at things but gaze at God. Seeing Him clearly will enable us to see all other things clearly."[3]

It is so easy to lose focus in life, to lose our center. Life conspires to drag our eyes away from the face of the Savior, hypnotizing us with the unending sway of our problems.

"I can't spend time with God today," I may rationalize. "I haven't the time." But the truth of the matter is this: The rougher the day, the *more* time I need to spend with my Savior. The more hoops I have to handle, the more I need to keep my center.

I think it's important to remember that if Mary hadn't chosen to take time out of her busy Martha-run schedule to sit at Jesus' feet, the whole encounter wouldn't have happened. The Gospels would have moved right along without recording this intimate pause between a woman and her Savior. And we wouldn't have seen the difference Living Room Intimacy can make in a life—in a family—surrendered to God.

MAKING ROOM

I've found I need solitude, a daily quiet time alone with God, if I am to have any hope of keeping my center. Left to my own devices, I am fickle and ever-changing. One day I'm hot: "O Lord, I love you! Be glorified in me." The next day I'm lukewarm: "Sorry, God, have to run." I have found the words of the hymnist so true:

Prone to wander, Lord I feel it,
Prone to leave the God I love.[4]

The only way I've found to fight this wandering tendency in my life is to keep my heart centered on Christ, to keep my gaze fixed on him. But that takes time and an act of my will. I have to be willing to make room in my life if I want to experience the Better Part.

In his book *First Things First*, Stephen Covey tells the story of a man teaching a time-management seminar. In order to make a point, the man pulled a wide-mouthed gallon jar from under the counter that served as his podium. He picked up some fist-size rocks and put them in the jar. Then he looked out at the class and asked, "Is the jar full?"

Some of the students, not knowing where he was going, blurted out, "Yes." The teacher laughed gently and said, "No, it's not." He pulled out a bucket of pea gravel and began to pour it in the jar. The class watched as the pea gravel filtered down between the rocks, filling the spaces until it reached the top.

"Now, is the jar full?"

The class was a bit reticent to answer. After all, they'd been wrong before. Instead of waiting for their response, the man poured a bucket of sand down among the pea gravel and the large rocks. He shook the jar gently to let the sand settle, then added more, until finally the sand reached the mouth of the jar. Then he asked again, "Is the jar full?" And they said, "Probably not."

Now the teacher reached for a pitcher of water and slowly poured the water in the jar. It filtered down until it was running out of the jar at the top. "Is the jar full?" the time-management consultant asked. The class answered, "We think it is."

"Okay, class," he said. "What is the lesson in this visual aid?"

Somebody in the back raised his hand and said, "No matter how busy your life is, there is always room for more!"

"No," the teacher said as the class broke into laughter. "That's not it!"

"The lesson is, class," he said when the chuckles subsided, "if you don't put the big rocks in first you'll never get them in later."[5]

What a powerful picture of a powerful truth! It sounds like the same point Jesus made when he said, "Seek first his kingdom and his righteousness, and all these things will be given to you as well" (Matthew 6:33).

First things first, the Lord was saying. Take care of my business, and I'll take care of yours. Make room in your heart for me, and I'll make room for everything else.

TOO FULL FOR COMFORT

You see, we were created for fullness. According to Ephesians 3:17-19, when we come to know Jesus as our Lord through faith, we begin to understand the incredible love of our Savior. And as we come to know this love better, we are "filled to the measure of all the *fullness* of God" (v. 19, emphasis mine).

We were created for the fullness of God, not an ounce or liter less. But are we ready for that? After all, being filled to the measure with all the fullness of God will most likely require our being stretched. At the very least, it is sure to disturb our comfort.

Are we willing to let God explode our comfort zone and expand our capacity for him? Or do we want a God we can manage?

Unfortunately, a lot of the time that is exactly what we want—enough of God to make us happy, but not enough to make us change. We'd never say it, but our attitude is just what Wilbur Rees had in mind when he wrote:

> I would like to buy $3 worth of God, please, not enough to explode
> my soul or disturb my sleep, but just enough to equal a cup of warm
> milk or a snooze in the sunshine. I don't want enough of Him to make
> me love a black man or pick beets with a migrant. I want ecstasy, not
> transformation; I want the warmth of the womb, not a new birth. I
> want a pound of the Eternal in a paper sack. I would like to buy $3
> worth of God, please.[6]

The trouble, of course, is that God doesn't work that way. He's not on the market in manageable, bargain-size portions. He's not on the market in the first place. And he's not looking for buyers; he's looking to *buy*—you and me. He wants a people who are sold out to him. All the way. Total liquidation. He's not willing to barter. He's not looking to please. He has already paid the price. His Son died on the cross to pay our debt and ransom our souls.

But the transaction is never a forced sale—and that's crucial to realize. God is a gentleman, not a robber baron. He will court us and pursue us, but he'll never push himself on us. We can actually say no to the Maker of the Universe. We can choose to keep him in a corner of our lives.

Author and teacher Cynthia Heald puts it this way, "We are as intimate with God as we choose to be."[7] The only limitations of God's presence in our lives are the limits we ourselves set—the excuses we set up to avoid being filled to the measure with God.

Martha's excuse was duty. She had cleaning and cooking to do. She didn't think she had time to sit at Jesus' feet.

Perhaps your excuse is children or work. Or maybe like me, the only excuse you really have for devotional delinquency is sheer laziness. But whatever it is—whatever keeps us from spending regular time with God—it is sin.

Does it sound harsh to say that cooking or cleaning or taking care of children or doing your job might be sinful? But think about it. The very *definition* of sin is separation from God. So no matter how important the activity, no matter how good it seems, if I use it as an excuse to hold God at arm's length, it is sin. I need to confess and repent of it so that I can draw close to the Lord once more.

Because the longer I go without being filled with God's presence, the drier and emptier and more frustrated I'm going to become.

THERE'S GOT TO BE MORE

When my husband and I left Montana so he could serve as music pastor in Grants Pass, we were exhausted. The oil boom of the late 1970s had gone bust in eastern Montana, leaving a trail of bankruptcies, foreclosures, and hopelessness. In one month alone, fifty families in our church had left town looking for work. It had been a hard time for us both, emotionally and financially. But I had no idea it had drained me so much spiritually.

Someone commented recently, "I didn't know I was 'dry,' until I got around people who were 'wet.'" I knew what she meant, because that's exactly what happened to me when we got to Oregon. The people in Grants Pass were "all wet"! Soaking wet, drenched with God. The presence of the Lord was so sweet in our services, the people so mature in their faith, that all I could do was weep.

I'd known the Lord for years. I'd been a pastor's wife for nearly a decade. But I was spiritually dry. Dry-bone dry.

Who were these people? I wondered. How could they be so happy? What did they have that I didn't have? How could they sit there enjoying the presence of the Lord when I always felt compelled to be in a state of constant motion, busy but exhausted from the effort of keeping my Hula-Hoops in the air?

Sometimes we have to slow down in order to take spiritual inventory and see where we stand with God. Sometimes we have to realize how empty we are before we're willing to be filled. During that first year in Grants Pass, I did both.

As I looked back at my life, I could see a series of mountaintop experiences where the rain had fallen rich and deep, but there were quite a few dry valleys as well. Famine times when I was so dry and so low emotionally that I barely felt alive. I had the classic sanguine personality when it came to my walk with God. Big, big, highs. Big, big lows. And now, more recently, I felt lost in a barren, featureless desert.

"Tear down the mountaintops if you have to, Lord," I cried one night. "But fill in my valleys! Bring a steadfastness to my life so I can walk faithfully in the good times as well as the bad. I want to know you! I want to be filled with you—and stay filled."

What was wrong with me? When I stopped to think about it, I knew part of the answer. My personal times of devotion were erratic at best. My prayer life was quirky, my reading of the word sporadic. And because I was not spending regular quiet time with God, I was not putting myself in a position to be filled and refilled.

No wonder I was running on empty!

What it really came down to was I only met with God when I felt like it. And that, I was learning, just wasn't enough. If I wanted to be filled with God on a more consistent basis, I had to determine to let myself be stretched, to make room for the Better Part on a daily basis in my life. And that would mean learning to abandon my emotions as a compass and start exercising my will.

AN ACT OF THE WILL

Making room for the Better Part in our lives isn't easy. Many great men and women of God have struggled to hammer out time alone with their Savior. I love the candor and the humor of J. Sidlow Baxter as he describes his battle to reestablish a regular devotional time after a "velvety little voice told him to be practical...that he wasn't of the spiritual sort, that only a few people could be like that."

That did it. Baxter was horrified to think he could rationalize away the very thing he needed most, so he set about to make some definite changes. He writes:

> As never before, my will and I stood face to face. I asked my will the straight question, "Will, are you ready for an hour of prayer?" Will answered, "Here I am, and I'm quite ready, if you are." So Will and I linked arms and turned to go for our time of prayer. At once all the emotions began pulling the other way and protesting, "We're not coming." I saw Will stagger just a bit, so I asked, "Can you stick it out, Will?" and Will replied, "Yes, if you can." So Will went, and we got down to prayer.... It was a struggle all the way through. At one point...one of those traitorous emotions had snared my imagination and had run off to the golf course; and it was all I could do to drag the wicked rascal back....
>
> At the end of that hour, if you had asked me, "Have you had a 'good time'?" I would have had to reply, "No, it has been a wearying wrestle with contrary emotions and a truant imagination from beginning to end." What is more, that battle with the emotions continued for between two and three weeks, and if you had asked me at the end of that period, "Have you had a 'good time' in your daily praying?" I would have had to confess, "No, at times it has seemed as though the heavens were brass, and God too distant to hear, and the Lord Jesus strangely aloof, and prayer accomplishing nothing."
>
> Yet something *was* happening. For one thing, Will and I really taught the emotions that we were completely independent of them.

Also, one morning, about two weeks after the contest began, just
when Will and I were going for another time of prayer, I over-
heard one of the emotions whisper to the other, "Come on, you
guys, it's no use wasting any more time resisting: they'll go just the
same."...

Then, another couple of weeks later, what do you think happened? During one of our prayer times, when Will and I were no more
thinking of the emotions than of the man in the moon, one of the
most vigorous of the emotions unexpectedly sprang up and shouted,
"Hallelujah!" at which all the other emotions exclaimed, "Amen!" And
for the first time the whole of my being—intellect, will, and emotions—was united in one coordinated prayer-operation. All at once,
God was real, heaven was open, the Lord Jesus was luminously present,
the Holy Spirit was indeed moving through my longings, and prayer
was surprisingly vital. Moreover, in that instant there came a sudden
realization that heaven had been watching and listening all the way
through those days of struggle against chilling moods and mutinous
emotions; also that I had been undergoing necessary tutoring by my
heavenly Teacher.[8]

When I first read Baxter's words, they unlocked something deep within my
soul. So I wasn't alone! Other people struggled as well. Suddenly I felt hope—
hope that I, too, could experience the joy of the Better Part. I didn't have to wait
until I felt spiritual to spend time with God. I just had to make a decision of the
will, and the spiritual feelings would eventually come around.

So I began to try it, but it wasn't easy. Sometimes I had to struggle like J.
Sidlow Baxter. Sometimes God seemed far away and my heart like cold steel.
Sometimes I just felt irritable and impatient. But I persisted, and gradually
things began to change. Like a patient waking from a long coma, I began to
experience a hunger for God like I'd never known before—a kind of "unsatisfi-
able satisfaction" that grew and grew.

AMAZING GRACE

As I began to understand grace—God's marvelous, amazing, abundant grace—in a brand-new way, I began to recognize the Holy Spirit at work within me, giving me the power and the desire to do God's will as never before.

I found myself at the altar praying after the services had ended—seeking the Lord. I found myself waking in the middle of the night to spend time in his Word—seeking the Lord. I found myself turning to books and tuning in religious broadcasts in the middle of the day—seeking the Lord.

I wanted everything that Jesus Christ had to offer. And as I sought his face, I found that he'd been there waiting all the time, with a pitcher full of his presence, ready to pour. Wanting to fill me "to the measure of the fullness of God." Just waiting for me to choose the Better Part and meet him there in the Living Room.

Living Room Intimacy, you see, is not some mystical state of being (or non-being) like the Hindu idea of nirvana. We need not trek to the mountains of Nepal to find it, nor go on a spirit quest like the native Americans of old. We won't find it on a shelf, in a dusty old cave, or in a museum under lights.

The Better Part is not out there somewhere. It is inside us, where Christ dwells by his Holy Spirit. Isn't that wonderful? We can't misplace the Better Part. No one can take it away from us, though unfortunately we can choose to ignore it.

Remember the painting of Christ knocking at a door? The beautiful scene hung above my grandmother's dresser for years, a gentle reminder to this little girl that Jesus longed to come into her heart. There was no latch on the outside of the wooden door where the Lord stood waiting. It could only be opened from the inside.

So it is with the door of my will. Jesus didn't force his company upon the sisters of Bethany, nor will he force it upon me. I have to let him in before we can enjoy our Living Room time together. And the door isn't always easy to open, even from the inside. But three little keys, I've discovered, can make all the difference. They are three simple truths—so simple they tend to be disregarded, but powerful enough to click open stubbornly willful doors. They have made all the difference in keeping my life centered in Christ.

What are these three little keys? They're easy to remember because they each begin with *C:*

- Consistency
- Creativity
- Conversation

CONSISTENT PRACTICE

As a young teenager, I read a book about Andraé Crouch, a popular gospel artist at the time. Andraé's preacher father had prayed over his twelve-year-old son's hands when their church needed a pianist, and God had answered his prayer. Andraé not only became the church pianist, but also went on to bless thousands with his music and powerful songs.

Well, that definitely inspired me. "Dear Jesus," I prayed the next afternoon as I sat down at the piano, "you know I'm not very good at this piano stuff. Would you do for me what you did for Andraé?"

I waited, but nothing happened.

Instead, the word of the Lord came to me saying...well, to be honest, I didn't actually hear the audible voice of God. I never have. But at that moment it was almost as if I did. Somewhere up in the region of the right side of my heart, the voice of the Lord came to me, saying:

"Practice, Joanna, practice."

Practice. I have an idea that's what God wants to whisper to our hearts when we ask for the Better Part. "You've got to invest time, darling. You need to do a little every day." If we want to be accomplished Christians, and if we want to know God in all his fullness, there is something crucial about the act of seeking Jesus on a regular, day-by-day basis.

I've learned in my own life that if I want to develop a consistent quiet time with God, I have to set aside a certain portion of my day just for him. And then I need to guard it well—even scheduling it in my Day-Timer. Because if I'm not careful, the Better Part can get shoved so far to the side of my plate that it ends up on the floor rather than feeding my soul.

It doesn't really matter *what* time of day I choose. People of faith over the centuries have had good success with a variety of times. Daniel, for instance, prayed three times a day: morning, noon, and night (Daniel 6:10). David must have been a morning person, according to Psalm 5:3: "In the morning, O LORD, you hear my voice; in the morning I lay my requests before you and wait in expectation." Jesus tended toward morning as well, according to Mark 1:35: "Very early in the morning, while it was still dark, Jesus got up, left the house and went off to a solitary place, where he prayed."

As for myself, I've fluctuated between morning and night but have finally settled for morning once again. Not only is it easier for me to find uninterrupted time then, but I've found it is a wonderful way to start the day.

But again, it's not really important *when* I choose to meet God every day. What really matters is that I show up regularly—and to be honest, that's where I've always fallen short. Because of my all-or-nothing temperament, missing a day or two of devotions was enough to throw me off track for days, even weeks. Out of sight became out of mind, and I'm ashamed to admit, there were entire months when I went without having a formal, that is, a sit-down-with-my-Bible-and-pray alone time with God.

But consistency, after all, doesn't mean perfection; it simply means refusing to give up. And that's what has saved me. Like Sidlow Baxter, I refused to give in to the possibility that I wasn't "of the spiritual sort." So with a huge amount of God's grace and a stubborn will to keep trying, I've been able to get back on track with my quiet times.

And somewhere in that dailiness, in that everyday familiarity that comes from time spent together, I have felt myself grow closer to the Lord. Steadily, consistently closer. And also, in the process, more filled with his presence. More calm and serene. More practically centered.

It's amazing what a little time-out can do for you. Especially when you spend that time with Jesus.

SOME CREATIVE STRATEGIES

In college and the years that followed, I tried many times to read the Bible systematically, but I would inevitably give up, usually around Leviticus and Numbers. Somewhere between the laws and the begats, I'd end up falling asleep. Then I'd lose momentum. And then I'd be back to my old slapdash habits of diving here and there among my favorite passages and not really learning anything new.

But when I began using a reading guide that switched back and forth from the Old Testament to the New Testament, everything changed. The variety sparked my interest as I began to see Christ in the Old Testament and the beauty of the blood covenant in the New Testament. I could hardly wait to get back to my Bible reading each day to see what would happen next in the epic story of God's plan for humanity.

The *NIV Study Bible* my husband bought for my birthday enlivened my study time even more. I loved the contemporary language of the *New International Version*. And having everything I needed at my fingertips—a thorough concordance and cross references, as well as study notes to help when I didn't understand—kept me from getting stalled in my study.

In those two simple changeovers—switching between books of the Bible and reading a more contemporary version—I discovered a bit of the power creativity can have in our quiet times.

It is so easy to fall into habits and rituals—the ones that are imposed upon us as well as those we ourselves impose. But while the consistency of habit and the beauty of ritual can be empowering and enriching, they can also lead to dullness. *Three more chapters,* we yawn. *Then I can go to sleep…* And while the dullness of routine is really no excuse for abandoning our devotional times, the reality is that we stand a better chance of sticking with our quiet times when we have interest as well as will to spur us on.

There's more than one way, in other words, to enjoy a quiet time with the Lord. There's more than one approach to studying Scripture. There's more than one way to mediate and pray. The practical truth is that if we don't learn how to feed our souls so they will eat, our souls will wither and slowly die. And that may require a little variety in our spiritual diet—a little creativity in the way we approach our quiet times.

A LITTLE CONVERSATION

The last "C key" to the Better Part is conversation. Now that may sound a little strange to you. What does conversation have to do with quiet time?

Creative Quiet Times

If you've found yourself yawning during devotions—or just eager for a change—you may want to consider the following suggestions for creative intimacy with God.

1. *Take God out for coffee.* Find a quiet corner in a café or even McDonald's and meet with God. Take your Bible and a notebook. Grab a cup of coffee and you're set for a heart-to-heart with your very Best Friend.

2. *Add a spiritual classic to your devotional diet.* Though nothing should replace the Word of God, Christian books provide delicious and enriching side dishes!

3. *Put feet to your faith.* Take a walk with God! Praise him for his handiwork. Listen to the Bible or a sermon on tape. Pray. Your body and spirit will appreciate the workout.

4. *Journal your journey.* Keep a spiritual diary. Record thoughts as you meditate on Scripture. Write love notes to the Lord. List prayer requests.

5. *Come before him with singing.* Add music to your devotions. Use a praise tape or sing a cappella. Read a hymn out loud.

6. *Let faith come by hearing.* Order tapes from favorite speakers or plan your prayer time around a radio speaker.

7. *Dig a little deeper.* A good Bible study will take you beyond just reading the Word. It will help you rightly divide the Word of Truth and apply it.

8. *All the King's versions.* It is important to find a Bible translation you understand for your regular devotions. But occasionally read from other versions to get a fresh perspective. Read the text out loud.

9. *Hide the Word.* Memorizing Scripture plants the Word of God deep in your heart. Then write down verses on index cards or sticky notes and take them with you to practice.

10. *Spend a half-day in prayer.* It may seem impossible, but as you set aside a large portion of time to spend with the Lord, he will meet you there in amazing ways. You'll find a plan for a half-day of prayer in Appendix E.

As the deer pants for streams of water, so my soul pants for you, O God

PSALM 42:1

But our relationship with God is supposed to be an intimate, loving relationship, and what relationship can thrive without dialogue—good, honest, back-and-forth communication? We need it in marriage, and we need it in our walk with God.

A few years back I looked at my relationship with God and realized that my quiet-time communication style involved a series of monologues with very little dialogue. I'd read about what God thought. Then I'd spend a few minutes telling God what I thought. But I never allowed us to get to the point of conversation, of give-and-take discourse, of the questions and answers that bring life to a relationship.

But that changed when I began to read the Bible as God's love letter to me. I started to hear his own voice calling out to me in the pages of Scripture, and I began to respond to it from my own heart. I started a Bible-reading highlights journal in which I recorded what I felt the Lord was saying to me from his Word. (The format I used is found in Appendix D.)

Instead of the two or three chapters of Bible reading I'd tried to cram in before, I read smaller portions this time, usually one chapter. Instead of simply reading a passage, I'd meditate on it, underlining important verses as I went. Then I'd choose the verse that seemed to speak most clearly to me and respond to the verse in my journal. Sometimes I would paraphrase it into my own words. Sometimes I asked questions. But usually the verse became a prayer as I asked the Lord to apply the truth of his Word to my life and my heart.

Eventually my Bible-highlights journal became a prayer journal as well. Pouring out my heart to the Lord on paper allowed me to be honest about my struggles, my hopes, and my needs. I tried to make a point of recording answers I received as well—both the words the Lord spoke to my spirit and the answers I saw unfold in events around me. In this way my journal served as both a record of my relationship with God and my living dialogue with him. And out of that simple conversation, some amazing things began to happen.

In the first place, I wasn't just reading through the Bible; the Bible was getting through to me. It came alive as I began to study and dig deeper.

My prayer life, too, took on fresh life. No longer was I just presenting God with my wish list and some suggestions about how I thought he should handle it. I was conversing with God—both talking and listening.

No longer was I the "man" in James 1:23-24 "who looks at his face in a mirror and, after looking at himself, goes away and immediately forgets what he looks like." This newfound conversation with God wouldn't allow it! The written record sketched a pretty detailed picture of my condition—a picture hard to ignore.

As I acknowledged what I saw, I repented and applied the truth I'd found. And gradually, in the process, the Holy Spirit began changing me into the "man" of verse 25 "who looks intently into the perfect law that gives freedom, and continues to do this, not forgetting what he has heard, but doing it."

Consistency. Creativity. Conversation. I can't tell you how much these three Cs have done to help me keep my life centered in Christ. Oh, I still have a long way to go! I'm far from perfect when it comes to my spiritual diligence. But I'm far from where I used to be. I'm more stable. More centered. More steadfast. Less likely to skip my quiet times with Jesus and quicker to get back on track when I do.

Most important, my capacity for God really is bigger. I'm no longer empty, no longer dry. I know where to go to be filled, and I'm in more of a hurry to get there. More eager than ever to choose the Better Part…to be filled with the full measure of God, to be centered and established in Christ.

A STABLE CENTER

Remember the Hula-Hoop girl from my birthday card? She knew the secret. She'd found her center, and so can we if we keep on choosing the Better Part on a daily basis.

In fact, we can find the kind of stability exemplified by another set of hoops I'd like to tell you about. Another childhood toy. Perhaps you remember it. It's a contraption of metal rings called a gyroscope. *Encyclopedia Britannica* defines it as "a spinning wheel mounted in such a way that it is free to turn about any of three possible axes." It's like a supertop. Once you set it in motion, it just keeps on going, and it's very hard to knock over. In fact, if you try to push it over, it stubbornly holds its original position, continuing to spin in the same direction.

"When I was a little boy, gyroscopes fascinated me," recalls Howard E. Butt Jr. in *Renewing America's Soul.* "A gyroscope looked to me like a dancing circle:

spinning freely, yet perfectly balanced and steady, held upright by some mysterious inner power."

Later, as a young adult, Howard learned that gyroscopes are more than scientific spin toys; they have numerous practical applications as well. "They stabilize our planes in turbulent weather, steady our ships as they sail through raging seas, and guide them automatically by their compasses."

What a picture of the life we are to have in Christ! As we surrender our hoops to the Lord Jesus, as we center ourselves in him, something wonderful happens. He takes those hoops and makes them dance. He turns the spinning circles of our chaotic lives into a steady, stable gyroscope mounted and held up by him alone.

He stabilizes us in the turbulence of life. He steadies us in the midst of raging seas, and he guides us by the compass of his eternal love. As we partake of the Better Part, Jesus Christ becomes the steady balance in our life of constant motion.

"The little boy in me still says: that looks like fun!" Howard writes, both of the gyroscope and the lovely application to a centered life in Christ. "And the open-eyed adult in me, looking around, whispers, 'We've never needed it more.'"[9]

I agree. On those crazy, loopy days when I don't feel so "hoopy," I'm learning to reach for the Lord instead of chocolate-chip sedatives. I'm learning how to leave the Kitchen and head for the Living Room where Jesus waits, because that's where I'll find everything I need and everything I want.

After all, it's not more Hula-Hoops I need to master.

What I really need is more and more of the Master himself.

8

Lessons from Lazarus

Now a man named Lazarus was sick.... So the sisters sent word
to Jesus, "Lord, the one you love is sick."

JOHN 11:1,3

I love a good story. There's nothing like sipping ice tea under a shade tree and losing myself in an intriguing book on a warm summer day. I can involve myself for hours in the twists and turns of someone else's life. Suspense, mystery, romance—they are the elements of great fiction as far as I'm concerned. The obstacles and overwhelming odds make me turn pages and buy sequels.

When it comes to real life, however, I'd rather go straight to the happy ending. Let's skip the poisoned apple; I'm more interested in Prince Charming and the kiss. Happily ever after—that's the kind of story I prefer for myself.

But life rarely works like that. Most of us spend the bulk of our lives cleaning up after dwarves rather than romancing handsome princes. And, unfortunately, when dark times come and the plots of our lives thicken, we can't just flip to the back of the book to satisfy our curiosity or ease our suspense.

There's no easy way to find out how the story ends.

We just have to hang on tight as the plot line unfolds.

A PUZZLING PLOT

I can only imagine how Mary and Martha must have felt when their brother, Lazarus, fell ill. Everything had been going so well. Since Jesus had come to visit them, nothing had been the same. There was a new peace. A new joy. A new sense of love that permeated the whole household. The incident recorded in Luke 10:38-42 had been more than just a couple of small paragraphs. That meeting had completely rewritten the story of their lives. But now, it seemed, the plot was taking a puzzling turn.

Perhaps it all started with a fever. "A little bit of my chicken soup, a good night's sleep, and you'll feel just fine," Martha probably told her brother matter-of-factly as she spooned the tasty broth into his waiting lips. Mary probably nodded and smiled as she sat beside him with a wet cloth, cooling his brow.

"I'm sure you're right, Martha," Lazarus may have said, gratefully sinking back into his pillow and the capable ministrations of his sisters. "I'll be fine."

But as you probably already know, Lazarus wasn't.

John 11:1 doesn't go into detail about his ailment, telling us only that there was a man named Lazarus who was sick.

But through the account that follows, it's obvious Lazarus must have been a very special man. He was dearly loved—not only by his sisters, but also by Jesus. The message sent by Mary and Martha said it all: "Lord, the *one you love* is sick" (11:3, emphasis mine). Their relationship must have been exceptionally close. This wasn't a stranger. This was a friend.

So I can imagine the hope the two sisters clung to as they sent the messenger. Surely everything would be all right. The illness seemed severe, but Jesus would come. Lazarus would be made well, and their life would continue as they'd always known it.

Jesus' disciples probably assumed the same thing. After all, when the news about Lazarus came, Jesus told them specifically that "this sickness will not end in death" (11:4). "No," he added, "it is for God's glory so that God's Son may be glorified through it."

Good news, the disciples must have thought. Lazarus will live!

But God had other plans for Lazarus and his sisters. For they had a place in a story bigger and richer than Michener's, more exciting than Clancy's, more mysterious than King's and more romantic than Steele's—with more twists and dips than any novelist could ever dream up on his or her own. It's the story of God's ongoing relationship with the human race. And it's a tale the Master Storyteller has been working on ever since the dawn of creation.

THE PLOT THICKENS

The Bible provides the basic outline. God's first draft was designed to be a perfect love story. He created a man and a woman to live in fellowship with him and with each other in fairy-tale bliss. The setting was so beautiful it defied description. And the story was sweet. Long walks in the evening. New discoveries in the daytime. No tears. No death. No sorrow.

That was God's original purpose—not only for Adam and Eve, but for you and me as well. Then a serpent slipped in, and sin spoiled Paradise. Disobedience destroyed God's manuscript and tossed the man and the woman out of Eden. The story was over, or so it seemed.

But instead of writing a cruel conclusion, Satan's attempt to interrupt God's epic tale served only as an introduction. For "the moment the forbidden fruit touched the lips of Eve," Max Lucado says, "the shadow of a cross appeared on the horizon."[1] With the fall of man, God began unfolding the greatest story of all—his incredible plan of redemption.

And so the saga continues, right down to this very day. Good and evil still war for the human soul. The conflict between love and hate remains the central theme. What Satan intends for evil, God still turns for good.

But go ahead and flip the pages.

You'll see this story has a happy ending. An incredible out-of-this-world happy ending! A glorious finale complete with trumpets and fanfare and an old-fashioned camp meeting in the sky!

But in the in-between part—well, that's where you and I come in. For though we already know the ending, we don't get to skip ahead to the end—at least not yet. And that, I believe, is because God has a lot he wants to teach us as the story unfolds. For tucked among the twists and turns of the everyday plot are valuable lessons about who God is and how he works and how we fit into the tale.

Lessons like the ones Mary and Martha learned the day they feared their brother's story had ended and all hope was gone.

A GREATER GLORY

I've always loved dot-to-dot puzzles. Looking at the dots, I have a sense of what the picture will eventually look like. But that's not the way things always work in God's scheme of things, as Mary and Martha found out that tragic day in Bethany. What they learned from painful experience was the first of the lessons we can learn from the story of Lazarus:

- *God's will does not always proceed in a straight line.*

That means I will not always see a clear connection between point A and point B. I won't always see the pattern in what happens to me. I won't always understand the plan.

One reason for this is that God is weaving together a greater glory than just my own. As Paul explains in Romans 8:28, "We know that in all things God works for the good of those who love him, who have been called according to his purpose." It is God's purposes, not mine, that must prevail. He is concerned not only with the individual need, but with the corporate need as well.

God wraps up my good with your good and the good of both of us with the good of others. The plot lines of our individual stories weave together to form his master plan. Nothing is wasted. Nothing is left out. There are no dead ends or red herrings; every story line is given his greatest attention, his diligent care. Your story matters to Jesus, just as the individual stories of Mary, Martha, and Lazarus mattered to him. But he always has the big picture in mind as he handles the stories of our lives. He knows the beginning from the end, and he operates accordingly.

So don't be surprised if your personal plot takes a couple of twists now and then. Don't get upset when point A doesn't automatically lead to point B. There are no detours in God's story line, not really. Just complications that he's more than able to resolve.

Satan does his best to foul things up, but God just counters his devilish ploys with moves of his own. I can only imagine what it looks like in the spiritual realms when he does. "Take that!" I can hear Satan chortle as he pencils in a diabolical plot change. "Okay," God says, "I think I will." Then with a smile that brightens the ages, God takes Satan's worst and transforms it into our best. And with each jog and twist, our story grows clearer and richer and more divine. The Author of our salvation really does know what he's doing, even when we can't figure it out.

When God gave Joseph a dream of the moon and stars bowing down to him, Joseph assumed that great things were in store for him. He didn't expect a side trip to Egypt. But God's plan was far greater than anything young Joseph could have imagined. He used those years of slavery and prison to shape a man who would eventually save not only his family and Israel but the entire known world from starvation.

When King Darius was forced to throw Daniel into the lions' den, I'm sure Daniel must have wondered if he was about to meet his Maker as kitty chow. He had no idea his miraculous rescue would serve as a catalyst for the conversion of a nation. But God had a plan.

God always has a plan. But it may not follow human logic. In fact, it may often seem to go directly against what we believe about God.

WHEN BAD THINGS HAPPEN

"The hardest problem I have to handle as a Christian," pastor and author Ray C. Stedman once said, "is what to do when God does not do what I have been taught to expect him to do; when God gets out of line and does not act the way I think he ought. What do I do about that?"[2]

These are the hard questions we must wrestle with in the story of Lazarus. Why would Jesus allow such sorrow to come to a family who loved him so much? Why would he withhold his power to heal when he'd healed so often before?

These aren't easy subjects to understand. They're not easy realities to endure—and some of you reading this book have endured more tragedy and pain than I can even imagine. Some of you have lost children. Some of you are facing a diagnosis you've always dreaded. Some of you have experienced a broken marriage and are facing life alone.

Why? There are no easy answers. The fact is, we may not know the purpose behind our pain until we see Jesus face to face. Even then, we aren't guaranteed any explanations. We are given only a promise: "He will wipe every tear from their eyes. There will be no more death or mourning or crying or pain, for the old order of things has passed away" (Revelation 21:4).

Because we live in this world, trapped in the old order of things, tragedy will touch our lives. That's simply a fact—for Christians and non-Christians alike. We will all lose loved ones. We will all eventually die. Romans 8:28 is often distorted to mean "only good things will happen to those who love God." But Paul meant just the opposite. In the very next paragraph he spells out the kinds of "things" we can expect in this world:

> Who shall separate us from the love of Christ? Shall trouble or hardship
> or persecution or famine or nakedness or danger or sword?... For I am
> convinced that neither death nor life, neither angels nor demons,
> neither the present nor the future, nor any powers, neither height
> nor depth, nor anything else in all creation, will be able to separate us
> from the love of God that is in Christ Jesus our Lord. (Romans 8:35,
> 38-39)

Trials are real. Bad things happen—to good people and bad people alike. And we who are Christians don't escape life, Paul says. We overcome life: "In all these things we are more than conquerors through him who loved us" (8:37).

This promise anchors our all-too-shaky world to his unshakeable kingdom.

And so do the lessons of Lazarus. For while life may shake, rattle, and roll, this rock-solid truth from John 11:5 remains: "Jesus *loved* Martha and her sister and Lazarus."

Love. That's a dependable anchor. Go ahead. Put your name in the blank: "Jesus loves _____."

The love Christ has for you is a love you can cling to, for it will hold you. Though we may not understand God's methods, that doesn't change the fact of God's love.

Even when it seems to tarry.

WHEN GOD'S LOVE TARRIES

Common sense seems to dictate that Jesus would drop whatever he was doing when he heard Lazarus was sick and travel immediately to Bethany. Instead, when the bad news came, "he stayed where he was two more days" (John 11:6).

In retrospect, we can see God's purposes in this delay. After all, we have the gospel account. We know that everything turned out all right.

But what did Mary and Martha think at the time? What did the disciples think?

And what about my life—and yours? What do we do when God doesn't act or move the way we think he should?

If we're paying attention in those times, we may understand better the second lesson the story of Lazarus has to teach us:

* *God's love sometimes tarries for our good and his glory.*

As human beings, we tend to want rational reasons for everything. The Jews of Jesus' time were especially interested in the whys and what-fors of life. That's why, when they encountered a man who had been born blind, the disciples immediately wanted to know what had gone wrong. "Rabbi," they asked Jesus, "who sinned, this man or his parents, that he was born blind?" (John 9:2).

A reasonable question. After all, the religious teachers of the day had developed the principle that "there is no death without sin, and there is no suffering without iniquity." It followed, then, that where there was affliction there had to be sin. Perhaps the man had done wrong in the womb or in a preexistent state. Perhaps the man deserved his blindness. Or perhaps he was the innocent victim of his parents' sin.

The religious elite as well as common folk were big on cause and effect, much as we are today. We want explanations. We want to know why.

With one short sentence, Jesus ripped through their reasoning and shredded their shame-based philosophies. "Neither this man nor his parents sinned," Jesus answered in verse 3, "but this happened so that the work of God might be displayed in his life."

What hope must have sprung up in the blind man's heart as he heard Jesus speak those words. It wasn't his fault! He wasn't the victim of bad parenting or bad karma. God had a plan!

With spit and plain dirt, Jesus made a mud compress and placed it on the man's eyes, telling him to go and wash in the Pool of Siloam. The man was healed, and his neighbors were amazed. The Sanhedrin tried to discount the miracle, but out of one man's tragedy came another divine triumph.

Because of a fallen world, a man was born blind. But because of that man, Jesus Christ was glorified.

We are not pawns on some celestial chessboard, expendable and unimportant. We are cherished and highly loved. "Are not five sparrows sold for two pennies?" Jesus reminds us gently in Luke 12:6-7. "Yet not one of them is forgotten by God.... Don't be afraid; you are worth much more than many sparrows."

While we may never fully understand why God's love sometimes lingers, we can rest assured that God's love is always at work. He may not move according to our schedule, but he is right on time for what is best. And he has our ultimate good forever in mind.

TRUSTING GOD'S CHARACTER

The third lesson of Lazarus underscores this hope:

- *God's ways are not our ways, but his character is still dependable.*

In other words, we don't need to fret, even when it looks like hope is dead. We might not be able to see the end of the story. But we can trust the Storyteller.

Martha and Mary, while they were sitting at Lazarus's deathbed waiting for Jesus to arrive, had nothing to hang on to except what they knew about the character of Jesus. But what they knew was enough to sustain them. They knew Jesus loved their brother. They knew Jesus had the power to heal. They knew Jesus would know what to do. Even though they must have struggled with fear and doubt, I believe they had the underlying assurance that Jesus would eventually make everything all right.

If you are struggling to hang on in the midst of your difficult circumstances, let me remind you to go back to what you know about God. Open the Bible and find scriptures to cling to—scriptures that reveal the heart and faithfulness of God. Remind yourself that God is your strength. That he is your source of comfort. That he won't let you fall. That he loves you passionately and only wants the best for you.

"We only trust people we know," says Martha Tennison, a popular women's conference speaker. "If you're struggling to trust God, it may be because you don't really know God."

Martha Tennison has experienced this truth firsthand. On the trip home from a weekend at an amusement park, the bus that held sixty-seven members of her church youth group was hit head-on by a drunk driver. Twenty-four teenagers and three adults died in the inferno that resulted from a punctured gas tank. In the hours that followed, Martha and her pastor husband had to tell all the families that the children and the mates they loved were gone. The pain was nearly unbearable. Time and time again Martha found herself going to the Word, calling out to the God she knew was faithful.

"You find out what you really believe in the darkest hours," Martha says. "You find out that the God you *know* is the God you can hold on to."[3]

Even when his stories don't unfold the way we think they should.

GOD'S GRAMMAR LESSONS

My background in grammar is spotty to say the least. My seventh-grade English teacher was a lovely woman, but her heart wasn't in choosing correct pronouns or tying up dangling participles. So instead of analyzing sentences and conjugating verbs, we spent our afternoons painting with watercolors and baking soufflés. Really.

Until the end of each quarter, that is, when it seemed necessary to hand out a grade for English rather than home ec. Then our teacher would tape a large strip of butcher paper around the room with 150 grammar questions printed neatly in Magic Marker. It was an open-book test. She encouraged us to peek inside our pristine, nearly-never-opened English books for the answers. There was no drilling to see if we'd learned anything, just information transferred from the book to our college-ruled paper.

We all got impressive grades. But it wasn't until high school that I learned what a preposition was for. Or that you should never end a sentence with one.

It's taken me even longer to learn the rules in God's school of grammar.

You didn't know God taught grammar? Well, he does. Everything we need to know is spelled out in his Word, which is good, because this course involves an open-book test as well. But this Teacher doesn't wait until the end of the quarter to print out the questions and tack them up around the room. Instead, God allows us to face them every day. The questions come out of our lives. The answers are found in him and his Word.

I wonder what Mary and Martha felt when they finally received word from Jesus. They'd been waiting for days. But instead of the Master, the only person they saw walking up their path was an out-of-breath courier with a message that must have rung hollow in their ears: "This sickness will not end in death."

It's hard to hope when hope is dead. It's hard to believe God's promises when your brother's body is lying in your living room.

However, God's ways are not our ways. His plots often don't take the direction we think they should. And even his grammar is not our grammar. For it is against this backdrop of despair that we find God's grammar rule number one. Listen carefully. There will be a test.

- *God's Grammar Rule #1: Never put a period where God puts a comma.*

Too often, according to Ray Stedman, we interpret God's delays as God's denials. But the story of Lazarus tells us that "a delay in answer is not a sign of God's indifference or his failure to hear. It is a sign of his love. The delay will help us. It will make us stronger."[4]

Jesus could have spoken the word and made Lazarus well. He did it with the Roman centurion's servant (Matthew 8:5-13). He did it for a Syrophoenician woman's daughter (Mark 7:24-30). Without physically being present, Jesus healed with just a word. He could have done that with Lazarus—as Mary and Martha well knew.

But God's ways are not our ways, and his timing rarely coincides with our own. While God is never late, I've found he's rarely early. That is why we must trust his schedule as well as his character.

CeCe Winans writes in her book *On a Positive Note:*

Faith is about how you live your life in the meantime, how you make decisions when you don't know for sure what's next. What you do with yourself between the last time you heard from God and the next time you hear from God is the ongoing challenge of a life of faith.[5]

Waiting four days may have made Jesus late for a healing, but it made him right on time for a resurrection. So never put a period where God puts a comma. Just when you think the sentence is over, the most important part may be yet to come.

Simon Peter learned God's second rule of grammar the hard way. The disciple with the foot-shaped mouth meant well, but when Jesus rebuked him, Peter got the message loud and clear.

- *God's Grammar Rule #2: Don't put a comma where God puts a period.*

Throughout the Gospels, Jesus had spoken of his death. In Matthew 16:21 the Bible tells us that "Jesus began to explain to his disciples that he must go to Jerusalem and suffer many things at the hands of the elders, chief priests and teachers of the law, and that he must be killed and on the third day be raised to life."

But Peter wouldn't hear of it. He took his Master aside and began to rebuke him. "Never, Lord!" he said in verse 22. "This shall never happen to you!"

Peter probably thought he was being valiant, protecting and correcting the Lord. He must have felt pretty good about himself...until Jesus rebuked Peter's rebuke.

"Get behind me, Satan!" Jesus told Peter in verse 23. "You are a stumbling block to me; you do not have in mind the things of God, but the things of men."

Ouch. It's not every day the Son of God calls you "Satan," and when he does, it has to hurt. But if you are trying to put a comma where God intends a period, don't be surprised when Jesus pops your pretty bubbles. Because when you attempt to breathe life into something God intends to die, you become a stumbling block to Christ.

There are times in every life when God writes the end to a chapter, when he asks us to say good-bye to something or someone who has been important to us. It might be a spouse, a parent, or friend. It might be a job we've loved, a city we've enjoyed, a prejudice or an assumption that we've always thought was true.

Endings, in a sense, are inevitable. Dead ends, failed possibilities, and brick walls will disappoint us all. And when those endings come, we can fight them as Peter advised Jesus. Or we can accept them as Jesus did, as coming from the Father's hand.

Laura Barker Snow writes beautifully about these times:

My child, I have a message for you today; let me whisper it in your ear, that it may gild with glory any storm clouds which may arise, and

Relinquishing Control

Do you ever find yourself clinging to the pencil, refusing to let God write on the pages of your life? I've discovered that the Lord is infinitely kind and patient in his dealings with us. He will show us how to relinquish our rights for his best. If you're struggling in this area, maybe these steps will help you:

1. *Ask God to make you willing.* Sometimes this is the necessary first step. If you just can't muster up the willingness to surrender control to God, then pray first for a change of attitude.

2. *Recognize you have an adversary.* The last thing Satan wants is for you to totally surrender your life to God. Pray for the wisdom and strength not to listen to his lies.

3. *Let go one piece at a time.* Sometimes we cling to control because we fear we'll be asked to make drastic changes we're not ready for. But God, in his kindness, takes us at a pace we can handle. If we simply obey what he asks of us at the moment, he'll lead us to the next step when we're ready.

I have lost all things. I consider them rubbish,
that I may gain Christ and be found in him.

PHILIPPIANS 3:8-9

smooth the rough places upon which you may have to tread. It is short, only five words, but let them sink into your inmost soul; use them as a pillow upon which to rest your weary head.… This thing is from ME.[6]

And that, of course, brings us back to the fundamental truth behind all God's grammar lessons. The Father knows best.

His periods may not be our periods. His commas may not be our commas. His ways may not be our ways. But God is the One telling the story, and we can trust him to take the tale in the right direction. We can have faith that everything really will turn out all right.

And it is that very faith that takes us to the next lesson Lazarus's story has to teach us.

DEVELOPING FAITH

The house in Bethany was most likely filled with people following Lazarus's death. Jewish faith considered expressing sympathy a sacred duty. Mourning was so important to the Jews that an entire industry had grown up around it. If the deceased hadn't enough friends to mourn, the family would hire wailers to make sure the dead departed properly. The louder the better.

But Mary and Martha didn't have to hire anybody when Lazarus died. They had mourners aplenty, according to John 11. Friends and family flocked in to support the sisters in their grief, even from out of town (verse 19).

This means Martha once again had a houseful of company when Jesus finally arrived in Bethany. But when someone brought the news that Jesus was coming, it was Martha, not Mary, who ran to meet him. The guests, the duties, all the distractions—nothing mattered but seeing Jesus.

She met him somewhere on the road into Bethany, and with all the anguished honesty of deep sorrow, Martha poured out her grief. "Lord," she cried, "if you had been here, my brother would not have died."

Her response was natural and heartfelt. But then Martha added something I find remarkable, something that revealed just how much she had changed since the last time they'd met. "But I know," she continued, "that even now God will give you whatever you ask" (verse 22).

No longer do we see a woman trying to manipulate God. Instead of trying to rewrite the story of her brother's death—instead of putting a comma where there was a period or a period where there could be a comma—Martha was placing the quill of their lives in Jesus' hands.

Do whatever you want, she was saying. Punctuate as you please. Thy will be done.

It is that kind of surrender and that kind of resolve that sets in motion the miraculous. I can almost see the glory on Jesus' face as he declared his purpose to Martha that day on the road outside her home. "I am the resurrection and the life. He who believes in me will live, even though he dies; and whoever lives and believes in me will never die. Do you believe this?" (John 11:25-26).

How precious Martha's response must have sounded in Jesus' ears. "Yes, Lord," she told him, "I believe that you are the Christ, the Son of God, who was to come into the world."

I believe. Could there be two sweeter sounding words? In Martha's great declaration of faith and the miraculous events that followed it, we find the fourth lesson from the story of Lazarus:

* *God's plan is released when we believe and obey.*

This is one of the most exciting lessons of all, because it means that God's story, in a sense, is interactive. We are an integral part of the writing process. Our choices play a part in the unfolding of the plot. Just as Adam and Eve's disobedience blocked God's purpose, our obedience releases his plan.

Faith and obedience go hand in hand. It takes faith to choose obedience, and if you're like me, it takes obedience to choose faith when you're quaking with fear. But when God speaks a promise to our hearts, we can take him at his word. That's what Martha did. And as she did, faith arose to help her take the next step: to obey him when he spoke, even when what he told her to do seemed completely impractical.

RESURRECTION POWER

By the time Jesus came to Bethany, Lazarus had been dead and buried for four days. The time span was significant to the Jews. "Many Jews believed the soul remained near the body for three days after death in the hope of returning to it. If this idea was in the minds of these people, they obviously thought all hope was gone—Lazarus was irrevocably dead."[7]

For centuries, the two primary groups of Jewish religious leaders, the Sadducees and Pharisees, had argued about the afterlife. The Sadducees said there was no resurrection, no future life, no hell nor heaven. Life on earth was all there was. (That's why they were "sad you see."[8]) The Pharisees, on the other hand, believed there was a future for the dead. They believed in the immortality of the soul and in reward and retribution after death.

But neither sect understood the concept of resurrection. Certainly not the type of resurrection they were about to witness.

I can only imagine what went through everyone's mind when Jesus asked for the stone to be taken away. We all chuckle at the *King James's* translation of Martha's response, "Lord,…he stinketh!" She only dared to speak what everyone else was thinking. There was a dead body behind that stone—a rotting one at that. "Grody hody," as my son used to say. Yuck.

Martha wasn't getting the picture. No one was. Why on earth did Jesus want to open the grave of a man who had been dead four days? To pay his last respects?

You see, Martha had faith for *what could have been:* "If you had been here, my brother would not have died" (John 11:21).

Martha had faith for *what would be:* "I know he will rise again in the resurrection at the last day" (11:24).

What Martha needed was faith for *what was happening now:* "Did I not tell you that if you believed, you would see the glory of God?" Jesus asked her in verse 40.[9]

It is the same question Jesus asks of us today: "Will you believe?" Martha's response of faith was quick, her obedience certain. "So they took away the stone," verse 41 tells us. And the rest is history. Incredible, life-changing, never-to-be-looked-at-the-same kind of history.

For when Jesus stood outside the tomb and said, "Lazarus, come out!" hell trembled. In a matter of weeks, death's grip on humanity—past, present, and future—would be completely broken. The dark shadowland of death would be filled with glorious light. And never again would we read the story of eternal life the same way again.

The final lesson from the story of Lazarus still echoes today:

- *The "end" is never the end; it is only the beginning.*

When Jesus came late to Bethany, his lateness was an act of love. A gift of perspective. A foreshadowing meant as a mercy, not only for Mary, Martha, and Lazarus, but for his disciples and for you and me.

Jesus knew we would struggle with the concept of resurrection. He knew we would have doubts when his tomb turned up empty. He knew there would be conspiracy theories and chat rooms jammed with people wanting to debate the likelihood of the dead coming back to life. So the Author of our faith, our great storytelling God, prefaced his Son's death with an act that would foreshadow the resurrection. When Jesus raised Lazarus from the dead, he put to death Satan's lie that the end is the end.

The truth of Lazarus and the secret of the resurrection is this: If Jesus Christ can turn death into life, sorrow into gladness, suffering into triumph—then nothing truly bad can ever touch our lives again. Not really. Unfortunate things may happen. Difficulties may come. But it all becomes fodder for a greater work, a more glorious glory.

Philip Yancey points to the cross and the empty tomb as turning points in the scriptural view of suffering: "When New Testament writers speak of hard times, they express none of the indignation that characterized Job, the prophets, and many of the psalmists. They offer no real explanation for suffering, but keep pointing to two events—the death and resurrection of Jesus."[10]

As a result of Christ's work on the cross, Yancey says, "The three-day pattern—tragedy, darkness, triumph—became for New Testament writers a template that can be applied to all our times of testing."[11]

Looking back, in fact, we can see that pattern all through God's story. Joseph experienced it. So did Job, though he didn't understand it. The disciples felt it. So did our Lord. *Tragedy* may come. So will the *darkness*. But *triumph* is waiting just around the corner.

That's the lesson that Lazarus's resurrection hinted at—that's the truth Jesus' resurrection would triumphantly prove.

It may be Friday, suggested Lazarus's empty tomb.

But Sunday's comin'.

AN EMPTY SHELL

Philip wasn't like the other children at church. Though he was a pleasant, happy boy, he struggled with things that came easily to other kids. He looked different, too, and everyone knew it was because he had Down syndrome. His Sunday school teacher worked hard to get the third grade class to play together, but Philip's disability made it difficult for him to fit in.

Easter was just around the corner, and the teacher had a wonderful idea for his class. He gathered the big plastic eggs that pantyhose used to come in and gave one to each child. Then, together, they went outside into a beautiful spring day.

"I want each of you to find something that reminds you of Easter—of new life," the teacher explained. "Put it in the egg, and when we get inside we'll share what we found."

The search was glorious. It was confusing. It was wild. The boys and girls ran all over the church grounds gathering their symbols until finally, breathlessly, the eight-year-olds were ready to return inside.

They put their eggs on the table, then one by one the teacher began to open them. The children stood around the table watching.

He opened one, and there was a flower. Everybody oohed and aahed.

He opened another and found a butterfly. "Beautiful," the girls all said.

He opened another and out fell a rock. The kids laughed. "A rock?" But the boy who'd found it said, "I knew you would all get flowers and leaves and stuff, so I got a rock cause I wanted to be different. That's new life to me." The kids laughed again.

But when the teacher opened the next egg, the group fell silent. "There's nothing there!" said one child. "That's stupid," said another. "Somebody didn't do it right."

Just then the teacher felt a tug on his shirt and turned to see Philip standing beside him. "It's mine," Philip said. "It's mine."

The children said, "You don't ever do things right, Philip. There's nothing there!"

"I did so," Philip said. "I did do it right. It's empty. *The tomb is empty!*"

There was another silence. A very deep, unlike-eight-year-olds kind of silence. And at that moment a miracle happened. Philip became a part of that third-grade Sunday school class. They took him in. He was set free from the tomb of his differentness. From then on, Philip was their friend.

Three months later, Philip died. His family had known since the time he was born that he wouldn't live out a full life span. An infection that most children would have quickly shrugged off took the life out of his body.

The day of the funeral, the church was filled with people mourning Philip's death. But it was the sight of nine third graders walking down the aisle with their Sunday school teacher that brought tears to most eyes.

The children didn't bring flowers. Instead, they marched right up to the altar, and placed on it an empty egg—an empty, old, discarded pantyhose egg.[12]

THE GOD WHO WEEPS WITH US

We will all die. Lazarus eventually did. Little Philip did. You and I will.

But never forget: The end is not the end. It is only the beginning. When we belong to Jesus, we simply leave our empty shells behind and go to glory. "Where, O death, is your victory?" Paul writes to remind us in 1 Corinthians 15:55. "Where, O death, is your sting?"

And yet death *does* sting, even when we know better. It hurts to leave behind the people we love. It hurts to be left behind. We will all encounter many more hurts on our journey toward the grave. Sometimes the story of our lives seems like one painful episode after another.

And Jesus knew that.

Even though Jesus knew Lazarus was about to be raised from the dead, he understood Mary and Martha's pain. He did more than understand it. He felt it too. John 11:35 tells us, "Jesus wept." The word for *wept* denotes a deep sorrow with great emotion.

Because Jesus loved this family from Bethany, he wept, and he weeps with us as well. Though Jesus knows our triumphant outcomes, though he sees the joyful ending just around the bend, he still gets down in the middle of our sorrow and holds us close, mingling his tears with our own.

And that, I believe, is the essence of the story God writes throughout our lives.

Jesus Understands

"Jesus wept" is famous as the shortest verse in the Bible, but to me the real power of that two-word passage from the story of Lazarus is the reassurance that Jesus understands what life is like for us. He doesn't ask anything of us that he wasn't willing to do himself, and he promises to be with us in all we have to go through. For example:

- *Jesus knew temptation:* "He was in the desert forty days, being tempted by Satan" (Mark 1:13).
- *Jesus knew poverty:* "Foxes have holes and birds of the air have nests, but the Son of Man has no place to lay his head" (Matthew 8:20).
- *Jesus knew frustration:* "He scattered the coins of the money changers and overturned their tables…. 'Get these out of here! How dare you turn my Father's house into a market!'" (John 2:15-16).
- *Jesus knew weariness:* "Jesus, tired as he was from the journey, sat down by the well" (John 4:6).
- *Jesus knew disappointment:* "O Jerusalem, Jerusalem…how often I have longed to gather your children together, as a hen gathers her chicks,…but you were not willing" (Luke 13:34).
- *Jesus knew rejection:* "From this time many of his disciples turned back and no longer followed him" (John 6:66).
- *Jesus knew sorrow:* "My soul is overwhelmed with sorrow to the point of death" (Matthew 26:38).
- *Jesus knew ridicule:* "Again and again they struck him…and spit on him. Falling on their knees, they paid [mocking] homage to him" (Mark 15:19).
- *Jesus knew loneliness:* "My God, my God, why have you forsaken me?" (Matthew 27:46).

For we do not have a high priest who is unable to sympathize with our weaknesses, but we have one who has been tempted in every way, just as we are—yet was without sin.

HEBREWS 4:15

Today we suffer. Today we don't understand. But someday, in that eternal Tomorrow, that same Savior who weeps with us will wipe every tear from our eyes. He'll unbind our graveclothes of earthly flesh, and we'll be set free. Someday all the scattered, broken pieces will fall into place, and we will suddenly understand the hand of God has been upon us all the time. All the tragedy—all the darkness—will instantly be swallowed up by triumph.

What a perfect ending to our imperfect stories!

That's the love of our Master Storyteller God.

9

Martha's Teachable Heart

If you hold to my teaching, you are really my disciples.
Then you will know the truth, and the truth will set you free.

JOHN 8:31-32

"No previous experience required. We will train you," the advertisement said. It read like a help-wanted ad for the night shift at McDonald's. Except this ad appeared on the pages of one of America's leading business journals.

After decades of dog-eat-dog capitalism, it seems, Fortune 500 companies are beginning to look for a new breed of worker. While degrees remain important, many businesses are looking for more personal qualities in their personnel. "How do you interact with others?" they ask. "Are you a team player or a maverick?"

Bottom line: Are you teachable?

Companies are ignoring glowing résumés, bypassing corporate headhunters, and going straight to college campuses to recruit their workforce. Why? "We spend more time and money 'untraining' people than we would training them in the first place," said one executive I heard on a talk show. "We don't need know-it-alls; we need people who are willing to learn."

A TEACHABLE HEART

If Jesus would have taken out a classified in the *Jerusalem Post* at the start of his ministry two thousand years ago, I think it would have read much the same as that business ad. "No previous experience required. We will train." Jesus wasn't as interested in finding capable people as he was in finding available people. He was looking for teachable hearts.

Perhaps that's why Jesus said, "Let the little children come to me, and do not hinder them, for the kingdom of God belongs to such as these" (Matthew 19:14). Children learn quickly—mainly because they don't have preconceived ideas that keep them from hearing something new and receiving it.

Perhaps that's why Jesus called a group of ragtag men to come alongside him instead of a bunch of religious muckety-mucks. The minds of the educated scribes and Pharisees of Israel were loaded with false perceptions and man-made agendas; it would have taken years to reprogram their thinking to God's way of thinking. So Jesus chose men without résumés, without formal education, with no previous evangelical work experience.

To the rest of the world, they seemed unimpressive. Unwashed, untaught, and sometimes uncouth. But Jesus saw in them exactly what he needed—followers with the potential for transformation.

Unfortunately, though we all applaud the thought of transformation, most of us don't appreciate the process that gets us there. To be transformed means we have to change, and change too often hurts. But as Paul W. Powell writes, "God is more concerned about our character than our comfort. His goal is not to pamper us physically but to perfect us spiritually."[1]

I believe that's why Jesus chose to confront Martha's attitude after her little tantrum about help in the kitchen back in Luke 10. There was more at stake in the incident than met the eye. In Martha's outburst, Christ could see a fault line that ran deep down the woman's psyche, down to where her identity lay. Martha thought she had value because she was productive. Jesus wanted her to learn she had value simply because she was his.

I'm sure Martha's feelings must have smarted at Jesus' rebuke. After all, no one enjoys the exposure of his or her blunders. I wouldn't be surprised if there was a moment when Martha was tempted to pack up her bruised ego and stomp out of the room. She knew when she wasn't being appreciated. Let them cook their own dinner! Then they'd see how hard she'd slaved.

But instead, Martha stuck around and heard Jesus out. And if we want to be his disciples, we must be willing to do the same. Even when his words cross our will.

Are You Teachable?

Consider the following statements to give you an idea of your teachability quotient. Answer (U) for Usually; (S) for Sometimes; and (R) for Rarely.

	U	S	R
1. I feel comfortable asking for advice.			
2. I easily admit when I'm wrong.			
3. I enjoy reading for information rather than escape.			
4. I'm able to receive criticism without being hurt.			
5. I enjoy listening to other peoples' thoughts and opinions without feeling the need to express my own.			
6. When I read something in the Bible, I automatically think of ways to apply it.			
7. I enjoy church and Bible classes and usually take notes.			
8. I'm able to disagree with someone without feeling like I have to debate the issue.			
9. I'm willing to look at all sides of a situation before I form an opinion.			
10. I'd rather be righteous than always have to be "right."			

Give yourself 3 points for each U answer, 2 points for each S, and 0 points for every R. Then add the numbers. If you scored 24-30 points, you are well on your way to a teachable heart. If you scored 15-23, keep at it! You are definitely trainable. If you scored 0-14, you may need to make your teachability quotient a matter of prayer, because you'll find a teachable heart is one of life's greatest treasures.

Take firm hold of instruction, do not let go;
keep her, for she is your life.

PROVERBS 4:13 (NKJV)

CROSS MY HEART

My mind was in turmoil as I took the kids to school that cold winter morning several years ago. Angry clouds crowded the sky above as I fought my way through the unplowed side streets. Yesterday's slush had hardened into large, icy ruts that caused my van to lurch from side to side. I had to struggle to keep hold of the steering wheel. But the real struggle that morning was inside me.

What a picture of my life, I thought, peering through the frosty windshield at the gray landscape. Dark. Dreary. Icy cold.

A huge misunderstanding had erupted between a dear friend and me several months before, and nothing I'd tried had mended it. I'd made a mistake and I'd apologized. Why wouldn't she forgive me? The mental ruts of the frozen circumstance tossed my emotions back and forth, ripping away my joy and peace, leaving me empty, hard, and hollow.

Jessica's sweet voice drifted from the backseat as she sang along with a popular Christian song on the radio. Her voice matched the soft twang of the singer's question, "Has Jesus ever crossed your heart?"

The words were strangely familiar. They echoed the words I'd used the day before to pronounce judgment on my friend. "Well, I guess you find out what people are really like when you cross them," I'd told my husband in a moment of anger. But now I sensed the Holy Spirit turning my own words like a spotlight on the darkness of my soul.

"What about you, Joanna?" I felt the Lord prompt softly. "What has this 'crossing' of your heart brought out in you?"

What he showed me wasn't pretty. There were things in my life I'd left unsettled, core issues I'd refused to contemplate. But it was time to face them, and I knew it. For me, the simple fact that I was ready illustrates one of the most beautiful things I've learned about my Lord.

Jesus goes out of his way to prepare my heart to listen and learn. He waits for the moment I'm most ready to obey. And while I can still refuse him at any time, his rebuke is gentle. It woos me at the same time it disarms me, making me willing and open and ready to change.

If you haven't experienced this sweet aspect of our Savior's discipline, may I suggest you spend a little more time in the Living Room? Because when you're busy in the Kitchen, the rebuke sounds harsh and demanding, just one more duty to fulfill. But when you listen from the Living Room, you hear the love in God's voice and it sounds like life for your soul.

That's where Martha found it. In the Living Room. She received the rebuke of her Savior, and we've witnessed how she changed. Instead of exalting herself against God, she humbled herself, and she found the truth of King Solomon's words: "Open rebuke is better than secret love. Faithful are the wounds of a friend" (Proverbs 27:5-6, KJV).

Especially when that friend is Jesus.

TO LEARN OR NOT TO LEARN

"Mom?" John Michael's eyes were dark and serious. A brilliant child (of course!), my twelve-year-old had a mind that was constantly moving, exploring, and— occasionally—mixing up words.

"Yes, Michael?" I asked.

"I was just wondering. People who are really poor…," he began slowly. "They're like in puberty, right?"

Well, as you might imagine, I gently corrected his mistake, and then we had a meaningful talk about the plight of starving people around the world.

Okay, so that's what I should have done.

Instead, I burst out laughing. "Puberty!?" I howled, trying to keep my voice down. "You mean poverty?"

"Yeah. That." He looked at me. "What did I say?"

I explained the difference between the two words to my son, and we both had a good chuckle. In fact, we discovered a code word for his impending adolescence. "I think I've got a pimple," he said a few days later as he inspected a small white bump on his chin in the bathroom mirror.

"Cool, Michael." It was his first bona fide blemish. I patted his back and congratulated him. "You're finally entering poverty."

Teachable moments. Those times in life when truth pops up (pardon the pun), offering us a chance to grow. To learn or not to learn, that is the question. For when we are corrected, rebuked, or chastened, we have a choice. We can receive it, or we can refuse it.

John Michael could have been offended by my disregard for his feelings over his vocabulary mistake. He could have marched out the door. But he chose to receive my instruction with good humor, and in receiving it, he opened the door for a mother-son discussion on a topic not easily talked about.

As for me, I got a much-needed lesson in not taking myself so seriously. Michael has taught me how to laugh and learn from my mistakes instead of trying to hide from them.

The point is, we all get confused sometimes. Most of us are quick to admit we're not perfect—as long as we don't have to talk specifics. But when someone points out a flaw in our lives, we're not nearly as calm. And unlike my good-natured son, we're not all that likely to laugh off the criticism either. Instead, we go all stiff and huffy. Or we go ballistic, shooting off our mouths in an attempt to shoot down their theories. "That is simply not true," we say, listing the reasons. When that doesn't work, we go on the offensive, listing their faults. "Get the log out of your own eye, Paul Bunyan!" we shout, then run for cover.

But Martha, to her eternal credit, didn't do that when Jesus corrected her that day in the living room. Or at least I don't think she did.

When he observed, "You are worried and upset about many things.... Mary has chosen what is better, and it will not be taken away from her," there's no rebuttal recorded from Martha. No sputtering reply. In fact, the entire incident ends with the words of Jesus' rebuke.

The Bible doesn't tell us how Martha responded that day. But I'm convinced Martha received the rebuke of Jesus humbly and learned from it. I believe that Martha had a teachable heart—for nothing else could explain her mysterious transformation into the Martha of John 11 and 12.

In these two chapters we see a woman completely different from the one we last met in Luke 10:38-42. Oh, she was still pushy, a bit impatient, and too practical for her own good. But as we have seen, there was also a tender vulnerability that wasn't there before. A new faith. A new kind of intimacy with Jesus that only comes when we receive and apply correction from God.

We've already mentioned Martha's transformation in "Lessons from Lazarus." But I'd like to focus on the changes we see in John 11, for they paint a picture of a woman changed by a teachable heart. First, Martha left a house filled with guests and hurried to meet Jesus. This was a woman who used to be obsessed about entertaining. What would make her leave a house full of company?

Making that even stranger is the fact that Martha was most likely the first-born. She was accustomed to being the strong one. She'd held the family together before, and in the middle of this overwhelming grief, surely she would feel the need to hold it together again. But when Jesus arrived in Bethany, instead of holding down the fort, Martha threw aside her obligations and ran outside to meet her Master.

"Lord," Martha said to Jesus in John 11:21, "if you had been here, my brother would not have died." Her words dripped with grief and confusion. Mary would echo her pain moments later, using the exact same words. But only Martha had something additional to say. Without break, without pause, she added, "But I know that even now God will give you whatever you ask."

Faith. That's what was different. Instead of whining like a child, demanding that Jesus do things her way, Martha proclaimed her belief that Jesus could do whatever was needed. Gone was Martha's contentious "Tell her!" She wasn't ordering Jesus around this time. Instead, she humbly gave Jesus the authority and the room to decide what was best.

It was to this open, teachable heart that Jesus revealed himself in all his glory: "I am the resurrection and the life. He who believes in me will live, even though he dies.... Do you believe this?" Jesus asked Martha in John 11:25-26.

"Yes, Lord," she replied, "I believe that you are the Christ, the Son of God, who was to come into the world" (11:27).

Scholars call this declaration one of the most incredible statements of faith in Scripture, for it cuts to the very essence of who Jesus was and is. And this insightful proclamation came not from contemplative, sensitive Mary, but from organized, duty-bound—but teachable—Martha.

No longer blinded by doubt and self-interest, Martha was a woman whose eyes were open. She knew who Jesus was—not a just good man or a fascinating teacher, but the very Son of God. She proclaimed him the Christ, her Messiah.

But beyond Martha's theological understanding, I find in verse 28 the sweetest change of all: "And after she had said this, she went back and called her sister Mary aside. 'The Teacher is here,' she said, 'and is asking for you.'"

Wait a minute! What happened to the sibling rivalry we saw in Luke 10?

Gone now is the resentment. Gone is any form of competition. Martha could feel not only for herself, but also for her sister. And this time, instead of shooing Mary away from the feet of Jesus, Martha pointed her there.

Clearly, this was not the same woman we saw before in that Bethany home. The anxious, demanding Queen of Everything is gone. And in her place is a woman with a transformed heart. It's the kind of transformed heart we all desire but spend most of our lives wondering how to achieve.

I think we get a new heart from the Lord the same way Martha did—by being teachable. And being teachable, in essence, involves three things:

- being willing to listen
- acting on what we hear
- responding to discipline

DO YOU HAVE EARS?

"Hear, O Israel: The LORD our God, the LORD is one." Every morning for thousands of years, pious Jews have recited Deuteronomy 6:4. The verse opens the *Shema,* their main confession of faith, which instructs the Jewish people to: "Love the LORD your God with all your heart and with all your soul and with all your strength" (6:5).

Shema. The actual Hebrew word means "hear thou." And that's a word for us as well. The Scripture contains great truth. Powerful, life-changing words. If we're willing to *shema*—if we're willing to hear.

Unfortunately, it seems God's people have always been hard of hearing. Perhaps it's hereditary. Again and again, in the Old Testament we read about God's attempts to communicate with his wayward, hearing-impaired children:

So I told you, but you would not listen. You rebelled against the LORD's command and in your arrogance you marched up into the hill country. (Deuteronomy 1:43)

Although the LORD sent prophets to the people to bring them back to him, and though they testified against them, they would not listen. (2 Chronicles 24:19)

For many years you were patient with them. By your Spirit you admonished them through your prophets. Yet they paid no attention. (Nehemiah 9:30)

It's not hard to see a pattern here. Almost from the beginning of time, God's people have thwarted the Lord's transforming work by refusing to listen. By tuning him out. We do the same thing when we refuse to pay attention to the voice of his Spirit in our lives.

Sometimes the refusal to hear is deliberate; we don't want to face what we think God might have to say. Sometimes I think it's almost subconscious; we live in a state of denial because we just can't handle any demands the Lord might

How Does God Talk to You?

While we know God speaks clearly to us through the Bible, many of us are uncertain how to hear God's voice in our spirit. "How does God speak to you?" someone asked author and speaker Carole Mayhall. I have found her answer immensely practical and helpful:

For me, He speaks by a distinct impression in my heart. He's never spoken to me aloud, but sometimes the thought that He puts in my soul is so vivid that He might as well have! Many times it is just a thought or an idea that flashes into my mind and I know it is from Him....

Sometimes a thought pops into my mind—a thought so different from what I was thinking, or so creative I never would have thought of it, or opposite to what I *wanted* God to say to me. When that happens—and it lines up with God's Word—I know I've heard His voice in a distinctive way....

I pray frequently that I'll hear His voice more often and more clearly. When I don't, I know He hasn't stopped speaking; rather, I have stopped listening.[2]

My sheep listen to my voice; I know them, and they follow me.

JOHN 10:27

want to make. Sometimes we conveniently let God's voice be drowned out by the confusion of our daily existence; we avoid listening to him by being too busy to read the Bible or pray. It's almost like we're stubborn children who cover their ears and stomp their feet and hum loudly just to keep from hearing what their parents are trying to tell them.

Regardless of how we do it, the ultimate result is the same. When we refuse to listen to the Lord, we shut him out. We refuse him the opportunity to teach us, to transform our lives, and to work through us to transform the world.

Surely that's why Jesus put such a premium on listening. Over and over, Jesus' clarion call punctuates the Gospels, echoing the words of the *Shema:* "He who has ears, let him hear." And eight times in Revelation, Jesus instructs his Bride, the Church, to listen: "Let him hear what the Spirit says to the churches."

And make no mistake, the Lord still speaks today. Through the Scriptures. Through our circumstances. In our heart, by the voice of the Holy Spirit. We can hear him if we give up our rebellion and our denial. We can hear his voice, and when we hearken to him, he will teach us.

We who have ears...let us listen and hear.

DOING WHAT JESUS SAYS

Just hearing God's Word isn't enough, of course. The Bible makes that abundantly clear. God's transforming power in our lives is unleashed when we not only listen, but also *act* on what we've heard.

In fact, in our very refusal to apply God's truth to our lives, we may actually keep ourselves from hearing his voice in the future. Sin actually stops up our spiritual ears the same way excess wax plugs up our physical ones. When that happens, we may appear to hear, nodding and saying yes, yet have absolutely no comprehension. People with spiritually stopped-up ears are "always learning," Paul writes in 2 Timothy 3:7, "but never able to acknowledge the truth."

The sad fact is, we can grow so accustomed to God's voice that it no longer moves us. We can become like the people God warned us about through his prophet in Ezekiel 33:31-32:

My people come to you, as they usually do, and sit before you to listen to your words, but they do not put them into practice. With their mouths they express devotion, but their hearts are greedy for unjust gain. Indeed, to them you are nothing more than one who sings love songs with a beautiful voice and plays an instrument well, for they hear your words but do not put them into practice.

Sounds frighteningly familiar, doesn't it? So do the pointed words of James, the brother of Jesus, "Do not merely listen to the word, and so deceive yourselves. Do what it says" (James 1:22).

I've already said quite a lot about obedience in this book, mainly because I believe obedience is an essential ingredient in intimacy with God and the key to having a Mary heart. And obedience is exactly what we're talking about here. Either we take Jesus' words to heart and *change,* or we listen but disregard them. And to disregard the voice of God is worse than not listening at all. Especially if we say we love him.

When my children refuse to listen, I find myself wanting to quote the words Jesus used in John 14:21: "Whoever has my commands and obeys them, he is the one who loves me." *Don't tell me you love me,* I want to say when they come begging to watch cartoons after they've already been told to clean their rooms. *Obey my commands.*

Jesus doesn't mince words with us. He cuts to the heart of what really matters in each of our lives. He puts his finger on our sore spots, the sin-infected places we try so hard to hide. He points to our cluttered bedrooms and says, "Do this and live." Because if we want to live, we're going to have to obey.

Oswald Chambers has illuminated my life in so many ways, but perhaps none as penetrating as this simple truth about the importance of obedience:

All God's revelations are sealed until they are opened to us by obedience…. Obey God in the thing He shows you, and instantly the next thing is opened up…. God will never reveal more truth about himself until you have obeyed what you know already.[3]

Unfortunately, it's often easier to talk about obedience than to do anything about it. We'll dissect and analyze God's truth, debate it, and philosophize about it—anything but actually let it affect our lives.

"What did Jesus really mean?" we ask each other as we ponder the hard sayings of Christ at Wednesday-night Bible study. "Surely he didn't mean we need to sell everything we have and give to the poor," we conclude, then go on to explain why we need to cut back on our mission giving until we've paid off the new Lexus.

That's an extreme example, of course. But I do think there is something deep inside each one of us that rebels against God's authority in our life. Something deep that insists on doing things our own way. That's as true now as it was when Eve bucked God in the garden, when the children of Israel ignored the prophets' warnings, and when the Jews turned Jesus over to be crucified.

And so Pilate's question to the Jews still echoes for us today: What will you do with this man? Because to know him is to hear his words and lovingly obey him, or we know him not at all.

Kathleen Norris, author of *Amazing Grace: A Vocabulary of Faith,* describes a simple exchange that impressed this reality upon her and changed her life. The women's circle in her church had asked her to conduct the Bible study session on the Antichrist, a task for which she felt distinctly inadequate. The packet of study materials provided comfort but not much practical help, declaring that even St. Augustine had given up on the subject, claiming it was beyond him.

So Kathleen went to her pastor for help. "He quickly summarized and dismissed the tendency that Christians have always had to identify the Antichrist with their personal enemies, or with those in power whom they have reason to detest. It is an easy temptation," Norris writes. "In our own century, the Antichrist has been equaled with Adolf Hitler, Joseph Stalin, Pol Pot, and given the current state of political hysteria in America, no doubt Bill and Hillary Clinton as well."

But then, Norris writes, the pastor said something so simple it would stay with her forever: "'Each one of us acts as an Antichrist,' he said, 'whenever we hear the gospel and do not do it.' "[4]

RECEIVING REBUKE

What happens when we refuse to listen to God and act on what he says?

The Bible is clear that God, like a loving parent, will administer the appropriate correction in our lives. "For whom the LORD loves He reproves," states Proverbs 3:12, "even as a father, the son in whom he delights" (NASB).

The level of the discipline we receive depends mostly on the level of our teachability. When my mother was small, all her father had to do was look disappointed with her and she'd be in his arms, melting with tears, begging for his forgiveness. Suffice it to say, it required a little more force on my dad's part when it came to his eldest child. I was not only well raised, I was also well "reared." And quite often, come to think of it.

Spiritually, the same is true. If we are teachable, we come around quickly to obedience. As a consequence, the level of discipline is fairly minor, sometimes even painless. But if we are unteachable, if we refuse God's rebuke, the level of discipline increases in severity, just like my "rearing" did. Not because God is ruthless, but because our hearts are rebellious. Our loving Father will do whatever it takes to break that rebellion before that rebellion breaks us. Even if it means giving us a time-out (like having to wait for something we've wanted), taking away our toys (like the new computer that just crashed), or allowing some affliction to come our way.

"Before I was afflicted I went astray," the psalmist writes, "but now I obey your word" (Psalm 119:67). Before you think God cruel, read on. This is no trembling, abused child. This is a chastened son, who like me, can look back and say to his Father with full assurance: "You are good, and what you do is good; teach me your decrees" (119:68).

Jesus was direct in his rebuke of Martha. His words were gentle, but they pierced straight to the heart of her shortcomings. And Martha paid attention. She was teachable. All it took was a tender rebuke from the one she loved. Jesus didn't have to convince her. She didn't launch into a debate. She simply accepted his words, though I'm sure they were painful to hear.

Martha knew the secret every child who has ever been lovingly disciplined eventually learns. You shouldn't run away from your daddy. Though correction hurts and rebukes sting, at the end of the pain, there is great reward. Hebrews 12:11 tells us, "No discipline seems pleasant at the time, but painful. Later on, however, it produces a harvest of righteousness and peace for those who have been trained by it."

I, for one, am incredibly thankful for the discipline my parents gave me. Far from crying "child abuse," I call them blessed. Because of their diligence in correcting my childhood wrongs, I have much less temptation to deal with as an adult. For one thing, I'm not tempted to steal—not since my mother marched me back into Buttrey's at the age of five and made me return the candy bar I'd taken. And I don't struggle with swearing either. I swore off cursing at the first taste of Ivory soap.

And as an adult, I'm learning to welcome the discipline of the Lord in my life as well. Instead of running from his rebuke, I find myself looking forward to it. Even—dare I say it?—asking for it. The words of Psalm 23 play through my soul like a precious song: "Your rod and your staff, they comfort me."

Several years ago, a four-year-old named Joshua Wiedenmeyer taught me a lesson about receiving discipline I will never forget. When Josh's parents, Jeff and Tammy, dropped by on vacation, Glacier National Park was high on the list of must-sees. We loaded both families into the van the next morning and set off for a day of sightseeing. The kids chattered as we pointed out various points of interest. The van climbed the "Going to the Sun" highway through pine trees and ancient cedars until we were far above the valley floor. At the summit, we spent an hour touring the visitors center and then ate lunch in the sunshine, enjoying the incredible beauty around us.

It was nearly two o'clock when we headed back down the mountain. Nap time. Poor Josh was having a tough time. He didn't like the car seat. He didn't want a cracker. Tammy tried to comfort him. She tried to distract him. But nothing worked. Finally Dad stepped in. "Josh, do you need a spanking?"

Now I've asked my kids that question several million times, but until that day, I'd never heard this particular response. Josh paused for a moment, his eyes bright with tears. Collecting his breath between sobs, he said in a small voice, "Yes, Daddy. I do."

"John, will you please pull over?" Jeff asked my husband, who complied. Jeff got out of the front seat, opened the van door and waited as Joshua climbed over several legs and into his arms. They walked a few paces off where Jeff applied loving, but firm pressure to his son's backside, then hugged him and spoke tender exhortation. They came back to the van and Joshua climbed into the backseat, catching his breath like we all do after a hard cry, but with nary a whine.

Joshua got what he needed and the rest of the trip he was fine. What a lesson. Instead of avoiding discipline, he embraced it. At four years of age, Joshua had discovered a secret many of us live a lifetime yet never learn.

"Blessed is the man you discipline, O LORD;…you grant him relief from days of trouble" (Psalm 94:12-13).

A HOLY MAKEOVER

Do you want to know God? Do you really desire to have an intimate, heart-to-heart relationship with him? If you do, then respond to his rebuke. Don't refuse his correction. "If you had responded to my rebuke," the Lord says in Proverbs 1:23, "I would have poured out my heart to you and made my thoughts known to you." Respond to him with a teachable heart, and you'll be surprised at the holy makeover that happens in your own life.

I want that for my life. I want a holy makeover as transforming as Martha's. My deepest fear has always been that I might wake up thirty years from now and realize I haven't changed—that I still struggle with the same worthless habits, petty attitudes, and hidden sin that I did way back when.

What a terrible thing that would be. But unless I have a teachable heart, such spiritual stagnation is my destiny. Bitter and fearful, I'll be encrusted with things from the past that I should have let go of long ago. And all because I refused to be taught by my heavenly Father.

The purpose of Jesus' death on the cross wasn't to provide fire insurance or an all-expenses-paid trip to heaven. He died and rose again so we could be made new. So we wouldn't have to stay in our trespasses and sins, tangled up by our emotions, hurts, and past disappointments. He did it so we could be "transformed into his likeness," Paul says in 2 Corinthians 3:18. No longer must we hide behind a veil of shame. Instead, with "unveiled faces" we "reflect the Lord's glory…with ever-increasing glory, which comes from the Lord."

Don't be *conformed* to this world, Paul tells us in Romans 12, but be *transformed.* That is the result of teachability, of being open to the Lord's lessons, and when we choose transformation, we choose something magnificent. The Greek word for it is *metamorphoo,* from which we get our word *metamorphose,* meaning to be transfigured or changed. It is the same word used to describe what happened to Jesus on the Mount of Transfiguration.

Transformation. We can experience it as well.

All we have to do is be teachable.

Jesus will change us. All we have to do is lay down our old lives—and he'll make them new.

THE BUTTERFLY

Joanie Burnside glows. Brown, cropped hair frames a beaming forty-something face as wire-rimmed glasses magnify blue dancing eyes. Joanie is also a talented actress, and I had the privilege of watching her perform a monologue one Palm Sunday at Mount Hermon, a Christian conference center.

The pre-Easter service at Mount Hermon is always poignant. I inevitably go away shaken at the immensity of Christ's work on the cross. But Joanie's presentation that year reminded me of not only what Jesus did, but what he longs to do in you and me.

You see, Jesus didn't come to make bad people better. He came to transform us into something entirely new.

My words can't paint the power behind the images I saw that morning, but with Joanie's permission, I'd like to try. Imagine with me an old woman, center stage, clothed in a dark coat and carrying a dingy laundry-type bag over her shoulder. She clings tightly to an out-of-date purse. Dirty rags cover her feet. Stooped and bent over a cane, the old woman's face is twisted with suspicion, her voice sharp and brittle as she begins her story.

Listen closely. Now and then, I hear Martha speaking. Now and then, I hear me.

"I've come to tell you the story of a butterfly," the woman begins. Her only props are the clothes that she wears and a simple wooden cross that stands behind her. "She started out as all others, a lowly caterpillar, one who would have grown but never changed. Her life would have become old, ugly, and embittered had it not been for the grace of the Creator.

"*This* is what she would have become," the old woman says, pointing at her twisted, decrepit form. "Though she willed herself to change…she could not. Submitting to his power was her only chance.

"Here was her scarf, which covered her head, her precious brain, her above-average intelligence. The universities and degrees were hers to obtain, to flaunt and impress…to shrink others down to her size.

"The hair, the crown that should have been, was merely a reflection of the anxieties that riddled her life, for she was prematurely gray. She worried about everything—her future, her past, her mistakes, her dreams.

"Her teeth…" The old woman bites down for emphasis. "The guardians of her mouth, one of her most vicious weapons, were ever ready to bite, to cut others to the quick with sarcasm and barbs. For out of the overflow of the heart speaks the tongue. Sometimes it was as seemingly innocent as gossip, other times judgment, and at times, outright lies as she assassinated the characters of others.

"Her purse was her security, for it housed her beloved checkbook. She was born into affluence, and as long as there was money in the bank to protect her, she was safe. No one could touch her, no one could reach her. She walled herself in with material goods—none of them evil in and of themselves, but all of them evil when worshiped and adored instead of him.

"Her cane she used like a finger, to point accusingly at the sins of herself that she saw in others. It became a wonderful crutch, this overdeveloped superego, for whenever she felt bad about herself, she could easily find bad in the lives of others around her.

"Her shoes covered one of her saddest features, her feet. Those poor, beaten stubs. She had spent a lifetime wandering aimlessly. She had no purpose, no one to follow, nowhere to go. Each day meant only another twenty-four hours of hopelessness."

The woman shifts a large sack she carries on her shoulder, then points at it. "Here was her burden, the sin she bore that weighted her down, every year getting heavier and heavier. She stuffed those sins in her sack, hoping no one else would notice what was so obvious to all. Her life had become grotesque with the weight, her sins disfiguring the beauty she was meant to be.

"Lastly was her heart, a shriveled shadow of what the Creator had given her."

Pantomiming the movement, the woman takes a small, stony heart out of her chest and holds it between two fingers. "It was hard and unrelenting, not letting any love in…not letting any love out…protected from intruders by her head, her mouth, her purse, and her cane.

"Then one day this woman met some friends who had lives of sweet purity. They offered her the Living Water, and when she could bear the thirst no longer, she took a taste…just a taste, mind you, for she wasn't ready to really drink yet. But that taste was so sweet, and it made her thirst beyond compare. She took, and drank, and that Living Water filled her and satisfied her from her crown to her toes."

The face of the woman onstage now glows with the memory of that water and the new life she's received. Piece by piece she begins to remove the unnecessary articles of clothing that once bound her.

"The scarf was removed and her knowledge used for his glory. Her thoughts became his thoughts as she surrendered to his Spirit." The woman unties the scarf and drops it to the floor.

"The hair, once gray with concern was made new again, for the joy that was his was now hers." The woman ruffles her hair with glee.

"The mouth that had cut down others now began to build them up, to sing psalms and hymns and spiritual songs…to seek ways to soothe hurts rather than cause them.

"The purse became a tool, as a sheath is to a sword. It carried something of great power. Her moneys were used to advance his kingdom rather than protect her own," the woman says as she lifts the purse for all to see.

"The cane was no longer needed as her urge to judge faded in the light of his grace. She gave it to others that needed to be held up, as she sought to come alongside and bear others' burdens.

"Aaaah…" The woman pauses, smiling as she shakes her finger. "And her feet? At first they began to walk, then run, skip, leap, and dance with joy, for finally she had a reason to live. A Master to follow. A path that he prepared specifically for her. Such joy she'd never known.

"The burden of her sins he took," the woman says, her voice becoming stronger and younger sounding. Her posture straightens as she drapes her things over the Cross. "How, she would never really understand, other than he said that he'd died for the right to do so.

"Her heart of stone was transformed into a new, vital, living heart." With trembling hands she lifts the small, imaginary heart heavenward, receiving a large, beating one in exchange. With her face uplifted, her eyes filled with wonder, the woman pantomimes the act of placing the new heart inside her chest.

"Create in me a clean heart, O God," she whispers, "and renew a right spirit within me" (Psalm 51:10, KJV).

The words are soft, pleading, and thankful as they drift across the quiet auditorium. The moment is holy as David's prayer echoes through each one of us.

A clean heart, O God. A right spirit. Within me.

"Thank you for hearing my tale," the woman says finally. Her voice is low and tender as she unbuttons her coat. "For as you see...I am the butterfly."

She sheds the cloak, revealing a splendid purple leotard with flowing multi-colored wings. Sparkling and shimmering in the morning light, the costume is beautiful. Exquisite.

With arms extended, the woman exits reborn. Floating, dancing, skipping. Leaving all of her earthly garments behind. Inviting each one of us to do the same.[5]

New lives for old. That's what Jesus offers. Warm hearts for cold. And all for the price of being teachable.

As I've surrendered my life to Jesus' teaching, even his rebukes, I've learned the value of God's tender discipline. It is only when we struggle to break free from the chrysalises of our lower nature that the true beauty of the new life Christ offers can truly be known.

So don't be afraid to shed the familiarity of old patterns and old clothes.

Jesus, remember, came to make all things new.

So hear him and obey. Receive his discipline.

And then...get ready to fly.

10

Mary's Extravagant Love

Then Mary…poured it on Jesus' feet and wiped his feet with her hair.
And the house was filled with the fragrance of the perfume.

JOHN 12:3

He looks so tired. The face she loves is lined and drawn as she meets him at the door. His forehead is troubled, but when he sees her, the Master's eyes soften. He makes his way through the crowded foyer and takes her hands.

"Mary…"

"I'm glad you're here, Lord," she says. "It's been too long." His travels have taken him away from Jerusalem lately. Away from the temple courts. Away from the rumored price upon his head. "I worry for you," Mary whispers.

Jesus smiles and slowly shakes his head. "Be anxious for nothing, dear Mary. My life is in the Father's hands." His words are tender, yet intense; as though they hold hidden truth. A shiver runs down her spine as they walk toward the living room.

It's clear this visit will be nothing like the one so many months ago. Something is wrong. And yet, somehow, Mary senses something so right. It goes against logic. She can see the Master's weariness. The men are clearly worried and befuddled. And yet Mary feels a tremor within, like a single strum upon a stringed instrument. Like hope…or is it joy?

There is no sound, only an awaiting. As though all of heaven is standing on tiptoe listening for the song. As if all of eternity has been gathering momentum for this week…for this journey…for this Man.

A LITTLE PERSPECTIVE

No one can know what took place in Mary's heart when she met Jesus that day. However, the sweet sadness and the sense of destiny surrounding this final trip to Jerusalem seems evident. We know that Jesus had "set his face as flint" toward the Holy City. Toward certain arrest and certain death. Of all the people surrounding him, only Mary seemed to understand, for only she seemed moved to take the appropriate action.

This story found in John 12:1-8 is the last time the Bible mentions Mary, Martha, and Lazarus. (The same story, told in Matthew and Luke, doesn't mention this family by name, but the similarities of the narrative seem to indicate that those Gospel writers were speaking of the same incident.) Though religious tradition places all three at the cross, Scripture doesn't specify their presence there. It's clear, however, this family deeply loved the Lord, and he loved them. This trio from Bethany had provided something Jesus needed after leaving Nazareth three and a half years before.

They had given him a home. A family. A place to lay his head.

And for these sisters and their brother and all who loved Jesus, the mood must have been confused on that last journey to Jerusalem. According to Matthew 26:2, Jesus had told the disciples what awaited him: "The Son of Man will be handed over to be crucified." He had kept no secrets, but still the disciples seemed unable to comprehend fully what was happening.

They knew, of course, that Jesus was a wanted man. The fact had been well publicized. After raising Lazarus from the dead, he had risen quickly to the top of the religious mafia's hit list. And no wonder. Many of the Jewish community, it seemed, had had a real change of heart (John 11:45). After seeing Jesus bring their friend Lazarus back to life, they'd been convinced that Jesus was indeed something special—perhaps even the Messiah. If Jesus could do that for a *dead* man, think what he could do for someone still alive!

Temple attendance had declined as crowds flocked to hear the man from Galilee. Synagogue-growth experts were deeply concerned. Perhaps they needed to be more seeker sensitive. Perhaps they needed to focus on a feeding program—the Nazarene had had great luck with his potlucks. Clearly, they needed to do something—and fast. Everything was at risk. Especially for the religious elite.

"If we let him go on like this," the chief priests and some of the Pharisees had argued before the Jewish governing authority, the Sanhedrin (11:48), "everyone will believe in him, and then the Romans will come and take away both our place and our nation."

Loss of position. Loss of power. Loss of influence. At this point in the game, that was a risk the Jewish leaders were not prepared to take—especially not after they had worked so hard to secure just those things.

The Sanhedrin had only recently worked an uneasy truce with the Roman procurator, Pilate, and after a rocky beginning it was finally working well. When the newly appointed Pilate first paraded Roman flags bearing the emperor's image down Jerusalem's streets, the people had rioted in a frenzy against the idolatry. In the face of such opposition, Pilate had quickly retreated into a you-don't-bother-me-I-won't-bother-you understanding with the temple and its officials. The Sanhedrin had finally gotten the procurator right where they wanted him. Until Jesus showed up, that is.

"You know nothing at all!" Caiaphas, the high priest, erupted during the meeting. Like most members of the Sadducee sect, he was not known for his tact nor his kindness.[1] In his mind, he was thinking strategically, hoping to push the situation to its logical conclusion. "You do not realize that it is better for you that one man die for the people than that the whole nation perish" (11:49-50).

But it was Caiaphas who hadn't a clue. Unbeknownst to him, he had just "prophesied that Jesus would die for the Jewish nation," John writes in verses 51-52, "and not only for that nation but also for the scattered children of God, to bring them together and make them one."

So while the religious establishment plotted Jesus' downfall, God's plan to bring all humanity back to him was gathering speed. Heaven's gates began to open, ready to receive all who would come in through Jesus Christ the Son.

Eternity's song began to play. The Lamb "slain from the creation of the world" (Revelation 13:8) was about to die so you and I could know God.

Mary alone seemed to hear the echoes of that music. Only she seemed ready to respond to the extravagance of Jesus' love.

EXTRAVAGANT LOVE

Tucking my daughter, Jessica, into bed at night is always a special treat. But of all our misty-water-colored memories, perhaps none is as sweet as that of bedtimes when she was small.

"I love you, Jessica," I'd say as I pulled her pink rosebud comforter up around her chin and smoothed her glistening blond hair as it lay upon her pillow.

"I wuv *you* more!" she'd say with a twinkle in her eye, thus beginning our favorite game. "Well, I love you most," I'd say, then kiss her on the cheek and tickle her pink-pajamaed tummy.

"Well, I wuv you the most-est," she'd announce when she'd finished giggling. Then she'd fling her arms open wide before I could, and she'd add the final words, "I wuv you the *who-o-o-le* world!"

Wow. Game over. The whole world? Now that's love. Especially for a three-year-old. Especially when you consider how much there is out there to love. Loving me the whole world meant she loved me more than ice cream. More than her favorite dolly. More than a trip to the park. More than birthday presents and her new trike. More than bubblegum and a ride on the brown-spotted fiberglass pony at Kmart. She loved me—*me*—more than all that put together.

That's extravagant love. The kind of love that disregards everything else so it can focus on one thing alone: the object of that love. The kind of love that sacrifices everything, only wishing it had more to give. Nothing is too precious. Nothing is too exorbitant. The heart demands we give—and give all.

When Mary anointed Jesus at the banquet given in his honor, she gave her very best. In fact, she may have laid down her very future when she poured the perfume on his feet. For that jar of perfume—which Matthew and Mark describe as an alabaster jar, broken in order to be opened—may have very well held every hope and dream she'd ever had.

To be married ranked high on every Jewish maiden's wish list. Their culture, even their religion, made marriage and especially childbirth the highest form of honor. To be barren was a disgrace. But to be unmarried…well, that truly was a shame.

By age twelve, most young Jewish women had been promised in marriage, if they weren't already married.[2] Fathers usually arranged the unions, though the girls were given a say in the matter. Several factors were involved. One was the bride's price, the compensation paid to the bride's father by the groom. But the bride was often expected to bring something of value to the union as well.

When both sides agreed, the betrothal—the engagement part of the ceremony—was performed. An ornate document called the *ketubah* was signed by the future bride and groom, and the ceremony was sealed by a kiss. From that moment on, the couple were legally bound to wed, though the actual wedding ceremony might not take place for several years.[3] The agreement could be dissolved only by death or by divorce, the option considered by Joseph before being reassured by an angel.

As far as we know, Mary never had the opportunity to marry. Because she and Lazarus lived with Martha, it appears that their parents must have died several years before. The fact that it was called Martha's house is interesting as well, for the family estate usually went to a son. Some commentaries speculate Martha may have been married and widowed, the house an inheritance from her husband.

But what did Mary have? With no father to arrange her marriage, time was ticking away. The alabaster jar of perfume may have been a part, if not all, of Mary's dowry. Worth more than three hundred denarii, nearly a year's wages, this was no ordinary perfume. Though unromantic by name, *nard* was rare, made from the aromatic oil extracted from the root of a plant grown mainly in India.[4] It had to be imported. Mary couldn't get it over the counter at Wal-Mart. I'm not sure she would have found it at Saks Fifth Avenue. In fact, there is no perfume I know of today that can even compare in worth—approximately thirty thousand dollars a bottle.

Alabaster, on the other hand, was a common container in the Near East. The snowy gypsum shone smooth and translucent when polished. Easily carved, it formed ornate jars, boxes, vases, and flasks. Sometimes marble containers were labeled *alabastra* as well.[5] But the origin and type of the container wasn't really significant. It still isn't.

What mattered most—what matters still today—is the treasure the container holds. And the treasure Mary poured out that day was more than an expensive perfume. She was pouring out her very life in love and sacrificial service.

Unfortunately, not everyone present had Mary's kind of heart.

A VIEW FROM THE DARK SIDE

What a waste! What an extravagant, exorbitant, unnecessary display of emotion. Why a whole bottle when a few drops would have been more than adequate? Why break the jar when it could have easily been poured? And why the hair? The whole scene was messy, not at all proper or orderly. As Mary caressed the Master's feet, the perfume hung pungent in the air, her sobs the only sound breaking the stunned silence.

Why doesn't he tell her to stop? Judas thought as he watched the woman's shameful abandon. He turned away from the scene perturbed. He distrusted all forms of sentiment, anything that distracted from the cause of overthrowing the Romans and establishing the long-awaited kingdom. Following the Nazarene had been a roller coaster of emotional highs and lows for Judas, quite unsettling for a focused fellow like himself.

But Judas had hitched his wagon to a star, and he was committed to the ride no matter how rocky it got. It hadn't been easy. Certainly the Savior would establish his kingdom soon. Yet every time the crowds tried to crown Jesus king, he refused, ducking the opportunity.

Worst of all, the offerings had started to dry up. Jesus wasn't nearly as popular as before, judging by the weight of the moneybag Judas wore around his waist. It was getting more and more difficult to embezzle funds. Of course, that was such an ugly term. Judas preferred to call it "compensation for services rendered."

If something doesn't change fast, Judas thought, *I may have to consider switching careers.*

He wasn't like the rest of the disciples. The only non-Galilean of the group, this city boy from Kerioth was determined to make his mark on the world. But making a mark required money. Money he didn't have.

"Hey, Judas," one of the disciples leaned over and whispered. "How much do you think a pint of pure nard goes for these days?"

Pure nard? Judas hadn't recognized the fragrance. Why, it was worse than he'd thought. The world's most expensive perfume—someone had to say something. "Ahem...excuse me, Master?" he interjected. Judas pointed at the woman and her broken flask. "Why wasn't this perfume sold and the money given to the poor? It was worth a year's wages." A few disciples around him murmured agreement.

"Leave her alone," Jesus replied. His eyes bored through Judas as if looking into his soul. Judas shifted uncomfortably. "It was intended that she should save this perfume for the day of my burial," Jesus continued. "You will always have the poor among you, but you will not always have me."

Judas looked to the other disciples for support. But they diverted their eyes, looking away, around, anywhere but Judas or the Master.

Now Judas swallowed as he felt things shift and solidify inside him. Instead of piercing his heart, Jesus' words had somehow cemented the deal. Suddenly everything seemed crystal clear to him. Nothing would ever change. All this talk about dying...there was no kingdom to come. The whole thing had been a farce.

So much for being part of a new Jewish parliament. The gig was up.

Unless...

A TALE OF TWO FOLLOWERS

The story of Jesus' anointing is recounted in all four Gospels, as is that of Judas's betrayal. Whether or not Judas's thought process happened as I've speculated, the result was the same. Matthew and Mark both place Judas's dark turn of heart as happening immediately after Mary's extravagant act of love.

> Then Judas Iscariot, one of the Twelve, went to the chief priests to
> betray Jesus to them. They were delighted to hear this and promised to
> give him money. So he watched for an opportunity to hand him over.
> (Mark 14:10-11)

Only Matthew highlights the amount for which Judas sold Jesus—thirty pieces of silver, the exact amount prophesied four hundred years before in Zechariah 11:12-13. It was the standard price paid for a slave in Exodus 21:32— approximately 120 denarii.

Less than half the amount of money Mary had so lavishly spilled on Jesus' feet.

Life has a way of bringing to the surface who we really are, the deep hidden motivations of our heart. "For out of the overflow of the heart the mouth speaks," Jesus said in Matthew 12:34-35. "The good man brings good things out of the good stored up in him, and the evil man brings evil things out of the evil stored up in him."

It certainly happened in Judas. But it happened in Mary as well. While the situation caused the evil dormant within Judas to rise to the surface, it was the same instance that brought something beautiful up from the depths of the maiden from Bethany.

From all appearances, Mary seems to have been contemplative by nature. And while spiritual intuitiveness made her a wonderful worshiper, it also made her susceptible to despair. Instead of running to meet Jesus after Lazarus died, if you remember, she remained in the house. Downcast and alone amid the crowd of friends, she had sunk deeper and deeper into her grief, and even the news of Jesus' coming had not been able to lift her sorrow.

But—thank God!—Jesus meets us where we are. He comes into those dark, hidden corners of our lives and, if we're willing, he shines the sweet spotlight of heaven, his precious Holy Spirit. If we allow him, he offers to clean out our personalities, tempering them through the Holy Spirit so we won't fall to the strong sides of our weaknesses and the weak sides of our strengths.

And that, as far as we can tell, is what happened to Mary. Even though she sensed, with her keen intuitiveness, the graveness of her Lord's situation, this time she did not collapse. Instead of just sitting passively and listening to the Savior, instead of being overwhelmed by grief, this time Mary responded. She gave herself in worship to the One who had given so much to her and her family.

Not so with Judas, apparently. Though Jesus knew the disciple's weaknesses, he had given Judas chance after chance in the three years they had traveled together. According to John 13:29, Jesus had even made the man treasurer of the group.

"Sometimes," William Barclay writes in *The Gospel of John,* "the best way to reclaim someone who is on the wrong path is to treat him not with suspicion but with trust; not as if we expected the worst, but as if we expected the best."[6] That's exactly what Jesus had done with Judas. But Judas had remained unchanged.

Imagine spending three years of your life with the Messiah, yet walking away more or less the same—or even worse than when you started. Judas did just that. It can happen to any of us if we don't settle, once and for all, the question of Christ's lordship in our lives.

Until we determine whom we will serve, we run the risk of developing a Judas heart instead of a heart of sacrificial love. For whenever *our* interests conflict with *his* interests, we'll be tempted to sell Christ off as a slave to the highest bidder, rather than spend our all to anoint his feet.

EXTRAVAGANT LOVE VERSUS TIGHT-FISTED LOVE

"To know whom you worship," says Theodore Parker, "let me see you in your shop, let me hear you in your trade, let me know how you rent your houses, how you get your money, how you kept it and how you spent it."[7]

Jesus says basically the same thing in Matthew 6:21: "For where your treasure is, there your heart will be also."

Mary's treasure was not in her trousseau. Her hope didn't lie in what she could get from Jesus. Her joy lay in what she could *give*.

Judas, on the other hand, was after all he could *get*. That is the first difference between a love that is extravagant and a heart that is mean and tight-fisted.

Consider the following:

• *Mary had a heart of gratitude.*

Her brother had been raised from the dead. The Messiah had come, and he'd called her friend. What greater honor—what greater joy—than to give her all to the One who had given her so very much.

• *Judas had a heart of greed.*

Things weren't turning out the way he'd planned. One of Westcott's Laws of Temptations, quoted by William Barclay, is that temptation "comes through that for which we are naturally fitted."[8] Our strength can be our undoing. And Judas's strength was his ambition, his focus, and his commitment to getting ahead. It was also, of course, his greatest weakness. It caused Judas to care more about the political situation and his own bank account than the condition of his heart.

Greed is a tyrant. As women, we can fall prey to its lies as easily as men. "The leech has two daughters," Proverbs 30:15 says. "'Give! Give!' they cry." A greedy heart is never satisfied. It never has enough.

"But godliness with contentment is great gain," Paul tells the young preacher Timothy (1 Timothy 6:6). Discontentment can creep in so easily, making us unsatisfied with what we have. It isn't long before the discontentment hardens into determination to get what we deserve, no matter the cost. But the cost is often extremely high.

"Some people, eager for money, have wandered from the faith," Paul warns Timothy in verse 10, "and pierced themselves with many griefs."

The secret to happiness lies not in getting what you want, but in wanting what you have. Judas came to his senses too late. His greed caused him to do the unimaginable—to betray a friend. To betray the Son of God. But the grief that soon replaced the greed could not heal his soul. Nor his mind. After trying to give the money back, Judas went out and hung himself, his body buried in a field bought by Jesus' blood.

Without gratefulness, we are prone to the same hardness of heart and darkness of mind that drove Judas's treachery. If we refuse to recognize the immensity of God's grace and its incredible cost on Jesus' part, sooner or later, we will take it for granted. And once we begin to presume on God's grace, we begin to abuse God's grace—trampling it under our careless feet in a maddening rush for yet another blessing.

Without gratitude we become like the people Romans 1:21 describes: "For although they knew God, they neither glorified him as God nor gave thanks to him, but their thinking became futile and their foolish hearts were darkened." Dark minds do dark things. Look at Judas.

How sad that it is possible to *know* God but never truly *experience* God. If we want intimacy with God, we must nurture a grateful heart that glorifies Jesus.

TWO KINDS OF HEARTS

Consider the following additional differences between the hearts of Mary and Judas. Which kind of heart do you have? Is it extravagant with gratitude or tight-fisted with greed?

- *Mary came with abandon.*
- *Judas came with an agenda.*

- *Mary heard what Jesus was saying—and she responded.*
- *Judas heard but did not understand.*

- *Mary held nothing back.*
- *Judas gave nothing up.*

Instead of being shamed by Mary's extravagance, Judas became critical of what she gave. His greed warped his perception. "If we find ourselves becoming critical of other people," Barclay says, "we should stop examining them, and start examining ourselves."[9]

Extravagant love is still rarely understood. "Don't you think you're going a little overboard with this 'God stuff'?" a friend may ask. "Why spend so much time in prayer? After all, God knows your heart," another may reason.

But true love always costs the giver something. Otherwise, the giving remains only a philanthropic contribution. At best, kind. At worst, self-serving. In the light of Mary's total abandon, halfway love is truly the "least" we can do.

Do we love Jesus the who-o-o-le world? Or only when it's convenient?

EXTRAVAGANT SACRIFICE

When a forty-nine-year-old Canadian mining executive walked into the Colombian jungle in October 1998, he went hoping to walk back out with one of his employees. Instead, he didn't walk out at all—at least, not right away.

For more than three months, Ed Leonard, a sixty-year-old driller who worked for Norbert Reinhart's drilling firm, had been held by the rebel group known as the Revolutionary Armed Forces of Colombia.

Kidnapping was, and is, big business in Colombia. In 1998 alone, more than twenty-one hundred people were abducted, though most were later released on ransom. And that's what Reinhart was hoping for. Along with a toothbrush, some books, and a camera, he reportedly stuffed one hundred thousand dollars in his knapsack to pay for Leonard's release. But there were no guarantees.

Reinhart's wife, Robin, begged him not to go. Sure, Leonard had a wife and kids, but they had two young children as well. Still, Reinhart had promised Leonard, a man he'd hired over the phone, that the job was safe. He was going to do whatever it took to get him home.

On October 6, the guerrillas took Reinhart's ransom money but demanded an exchange as well. The mining executive agreed. That afternoon on a desolate, rocky road, Norbert Reinhart met his employee for the first time.

"You must be Ed Leonard," Reinhart said, shaking the older man's hand. "Your shift is over. It's time for you to go home."

And with that he traded places with Leonard and became the rebels' captive.

The world was stunned. Some called Reinhart crazy. "Let the government and hostage professionals handle it," they said. But the negotiations had dragged on and on. When Reinhart was unexpectedly released several months later, he summed up the experience by saying, "I just did what I had to do."[10]

Extravagant sacrifice. Norbert Reinhart risked his life for the sake of his employee, not knowing what would happen to him. Though some close to the situation have pointed out less than altruistic motives, Norbert Reinhart's act is still impressive.

But Jesus laid his life down knowing full well he wouldn't walk away alive. This transaction would cost him everything, yet still he gave. And that's not just impressive; it's revolutionary.

Jesus laid down his life for you and me. He didn't have to do it. He could have spoken the word, and ten thousand angels would have flown to his rescue. But instead, he chose not to use his own power. He humbled himself and chose the way of sacrificial death. And there was never a hint of selfishness in his sacrifice—no self-interest, not a hint of mixed motives.

Why did he do it? He did it out of love—extravagant, lavish, life-changing love.

LAVISH LOVE

The apostle John writes in 1 John 3:1, "How great is the love the Father has lavished on us, that we should be called children of God!" What a wonderful picture—the lavish love of God. Love so wonderfully extravagant that, like a thick, rich hand cream, it must be spread around. So much love that the simple and the ordinary aren't enough.

Mary knew a little bit about that kind of love. So do a lot of Christians I know. They just give and give of themselves without seeming to tire. Compassion and service flow uninterrupted from their lives.

Sure they get weary. Sometimes they feel moody—but not for long. In fact, it seems the more they freely give, the more energized they feel.

I try to cuddle my life up close to people like that. I watch them and try to learn. Just how does Nita do all our church recordkeeping without complaining? How do Ed and Judy seem to know when people are hurting, though no one says a word? Why does Aunt Gert keep hosting the neighborhood Bible club every week? Her heart is weak, her body twisted with scoliosis, but still she loves and gives—then gives some more.

These are only a few of my heroes of faith. If you look, you'll find them all around you. They come in all shapes and sizes, ages and genders. They don't usually stick out in a crowd. Much of the time, their compassionate service is done unnoticed and unseen. But when you get up close, you'll find they have one thing in common. They know how to love—not just in word, but in deed.

That's what set Mary's love apart that day in Bethany. She not only loved Jesus; she did something about it. And what she did and how she did it point toward the secret for more fully loving God and loving people.

- *Mary loved with her whole heart.*

She didn't hold anything back. Instead, in sweet abandon, she poured everything she had into showing her love for Jesus.

LEAPING INTO LOVE

Do you ever feel yourself holding back parts of your life, wondering how much you can give and still have something left? Like Mary, you feel the call to total abandonment, but surrender like that makes you afraid. If you've felt that way, you're not alone. I think every one of us comes to a crossroads in our relationship with God where we're faced with the dilemma of total or partial surrender.

I remember the day God brought me to that crossroads. For nearly a month he had been dealing with my heart, asking me to sell out to him. Jesus had been my Savior, but he wasn't yet my Lord. He was telling me it was time to surrender.

I wanted to obey, but I was so afraid. What if I said yes? What would that mean? I was a young teenager with a lot of plans and dreams. If I gave myself completely to him, would he take them all away and make me go to Africa? At the time, that was the worst fate I could imagine—or almost… Come to think of it, what if he made me marry a short, fat, balding man with acne on his forehead and forced us to work among the pygmies for the rest of our lives? Why, that would be even worse!

But instead of answering my questions and calming my fears, the Lord kept pressing me for a decision. "Will you give me your all?" he asked. No negotiations. No promised stock options. Total abandonment was what he demanded, and nothing less.

The dissonant workings of my spirit and flesh finally collided that summer at youth camp. I still remember the night I totally surrendered. It felt as though I was standing on a hundred-foot-high diving board with nothing but blackness beneath me. "Jump," I could hear the Lord saying. "Jump. I'll catch you."

But I couldn't see his hands. To jump meant to leap into an absolute unknown. Would he really catch me? Or would I fall, endlessly fall, as in the dreams that often haunted my nights?

I stood there shivering in the darkness, my arms clasped around all my hopes and my dreams, and I realized there was no turning back. It was all my heart or nothing. To walk away from this decision would mean, for me, walking away from God. And that I could not, would not do. So I closed my eyes and took a breath and flung myself out into the dark unknown.

"I'm yours, Lord," my heart cried. "All of me! Nothing held back."

I waited for the unending fall. I kept expecting it to come. But instead, I felt strong arms around me. Arms that built the universe. Arms that held the world. Arms so gentle, they cradled children. Arms so strong, they shouldered every burden we'd ever bear. They were the everlasting arms of Jesus. Catching me. Embracing me. Receiving me as his own.

I think I know a little of bit of what Mary must have felt that day she stood at Jesus' feet. As she held her precious ointment, she must have trembled inside.

Making Jesus Your Lord

Perhaps like me, you've met Christ as Savior, you've repented of your sins, but something still seems to be missing. For me, that missing part was found when I made Jesus not only my Savior, but my Lord. Hannah Whitall Smith, in her classic book *The Christian's Secret of a Happy Life,* outlines the necessary steps:[11]

1. "Express in definite words your faith in Christ as your Saviour and acknowledge . . . He has reconciled you to God; according to 2 Cor. 5:18, 19.

2. "Definitely acknowledge God as your Father, and yourself as His redeemed and forgiven child; according to Gal. [4]:6.

3. "Definitely surrender yourself to be all the Lord's, body, soul, and spirit; and to obey Him in everything where His will is made known; according to Rom. 12:[1].

4. "Believe and continue to believe, against all seemings, that God takes possession of that which you thus abandon to Him, and that He will henceforth work in you to will and to do of His good pleasure, unless you consciously frustrate His grace; according to 2 Cor. 6:17, 18, and Phil. 2:13.

5. "Pay no attention to your feelings as a test of your relations with God, but simply attend to the state of your will and of your faith. And count all these steps you are now taking as settled, though the enemy may make it seem otherwise. Heb.10:22, 23.

6. "Never, under any circumstances, give way for one single moment to doubt or discouragement. Remember, that all discouragement is from the devil, and refuse to admit it; according to John 14:1, 27.

7. "Cultivate the habit of expressing your faith in definite words, and repeat often, 'I am all the Lord's and He is working in me now to will and to do of His good pleasure'; according to Heb. 13:21."

Hannah suggests we make all these things part of a daily act of our will: "And here you must rest. There is nothing more for you to do…you are the Lord's now."

He who began a good work in you will carry it on to completion,
until the day of Christ Jesus.

PHILIPPIANS 1:6

For no one gives her everything without a struggle. No one gives her all without somehow wanting to keep part of it back. Perhaps Mary had wrestled with the thought of surrender as I did. Perhaps she'd stared at the alabaster bottle in the night. *Can I? Should I? Will I?* Until she said, "Yes, Lord. I'll give my all."

So when she broke the bottle and poured the ointment, Mary didn't stop herself to count the cost or calculate how much of the ointment was actually needed. She spilled it all out. Lavishly. Extravagantly. Until her treasure ran down over Jesus' feet and soaked into the floor.

Then she did something I find disconcerting. She unbound her headpiece and wiped Jesus' feet with her hair. By that act, she laid down her glory and, in essence, stood naked before her Lord. For in that culture, no proper woman ever let her hair down in public. A woman's hair was her glory, her identity, her ultimate sign of femininity, an intimate gift meant only for her husband. But for Mary, nothing was too extravagant for Jesus; she was even willing to risk her reputation. Like a lover before her beloved, she made herself vulnerable and fragile, open for rejection or rebuke.

But neither came. Only the tender, silent approval of a Bridegroom for his bride. Jesus watched as Mary dried his feet, and I'm sure there were tears in his eyes.

The extravagance might be misunderstood by the others, but not by the one that she loved. "She has done a beautiful thing for me," Jesus said in the face of his disciples' disapproval.

Leave her alone. She belongs to me.

HOLY KISSES

Jessica and I have graduated to a new "good-night" bedtime game. It involves kisses. Multiple kisses. One on the forehead and each eyebrow. Another on the nose and each cheek. A soft peck on the lips and the chin, and then—if we can bear it—under the chin where it tickles. With giggled, whispered kisses on each ear and a great big hug to tie them all together, we say our prayers and then "good night."

I'm not sure about Jessica, but I sleep better when I know I am loved that many kisses' worth. Exorbitantly, foolishly, extravagantly loved. Covered with kisses.

Judas offered Jesus a single kiss. The kiss of betrayal. How that must have hurt the heart of God. All the time they'd spent together, all the teaching, all the love—and then to be rejected that way. Jesus knew it was coming, of course, but even he seemed surprised by the chosen signal that night in Gethsemane. Can't you hear the pain in Luke 22:48 when Jesus asks, "Judas, are you betraying the Son of Man with a kiss?"

Unlike Judas's stingy, mocking gesture, the loving attention Mary lavished upon the Savior's feet had nothing to do with manipulation or control. When Jesus foretold his death, instead of rebuking him as Peter did—"Lord, this will never be"—Mary prepared her Savior; she made ready the way of the Lord. And instead of sinking into depression, contemplative Mary made room for the sovereign will of God as she anointed the Lover of her soul for burial.

A Test of Love

St. Augustine once preached a sermon in which he proposed a kind of self-test to see if we truly love God:

> Suppose God proposed to you a deal and said, "I will give you anything you want. You can possess the whole world. Nothing will be impossible for you.... Nothing will be a sin, nothing forbidden. You will never die, never have pain, never have anything you do not want and always have anything you do want—except for just one thing: you will never see my face."

Augustine closed with a question:

> Did a chill rise in your hearts, when you heard the words, "you will never see my face"? That chill is the most precious thing in you; that is the pure love of God.[12]

What good is it for a man to gain the whole world,
yet forfeit his soul?

MARK 8:36

"I tell you the truth," Jesus said in Mark 14:9, "wherever the gospel is preached throughout the world, what she has done will also be told, in memory of her."

And still the story is told—the story of a woman who loved so much she gave up just about everything. The sweet scent of Mary's extravagant sacrifice still lingers today.

We sense the precious aroma of extravagant love rising once more to heaven each time one of God's children gives his or her everything to the One who gave his all.

11

Balancing Work and Worship

Whatever you do, work at it with all your heart.

COLOSSIANS 3:23

I love teetertotters. My sister and I used to play for hours on an old wooden plank clamped to a metal bar at the church camp we attended every summer. Being older, I was the heaviest, so I had to scoot up several inches while she sat on the very edge. Then we were ready to go. Back and forth, up and down, through sun-speckled July afternoons we'd teetertotter amid the pine trees of Glacier Bible Camp. But we especially enjoyed finding that perfect spot of synchronicity—scooting around until both of our ends were suspended in midair. Pure, exquisite balance.

"No bumpsies!" Linda would cry whenever I'd shift my weight backward. She knew what was coming. The slightest change in the distribution of weight caused my side to plummet, making the plank hit the ground and sending my sister's little rear-endski fifty-three feet in the air.

Well, not quite. But I always tried. It was great fun.

Until my cousin Chuckie showed up, that is. He'd climb up onto the center of the teetertotter and stand with one foot on either side of the bar. Now *he* controlled which side went high, which side went low. Which side got the bumpsies.

Linda and Chuckie have always been in a cruel conspiracy against me. Growing up, they locked me out of Chuckie's bedroom every Sunday afternoon so I couldn't play Lincoln Logs. When we played hide-and-seek during the summer, I'd search for hours while they'd be inside sucking Popsicles and watching *Captain Kangaroo*. Not that I'm bitter, mind you. I just want you to understand.

So when Chuckie's I'm-so-innocent blue eyes narrowed on those July afternoons, I always knew what was coming. A bit of fancy footwork on his part, and I'd be flying through the trees screaming, hanging on to the plank with both hands, my long legs flopping in the breeze before I returned to the plank with a spine-shattering thud.

I love teetertotters.

BALANCING TEETERTOTTERS

I wonder if God had teetertotters in mind when he placed Luke's story of Mary and Martha between two famous passages: the story of the Good Samaritan (Luke 10:30-37) and Christ's teaching on the Lord's Prayer (11:1-4). One deals with our relationship with people. The other deals with our relationship with God. One teaches us how to serve. The other teaches us how to pray. One breaks down the wall that divides cultures. The other breaks down the wall that divides God and humanity.

Perhaps that is why this tiny section of Scripture we first looked at is so important. In Luke's story of two women and one Savior we find the fulcrum, the pivot point of our spiritual teetertotters—the secret of balancing the practical with the spiritual, and duties with devotion. Without a fulcrum, these stories are two separate wooden planks. Both are important. Both are true. But when we place the fundamental truths of service and prayer on the pivot point of practicality—when we get down to the company's-here-and-what-do-I-do? application, the fun really begins.

I have to admit I struggle to keep that balance. We hosted a church banquet just a few months ago, and I found myself in the kitchen rather than in the worship service. I could faintly hear the speaker. He sounded dynamic. My husband even poked his head through the door and said, "You're really missing it!" But I was adamant. "These dishes have to get done," I said as I blew my wilted bangs out of my eyes. "We don't want to be here all night cleaning up."

I'm not sure at what point in the evening it hit me. Obviously, I'm a bit slow—especially when you consider I was in the middle of writing this book.

But *Having a Mary Heart in a Martha World* was the last thing on my mind that night. I was flying high on Martha Stewart cruise control! The dishes gleamed, the glasses glistened, and even our mismatched cookware looked nearly new. But when everything was said and done, I realized I'd missed something special. Jesus had showed up in our midst, and I had been so busy washing dishes, I'd missed the opportunity to sit at his feet.

I'd totally forgotten everything I'd been learning about balancing work and worship.

Ouch. Bumpsies again!

OUR SUPREME EXAMPLE

Jesus was the most balanced individual the world has ever known. In fact, that is part of why he came—to show us how to manage the tricky balance between work and worship, between what we do and what we are.

He gave us a picture of what our teetertotter should look like in Luke 10:25-28—just before Christ's parable of the Good Samaritan.

"What must I do to inherit eternal life?" an expert in the law asked after cornering Jesus one day (10:25). What can I do to ensure "safe passage" to heaven?

A good question to ask. But Jesus looked into the legal expert's heart and saw he was more interested in debates than in answers, more concerned about theory than practice. So Jesus turned the question around and let the "expert" give his opinion.

"What is written in the Law?" Jesus asked. "How do you read it?"

I can almost hear the lawyer's voice deepen as he gathered his robes around him and assumed the proper posture for quoting Scripture. Everyone stopped what he or she was doing. Babies quit fussing. Kids stopped chasing butterflies. For they recognized the familiar portion of the Torah as it thundered from the scholar's mouth: "'Love the Lord your God with all your heart and with all your soul and with all your strength and with all your mind'; and, 'Love your neighbor as yourself'"(Luke 10:27).

The final sentence drifted upon the afternoon air, the expert's voice trailing off as he lifted one hand toward heaven for emphasis. Everyone was silent. The crowd waited, spellbound, their eyes shifting from the legal expert to Jesus. What would the itinerant rabbi say in the face of such learning and wisdom?

I can almost see Jesus smile and nod as he said, "You have answered correctly. Do this and you will live."

End of discussion. The expert gets an A+. Next question?

You see, loving the Lord your God and your neighbor as yourself was and is the very thing God has always wanted us to do—it's a perfect picture of the perfectly balanced life. These two verses sum up all of the Old Testament and the New Testament combined.

God wants us to love him. Really love him.

And he wants us to love each other. Really love each other. That's how we can know we belong to him—if we have love one for another (John 13:35).

Love for God. Love for others. Worship and service. These are the two ends of our teetertotter. Though love for God comes first, the two can't be separated. One flows from the other—and back again. That's what it means to live a balanced life, a Christlike life.

But the legal expert didn't seem to get it. And if he did, he wasn't willing to give up. This rabble-rouser from Nazareth had come out of the exchange looking better than he did. So, wanting "to justify himself," the man challenged Jesus, "And who *is* my neighbor?" (Luke 10:29, emphasis mine).

Aha, the lawyer must have thought to himself. *I've got him now.* That very question had stumped religious scholars for centuries. Of course, when you make God your exclusive property and call anyone who wasn't born a Jew a *goy*—or Gentile dog—your list of acceptable neighbors shrinks dramatically.

When you're not really interested in truth and you just want a lively conversation, Jesus is definitely the wrong person to come to. For he is Truth. And when you knock, he opens the door. When you seek, he reveals. And when you ask, sometimes you get an answer you don't want to hear. This poor old lawyer certainly did.

What he got was a bad case of the bumpsies—as Jesus brought his legalistic and superspiritual outlook thumping back down to earth with a practical picture of what loving your neighbor looks like.

CORRECTIVE MEASURES

Jesus is like my cousin Chuckie, only nicer. He doesn't give us bumpsies to watch us fly. He counteracts our off-kilter beliefs and lifestyles for one purpose—to bring us back into balance. But for the legal expert, Jesus' approach had to have been jarring. After all, the story Jesus told challenged some long-cherished beliefs, and it shook his Jewish sense of religious superiority, dismantling the excuses he'd used not to get involved with those lesser than himself.

The hero of the story Jesus told wasn't Moses or Joshua. He wasn't a Jew at all—not a real one anyway. He was one of those despised half-breed Samaritans who lived up north. And Jesus didn't stop there. He not only glorified the Samaritan by calling him "good," but he also made an unflattering comparison between that man's generosity and the hypocrisy of the Jews who'd walked by the bleeding, broken man on their way to Jerusalem and church.

The expert probably squirmed along with the rest of the religious elite in the crowd. Maybe the story brought to mind the ragged blind man he'd passed on the way to the debate. "Alms! Alms for the poor," he'd cried. But the religious expert was out of change, and besides, he'd given at the temple.

Jesus was hitting pretty close to home. Stepping on the toes of people for whom the sandals fit all too well.

He has a way of doing that, you know—of highlighting discrepancies we'd rather ignore. And while we may be more comfortable with our little rear-endskis planted on one end or the other, balancing our life is exactly what Jesus calls us to do.

Love the Lord your God…and love your neighbor as yourself.

Love God? *No problem!* some of us think. *I'm really good at the spiritual side of my walk. You might even consider me an expert. Kumbayah, my Lord, kumbayah…* And so there we stay, sitting on one side of our teetertotter, happy to be worshiping in the Lord's presence.

But there is more—more to this balanced Christian walk than only worship.

Love people? *Sure I do!* others of us say to ourselves as we sit on the other end of the teetertotter. *I love serving people. I'm definitely a Martha. Why just the other day…* And so we recite our service record and list our sacrificial accomplishments, glad to be helping the Lord.

But there is more to this balanced Christian walk than only serving.

You see, Jesus wants *all* of us to be like my cousin Chuckie (only nicer). He directs us—if I might put it this way—to get off our religious duffs and do the hard but rewarding work of balancing our Christianity, spending adequate amounts of our lives both in the Living Room and the Kitchen, worshiping and serving, loving God and loving people.

Holy Sweat—that's how Tim Hansel refers to this balance. In fact, he wrote a book with that very title. *"Holy Sweat,"* Hansel writes, "is the active melding of the spiritual and the earthy, the holy and the physical, a profound paradox that lies at the very heart of this life we call Christian."

Hansel says, "The holy is here within us, waiting to pour out of us, and…it's much more accessible than we ever would have thought. It's grace with blisters; it's redemption in overdrive."[1]

I like that! While I have been justified by faith alone—saved not by my works but because of Christ's sacrifice—I must partner with the Lord in the process of being sanctified, that is, being made more like him. I must allow his holiness to affect the way I live and what I do.

God provides the holy, and I provide the sweat. That's part of what it means to balance work and worship. It's what we were made for.

Though we were created for worship, first and foremost, we were also "created in Christ Jesus to do good works, which God prepared in advance for us to do" (Ephesians 2:10). We were created for the intimate fellowship of the Lord's Prayer but also entrusted with the ministry of the Good Samaritan.

Created to say yes to the calls of both duty and devotion.

PRACTICE SAYING YES

Remember several years ago when the take-time-for-yourself experts were instructing all us overcommitted types to go to our mirrors and practice saying no? Some of us actually did it! Tip of the tongue to the roof of the mouth, long humming "nnnn," followed by a satisfying "oh." It wasn't easy at first, but eventually we conquered it. After a while, it actually became fun.

I suppose having two toddlers gave me extra practice, but it wasn't long before that two-letter word just flowed off my lips. No…No, no, NO! I could say it without even thinking: *No, I'm sorry, but I'm unavailable. No, I'm sorry, but that isn't convenient.* It was so effective, no one even bothered asking anymore.

No one except God, that is.

He wasn't impressed by my self-care or even my excuse of "family priorities." He knew my heart, and he was well aware that my no had become far too quick, a nearly thoughtless knee-jerk reaction. I was so busy protecting myself that I wasn't even stopping to consider that a request for my involvement might be part of God's call to me. So sometimes when I said no, it wasn't really to people or ministries. It was to God himself. And as I eventually discovered, you can't say no to God without suffering some major spiritual side effects.

It didn't happen all at once, but it did happen. Like the Israelites, I began to experience the spiritual consequence of prolonged self-interest: "They soon forgot His works; they did not wait for His counsel...[so] He gave them their request, but sent leanness into their soul" (Psalm 106:13,15, NKJV).

That's what happens, I believe, when no becomes our easy answer to anything outside our own personal agendas. Our souls grow skinny, starved, and weak. For we were created for abundant fullness, not for negative, ingrown inactivity. We were created to say an enthusiastic yes to the call of God in our lives—both his call to devotion and his call to service. Saying yes to him releases his power and his joy to our souls. It's what gives us the strength and the energy to do what he wants us to do.

At the same time, it's important to remember that saying yes to God doesn't mean saying yes to everything! When our lives are overbooked, it's easy for us to become spiritually dry and undernourished. We can barely hear God's voice above the busy noise, let alone say yes to what he is asking. In this case, we do need to learn how to say no, but only so we are able to say yes to God when he wants to give us an assignment.

"It's a great release to know that the secret to 'doing it all' is not necessarily *doing it all*," Jill Briscoe writes in her excellent book *Renewal on the Run*, "but rather discovering which part of the 'all' he has given us to do and doing all of that."[2]

As I've come to understand the impact that yes and no can make on my life, I've begun to look at each situation individually, even stopping to *pray* about the request before giving my answer, if you can imagine! That way, though I still have to say no sometimes, the purpose for the no is different.

Now I say no in order to say yes to God: *"No, I won't be able to be on the planning committee. The Lord is leading me to help with the nursing-home ministry."* And as I walk in this dependent obedience, I find the Lord not only blesses what I do, but he also raises up people to do the things I've had to decline. All because I've begun looking for ways to use the Y-word.

Go ahead! Practice saying it: "Y-y-y…" Same tongue, same roof of mouth, but instead of pointing the tongue up and inward, the tongue points up and outward—y-eh-sss! Why, it actually feels good after such a long string of downers. *Yes, I think I can help. Yes, I think it might be arranged—let me pray about it.* The effect can be absolutely euphoric! Especially when we make a conscious point of saying that yes to God.

THE RHYTHM OF A BALANCED LIFE

Here's something else I've discovered about balance. Being balanced is not so much a matter of staying in perfect equilibrium as it is a matter of finding the right rhythm for our lives.

You see, that pure spot of synchronicity my sister and I liked to find on the teetertotter never lasted very long. We spent a lot more time going up and down than we did hovering in the middle. In fact, that's partly what made it fun. As long as we kept ourselves going up and down, it all equaled out. We could teeter and totter to our hearts' content and still stay more or less in balance.

I've found that helpful to remember in my own life. Because, practically speaking, the balance between Living Room Intimacy and Kitchen Service more often resembles the up-and-down, back-and-forth motion of the teetertotter than it does that fleeting moment of synchronicity.

One side of my life may take predominance for a while, then the other. One day I may spend several hours in Bible study and prayer, settling softly on the side of intimacy with God, while the next day is given over to volunteering in my daughter's classroom, teetering over toward the service side. If you were to gauge those two days individually, they would appear totally out of balance. But not when you consider them together.

The same is true, I believe, of the seasons in our lives. For years, I spent most of my time chasing after two little toddlers. It was difficult to volunteer outside the home or even grab a few moments alone with God. Now that the kids are in school, I have more time to do both. And one day, in the sad not-so-distant future, when my time will be largely my own, I may actually be able to achieve that perfect symmetry of spirit and service

But I needn't worry too much if I don't. That's the beauty of dynamic, teeter-totter balance. As long as my heart is set toward both service and worship, I don't have to feel guilty when my life seems to settle longer on one side because I know I'll eventually push off from that spot and spend some time on the other.

Planning ahead helps. If I know I'll be spending a block of time in service, such as organizing an event or taking part in a Christmas musical, then I know I

Listening to Your Soul: A Balance Checklist

Because we were created for balance, we feel the difference in our souls when our lives tilt too far in one direction or another. The imbalance will show in our attitudes, our energy level, and in the way we interact with other people. Any of the following could be an indication that you need to tilt more toward either service or devotion.[3]

Signs That You May Need More Time in the Kitchen:

- *Slight depression.* You feel a vague unhappiness, a sense of being down.
- *Resentment of intrusion.* Rather than welcoming people into your life, you find yourself wishing they'd go away.
- *Frustration over direction of life.* You feel a sense of purposelessness and sometimes wonder, "Is this all there is?"
- *Increased self-indulgence.* You feel an itch to treat yourself with favorite foods or shopping.
- *Apathetic attitude.* You find that very little moves you. You know your compassion level is low, but part of you just doesn't care.
- *Low energy level.* Like the Dead Sea, you may have many inlets, but no outlets—and therefore you're growing stagnant.

need to build in time afterward for prayer, devotion, and adequate rest. If I know I'll be spending a block of time in concentrated worship—say a women's retreat or a week of special services—then I know I need to make sure my commitments to other people are covered and schedule in a few days of catch-up work.

But I don't need to look too far ahead. I don't have to keep a running account of hours spent in service and hours spent in worship and devotion or worry that every moment of every day is in perfect perpetual balance. What I need to do instead is submit my life to the Lord and let him help me "do the Chuckie." He'll show me how to attend to both sides of my life.

In fact, that very up-and-down rhythm can actually keep my life moving in

Signs That You May Need More Time in the Living Room:

- *Irritability and frustration.* You find yourself snapping at people, wound so tight you're about to "snap" yourself, and especially short-tempered with those you perceive as lazy or uncooperative.
- *Uncomfortable with quiet.* Silence makes you nervous, so you're quick to turn on the TV or the radio.
- *Low joy threshold.* It's been a long time since you've sensed that undercurrent of joy and abundance running through your heart.
- *A sense of isolation.* You feel all alone—as if no one is there for you and no one understands.
- *Increased drivenness.* You're haunted by a sense that you must do more and more. You keep volunteering for more projects and more committees, even though you know your plate is full.
- *Sense of dryness and emptiness.* No wonder! You have many outlets and demands, but no inlets or source of strength.

Test me, O LORD, and try me, examine my heart and my mind;
for your love is ever before me, and I walk continually in your truth.

PSALM 26:2-3

a positive direction. Our lives are meant to be dynamic, not static. Like a clock pendulum or the pump of an oil well, the rhythm actually generates energy for our lives. The truth is, we thrive on a life that is rhythmically balanced, not standing still.

Teetertotter. Up and down. Work and worship. Love the Lord and love other people. It's the dynamic rhythm that drives a meaningful, yes-centered, balanced life.

Your rhythm of life may be different than mine—Mary and Martha certainly had different patterns. But so basic is this need for balance in our lives, the Lord has ordained certain balancing principles that apply to everyone. They provide rhythm as well as rhyme to our haphazard lives, and we ignore them to our detriment. In recent years, the Lord has been bringing two of these principles to the forefront of my heart—perhaps because these two principles are so easy to forget in our frantic culture. One is a "teeter" principle of Sabbath rest. The other is a "totter" principle of hospitality.

THE GIFT OF SABBATH REST

The story is told of a migrant South African tribe that regularly went on long marches. Day after day they would tramp the roads. But then, all of a sudden, they would stop walking and make camp for a couple days. When asked why they stopped, the tribe explained that they needed the time of rest so that their souls could catch up with them.

Isn't that a great concept? Letting your soul catch up. When I read this little story, it resonated deep within me. I can get to running so fast that I leave everything behind. Not just God. Not just people. I can lose my own soul as well.

I think that's why God instructed us to observe a regular period of extended rest in the middle of our busy lives. That's why he gave us a Sabbath.

In Hebrew the word *Sabbath* literally means "a ceasing of labor." It refers specifically to a day of the week set aside for rest and for worship.

The Jews have always observed the Sabbath from sundown on Fridays until sundown on Saturdays. We Christians set aside Sunday, the day of Jesus' resurrection, for our Sabbath. But the chosen day is not as important as the chosen purpose—to bring balance and perspective to our work-weary lives on a weekly basis.

"If you call the Sabbath a delight and the LORD's holy day honorable," says the prophet Isaiah, "and if you honor it by not going your own way...then you will find your joy in the LORD" (Isaiah 58:13-14). Unfortunately, the Sabbath is being squeezed out by our nonstop culture, and that poses a big balance problem in the lives of many Christians.

In the first place, many of us find it hard to resist the business-as-usual mentality that's become the norm. Even if we block off Sunday morning and Sunday evening for church, it's hard to resist the lure of the mall in the afternoon. We may have business meetings or other responsibilities scheduled for Sundays—ball games and recitals, to name a few. It's increasingly hard to resist the temptation to use the Sabbath as a catch-up day instead of a day of worship and rest.

Second (and partly as a result), many people find themselves in a position of having to work on the Lord's Day. They're afraid to insist on having Sundays off, fearful of losing their jobs or simply getting behind. Although, legally speaking, employers can't deny workers time off to practice their faith except in extreme circumstances, the pressure is undeniably there. (See Appendix F for some resources on what to do if you're caught in this squeeze.)

But despite all the distractions, real and imagined, I really believe that if we want balance in our lives we must set our hearts toward obeying the fourth commandment (Exodus 20:8). The specifics of what that means for you and your family will be between you and God. But I believe that Sabbath-keeping as God ordained it must involve three things.

First, the Sabbath needs to be different, set apart; it has to contrast noticeably with the other six days. It shouldn't just be a day when we take care of errands we didn't get to on Saturday or finish paperwork we brought home on Friday.

Second, the Sabbath should be a day of devotion. It's meant to be spent in the Living Room. Kitchen duties can wait. This is a time to focus our hearts and our minds on God alone.

Finally, the Sabbath should be at least partially a family day—a time spent not only with our biological families, but also with the family of faith gathered for corporate worship and fellowship. "Let us not give up meeting together, as some are in the habit of doing," Paul wrote to the church in Hebrews 10:25, "but let us encourage one another—and all the more as you see the Day approaching."

How do these priorities translate into actual practice? Here are the Sabbath guidelines Elizabeth Stalcup and her family have decided on: "Our family attends church services on Sunday morning, no matter how tired or frazzled we feel, unless we are ill. We don't do laundry, clean house, go shopping, or cook elaborate meals. We take walks, read the Bible, visit with friends, nap, or putter in the garden."[4]

This kind of Sabbath-keeping requires a certain amount of discipline. Housework and homework must be done ahead of time. Family members may grow restless with the quiet. But those who have made Sabbath-keeping a priority testify that the balancing power of Sabbath rest is truly worth the sacrifice. After all, as Elizabeth says, "God gave us the Sabbath because He loves us."[5]

If for one reason or another, you cannot set aside Sunday as a Sabbath, may I encourage you to be creative and set aside another time each week? Some churches have midweek services or home groups, while others may offer worship services on Friday or Saturday nights. While I believe in letting the Lord's Day truly be the *Lord's* Day, I also believe that if we are sincere about seeking his face, God will help us set aside the Sabbath rest and worship we so desperately need.

I'd like to add another word of advice on this subject—one that applies specifically to those of us who "work on Sundays" for the Lord—whether it means teaching Sunday school, playing the piano for worship, or caring for children in the nursery. Although this work doesn't prevent us from gathering with the body of Christ, it is definitely work. We may need to find a separate time for Sabbath. A time when we, too, can open our arms and take advantage of God's gift of Sabbath rest, devotion, and fellowship.

GOD'S GIFT OF HOSPITALITY

The practice of keeping the Sabbath is not the only God-ordained balancing principle that seems to be lost these days. Another one, which tilts back to the service side of the teetertotter, is the practice of hospitality. And I'm not just talking about giving dinner parties. I am talking about the practice of opening up our arms to welcome others into our lives.

"Christian women just don't have a choice about whether or not they'll be hospitable," says Rachael Crabb, author of *The Personal Touch*. "It's a biblical command. Scripture tells us that in the last days, people will be lovers of themselves. We're called to be givers instead."[6]

Over and over in the Bible, we're encouraged to show hospitality by reaching out and giving of ourselves to others, welcoming them into our lives. We are given the example of Abraham, who entertained three holy visitors without knowing who they were. Jesus exhorted us to entertain those who can't pay us back (Luke 14:12-14). Paul lists hospitality as a requirement for office in the church (1 Timothy 3:2) and encourages all of us to "practice hospitality" in Romans 12:13. Peter adds the injunction to do it "without grumbling" (1 Peter 4:9).

Ouch. That last one hits home for me. But it is the verse in Romans 12 that brings me comfort because hospitality is definitely not an area where I feel gifted or proficient. Paul's exhortation to "practice" hospitality offers me hope that I may one day improve. At the very least, I must attempt it. *Practice, Joanna, practice.*

Genetically, I should be predisposed to hospitality. Growing up, my dad was always bringing home, if I may put it so indelicately, "stray" people. Far from objecting, my mother always welcomed them with a loving heart and something to eat. In fact, for quite a while, we jokingly referred to my parents' house as "Gustafson's Home for Wayward Boys and Girls." They made hospitality look easy.

But it isn't easy—at least not always. It's something I struggle with personally—partly because I'm not a very talented housekeeper, but mostly because I'm just so busy. It's a challenge to make space in my life to bring people in. So many times I've felt like the Benedictine monk Kathleen Norris tells about in her book *Amazing Grace: A Vocabulary of Faith.*[7]

Benedictine monks, you have to understand, are experts at hospitality. Their founder, St. Benedict, made caring for strangers one of the fundamental rules of the order. "Receive visitors as you would receive Christ," he instructed. No one is to be turned away. It's been that way with the Benedictines for centuries. And yet one busy monk, when approached by a visitor with questions concerning the abbey, replied brusquely, "I don't have time for this; we're trying to run a monastery here!"

Ouch. How easy it is to get caught up in our busy lives that we forget the reason Jesus came and the purpose for which we were called.

"Practicing" Hospitality

If you're like me, hospitality doesn't come naturally. Here are a few tips from Karen Main's classic book *Open Heart—Open Home* that have helped me a lot—plus a few I've discovered on my own!

1. *Never clean before company.* Instead, try to clean on schedule and clean up as you go, so you'll always be ready for unexpected guests.
2. *Keep the emphasis on welcome, not performance.* The purpose of hospitality is to open your arms to others, not to impress them. It's better to keep things simple and warm than to go overboard.
3. *Do as much ahead of time as possible.* Plan ahead for hospitality—even cook ahead. Karen says, "Hard work indicates I'm not managing my time well, not planning or preparing ahead, doing too much, not being dependent on the Lord's strength, but on my own."
4. *Include little touches of beauty.* A few candles and a jar of daisies picked from the yard can make grilled cheese a gourmet delight. (And they help hide the grease stain on the tablecloth as well!)
5. *Use all the help that comes your way.* When someone offers to help, say yes! Many hands make less work—and sharing the labor can be a great opportunity for fellowship.
6. *Keep records.* Karen has files of easy recipes and creative entertaining tips. Other women keep records of the guests and what was served. I've found that to-do lists organize my scattered thoughts and help me focus my energy more productively.[8]

Offer hospitality to one another without grumbling.

1 PETER 4:9

When we lived in the church parsonage, transients would come several times a week from the nearby railroad tracks searching for food or shelter. I'd be busy. They'd be scruffy or even smelly. I'm ashamed to admit that there were times I'd whisper inside, *Go away! We're trying to run a church here!*

But then, invariably, they'd say something like: "The guys at the gas station told me to come here. They said this church helped anybody."

Ouch and double ouch. As Christians, as a church, we are called to be a hospital, the very root of *hospitality.* Our lives should be a refuge for the hurting, not a country club for the comfortable.

"What good is it," James asks, "if a man claims to have faith but has no deeds?" Suppose someone is without clothes and daily food, the brother of Jesus ponders in James 2:14-17. "If one of you says to him, 'Go, I wish you well; keep warm and well fed,' but does nothing about his physical needs, *what good is it?*" (emphasis mine). James repeats the question, then concludes: "In the same way, faith by itself, if it is not accompanied by action, is dead."

Hospitality isn't an option for anyone who wants to say yes to Christ. It's part of his call to us, though it may be hard to work into our busy lives.

LEANING INTO OUR WEAKNESS

In my struggle with hospitality, I've discovered yet another thing about balance that's important to understand. In order to live the balanced life God desires, we may need to give more weight to the side we feel weakest in.

My sister and I would have never gotten around to actually teetertottering if I hadn't made the effort to scoot toward the middle. My "strength" would have outweighed her "weakness." I had to move toward her in order to achieve a workable balance.

The same is true of the balancing act of our lives. There are times when we have to make a concentrated effort to lean into our area of weakness, to give more weight to the area of intimacy or service that doesn't come easily for us.

That's what Martha did. She leaned away from the comfort of her Kitchen and shifted the weight of her attention toward the Living Room. Mary did the same thing when she left her place at the Lord's feet and leaned toward the active service of anointing her Lord. And I, too, am trying to learn this lesson of corrective measures, building up the weak sides of my life.

But I don't need to do it alone. Whenever I hear the sweet, convicting voice of the Holy Spirit pointing out my inconsistencies, I know he remains ready and willing to help me change. If hospitality is my weakness, he'll help me scoot toward that kind of service. When I need a little more weight on the side of Sabbath rest, he's faithful to help me lean in that direction, making me "lie down in green pastures." As I keep my eyes focused on the Lord, I'll have a passion for God and compassion for people—and the kind of balance the Lord intended for me all along.

BELOW THE WATER LINE

So how do we balance work and worship? All of the things we've talked about—keeping an attitude of yes, finding a rhythm, leaning toward our weaknesses—can help keep our teetertotters balanced. But it all comes right back to the same pivotal reality that changed the lives of Mary and Martha of Bethany. It's the same reality we've returned to again and again in this book.

The secret of balancing worship and work, devotion and service, love of God and love of people is maintaining our connection to Jesus Christ. Our relationship with him is the fulcrum, the anchor, the steadying point that makes balance possible in the first place. And the deeper that relationship goes, the more stable the balance will be.

"It all begins at the water line." That's how Jeanne Mayo puts it. I've come to appreciate not only the teaching of this incredible woman, but also the way she lives her life. She accomplishes more in twenty-four hours than I do in two weeks. But in the midst of her busyness, she has made a deep commitment to balance.

It isn't easy. Besides being the wife of a pastor in Rockford, Illinois, Jeanne leads a youth group of nine hundred and superintends the church school of thirteen hundred children, not to mention a wide speaking ministry.

How does she keep a balance? I asked her not long ago. "It takes a ruthless commitment to first things first," Jeanne said. "I'm constantly having to ask the Lord to do the Psalm 139 thing on me: 'Live in my heart. Search and examine me. Know my heart.'" Then Jeanne shared a story that has become a spiritual trigger point in her life. God is faithful to bring it to mind when her life begins to slip off kilter and out of balance.

In the autumn of 1992, a man named Michael Plant commenced a solo crossing of the North Atlantic. An expert yachtsman, Plant had made the trip several times before. His brand-new sailboat, the *Coyote,* was so technologically advanced there were few like it in the world.

Plant set off alone, leaving his support team to monitor his trip by satellite and radio. Everything was going well. Even when a storm disrupted communications, no one worried much. After all, this guy was one of the best sailors and navigators to be found. His boat was equipped with state-of-the-art navigational and emergency equipment. Plant would resume radio contact when everything settled down.

But Michael Plant was never heard from again. After numerous attempts to reach him by radio, the Coast Guard sent helicopters out to look for him. They found the *Coyote* floating upside down. Its captain and sole passenger was never found.

Why? How could this happen? the experts wondered. Everyone knows that sailboats are very hard to turn over. Their deep keels and massive rudders right themselves. But as the ship was examined, the cause of the tragedy became clear. For all its technological advances and beauty, the *Coyote* didn't have enough weight beneath the water line. There wasn't enough ballast below to outweigh the fancy gadgetry above. And so it flipped over as it lost its ability to balance in the water.[9]

"Our lives will capsize as well," Jeanne Mayo concludes, "if what lies below the spiritual water line of our lives doesn't outweigh what lies above." No matter how good we may look on the surface, no matter how balanced we may seem, it's what lies below that really counts.

If we want to live a balanced life, we must concentrate on the underpinnings of that life. Jesus did. He was in constant communion with his Father. We must do the same if we hope to sail successfully through life. And we *can!*—because the cross purchased the same privilege Christ enjoyed: an intimate one-on-one relationship with God.

As we spend time in the Living Room, walking and talking with him, we fill the hulls of our lives with the rich things of God. And out of that abundance will come both a steadfastness in the midst of storms and a surplus we can share with others.

We'll be loving God and loving our neighbor. Spending time in the Lord's Prayer and playing the Good Samaritan. Keeping the Sabbath. Practicing hospitality.

We'll be living in rhythm, but with a deep, solid anchor. Work will become worshipful. Worship will be a delight.

We'll be doing the "Chuckie"—and doing it with joy!

12

Having a Mary Heart in a Martha World

To him who is able to keep you from falling and to present you before his glorious presence without fault and with great joy.

JUDE 24

A Mary heart. A Martha world. Can the two parts of me ever come together? Will I ever find the pure, exquisite joy of being centered in Christ alone? Is it really possible to live a balanced life of Living Room Intimacy and Kitchen Service?

Now more than ever, I believe the answer is yes. Though I haven't "obtained all this, or have already been made perfect," like Paul, I, too, want to "press on to take hold of that for which Christ Jesus took hold of me" (Philippians 3:12). I haven't arrived, but I know where I'm headed.

Wainwright House sits on Long Island Sound like the movie set of some nineteenth-century romance. Ivy trails up and over its three stories of hand-hewn rock, curling around turrets and paned windows, before creeping back down into the gardens that surround the one-hundred-year-old mansion. It was my first time on the East Coast, and staying at this beautiful estate felt like a dream come true.

Along with fourteen other participants, I sat in Wainwright's massive library listening to Elizabeth Sherrill, the best-selling author of *The Hiding Place,* teach on how to write a personal experience story for *Guideposts* magazine.

It had been an exciting fall. Not long after receiving the workshop invitation, I'd received word that WaterBrook Press was interested in publishing

Having a Mary Heart in a Martha World. Wonderful news! Except for the fact that now I had to actually write it.

I was scared to death. Sitting in the dark-paneled room that first day, thoughts raced through my mind, criticizing and taunting me. *Who do you think you are, writing about intimacy with God?* I certainly wasn't an expert on the subject, though my heart longed to be. There were far more qualified people—of that I was sure.

"Above all…"—Elizabeth's voice broke through my musings as she spoke about writing in the first-person point of view—"the narrator must be the struggler."

She had my complete attention. "Rather than portraying the individual as an expert," she said, "we need to see the person grow through the story. We need to see him or her change." Something leaped inside me. Excitement. Hope.

I certainly qualified as a struggler when it came to intimacy with God. My downcast heart began to look up. Could it be that God was choosing me to write this book for the very reason I felt disqualified?

O Lord, I'm yours, I prayed silently as I scribbled down Elizabeth's words. *Take my struggles and use them for your glory. But whatever you do, please don't leave me the same. Change me. Give me a Mary heart in my Martha world.*

I had no idea how wonderful, nor how difficult, the Lord's answer to that prayer would be.

LORD OF THE PROCESS

Don't you wish your kitchen had a replicater? You know, the kind they have on *Star Trek,* where you say, "Coffee, Colombian, two teaspoons sugar, and a sprinkle of grated Belgian chocolate"…and *poof,* there it is!

Unfortunately, I'm still stuck with my Proctor-Silex drip coffeemaker and this fundamental reality: It takes a process to make a product.

The diamond ring I wear on my left hand didn't just happen. Before John and I picked it out of a jeweler's window, someone mounted it in a setting of gold. Before that, someone else saw promise in a lumpy, milky stone and chiseled facets to release the beauty locked inside. Before that, a worker found that rock deep inside a mountain. And multimillennia before that moment, a trillion pounds of rock, pressure, and steam worked together to compress ordinary carbon into a shape and substance that we call a diamond.

It takes a process to get a product. The car I drive didn't suddenly appear on the dealer's showroom floor. The house I live in took four months to build—and much longer if you take into account the growing season of the trees used to build it, the mining required to form the nails, and the mixture of sand and heat used to make the glass.

Get the picture?

A product requires a process. The same is true of our Christian walk. Becoming like Jesus requires a process as well.

That simple discovery has revolutionized my life in recent years. You see, I had spent most of my thirty-seven years waiting to arrive. To be perfected.

Somewhere deep in my heart I still harbored the hope that when I *really* gave my heart to Christ, I would pop out of a Holy Ghost phone booth completely clothed in blue and red—a sweet little skirt; a long, flowing cape; and a big *S* plastered across my chest for "SUPER CHRISTIAN!" I'd be able to leap tall stumbling blocks in a single bound. I'd be faster than the fiery darts of the enemy. More powerful than all of hell's temptations.

Can't you hear the music and see the breeze ruffling my cape as I fly along?

Well, it didn't happen. In truth, I've resembled a mild-mannered, albeit female, Clark Kent more often than I've looked like any spiritual superhero. Some days it's all I can do to get out of bed. And try as I might, I've never gotten the outfit down.

You can imagine how relieved I felt when I finally got it through my head that Christianity is a process and not an event. It is a journey, not a destination.

"I thought it had been an easy thing to be a Christian," Samuel Rutherford wrote several centuries ago, "but oh, the windings, the turnings, the ups and the downs that he has led me through."[1] It is the twisting tests of life that produce character and faithfulness to God, Rutherford concludes. And I've found that true as well.

It takes a process to produce a product—and that applies to sanctified Christians as well as diamonds, automobiles, and houses. It's certainly true of having a Mary heart in a Martha world. If we want to be like Jesus, we won't be able to escape the refining process.

But we can be "confident of this," Paul writes in Philippians 1:6, "that he who began a good work in [us] will carry it on to completion until the day of Christ Jesus."

What God started on the day I surrendered my life to him, he will complete as I continually remain surrendered. It takes a process for me to become the kind of Christian I want to be—but Jesus Christ is Lord of the Process, and the process is divine.

That doesn't mean we'll always understand his methods. It is a mystery to me how God can take something as imperfect as my life and turn it into an agent for his glory. In her book *When God Shines Through*, Claire Cloninger writes about this imaginative God who takes the broken, scattered pieces of our lives and turns them into kaleidoscopes:

> For me, one of the greatest frustrations of walking through the "daili-ness" of my life as a Christian is that I don't always get to see how the bits and pieces of who I am fit into the big picture of God's plan. It's tempting at times to see my life as a meal here, a meeting there, a car-pool, a phone call, a sack of groceries—all disjointed fragments of mothering in particular.
>
> And yet I know I am called, as God's child, to believe by faith that they do add up. That in some way every single scrap of my life, every step and every struggle, is in the process of being fitted together into God's huge and perfect pattern for good.[2]

Claire concludes that it is those very scattered pieces that God uses to make a kaleidoscope. Instead of waiting for us to arrive, God shines the Light of Christ through the fragments we place in his hands, transforming "the disorder into beauty and symmetry," splashing the colors of our brokenness like fireworks across the sky.

PARTNERS WITH CHRIST

Don't get the wrong idea though. This process of staying surrendered and letting Christ work in you is not as passive as that might sound.

Yes, the Lord has gone out of his way to make us his own. Yes, he died and rose again. He sent the Holy Spirit to teach and guide us. He's invested his own life to make us holy, and he'll take what we offer him and make it into something good. But we're still expected to partner in the process.

"When we all pull together, together, together, when we all pull together how happy we'll be." I always loved that song. Julie Olson and I would pair up in Sunday school and do the motions, our freshly pressed skirts swishing softly as we moved back and forth. Nicely. Sweetly. Not like Brian Larson and the other uncouth third-grade boys who turned the song into a wrestling match.

"For your work is my work," Julie and I'd sing, pointing at each other with a smile, while the boys thumped each other on the chest. "And our work is God's work," we'd continue, repeating the chorus, then clapping our hands to emphasize, "how happy we'll be."

It's amazing how well-behaved I used to be. Of course, it's easy to sing sweetly in Sunday school. Life, however, can be another matter.

As I've grown older, I'm ashamed to admit my song has taken on shades of uncouth boys and wrestling matches. I get confused and a little belligerent about what is my work and what is God's work. And every now and then, spiritually, I pull a Hulk Hogan: "It's your work, not my work," I thunder, thumping on heaven's door. "I'm tired of pulling together. It's your work, God!" I demand, trying to slip a full nelson around the Almighty. "It's your work!"

But when I settle down enough to listen, when I calm my heart to hear his voice, the Savior reassures me, "Yes, your salvation is my work. It *is* finished. I did it on the cross. But now I want to partner with you in living it out."

A LIFE OF EASE, PLEASE

I don't know what I expected when I began. *Having a Mary Heart in a Martha World* had simmered in my heart for two years. What an incredible message: Jesus longs to know us! Every one of us. Mary and Martha alike, with all our different personalities and gifts and worship styles.

It was big. So big. Jam-packed with grace-filled implications. But when I sat down to write it, my words kept getting in the way. Chapter 2 alone had six different versions and as many different starts. It wasn't anything like the Holy

Spirit–inspired free flow I'd imagined when I'd signed the contract. In fact, it strangely resembled work. Hard work.

I tried the All-Star-Wrestling prayer approach: "Hey! It's your work, God! I'm doing this for you—howsaboutta little help here?"

Silence.

I tried Job's "Where are you—and why don't you care?" approach.

Silence again.

I even contemplated Jonah's "Forget Nineveh—I'm headed for the Bahamas" approach.

But still I heard nothing except the soft sense of his presence. The sense that he was there but waiting—waiting for me to catch on to what he wanted to teach me about the process.

Henrietta Mears has said there is only one way to learn God's lessons. "On your face, with your mouth shut."[3] That's a tall order for the verbally prolific. But that's where the Lord kept taking me. Down on my knees. In the vicinity of where Mary found Jesus that afternoon in Bethany.

Sometimes I just waited and listened. Other times I poured out my petition and complaint. But most of the time I found myself going back to my original prayer. Whenever I was stuck, whenever I'd tell God I didn't understand, the Lord would gently remind me of what I'd told him at Wainwright. "Take my struggles and use them for your glory," I'd said. "Change me. Give me a Mary heart in my Martha world."

And with those words would come a quietness, an awareness that the Lord was working. I began to realize that if I was yoked to Christ, then I could trust him to set the pace. He knew what I needed and what had to be done. I could trust him to accomplish what he'd started. My part was to partner with him. So I'd get up from prayer and go back to working…and waiting…some more.

THE TESTING OF OUR FAITH

What I was experiencing, of course, isn't new. It has happened to every Christian at one time or another. It's the experience of sanctification—working hard beside

Christ as he does his transforming work in us. It's the process of perseverance—keeping on keeping on, obeying in the little and the big things, doing the best we can, and then continuing to march on, trusting God to do the rest.

Perseverance isn't a lot of fun. Yet it is perseverance that allows God to take our muddled messes and turn them into miracles. He delights in transforming the black-carbon pressures of our life into diamonds of radiant beauty. But doing all that requires a process. A process that takes time. A process that is sometimes painful.

You've probably already surmised that I am a slightly odd woman. So you might not be surprised when I tell you I loved being pregnant. But I was especially excited about labor. Contractions. Lamaze breathing. The whole bit. I couldn't wait for it to begin.

"It's pain with a purpose," I'd rhapsodize to anyone who'd listen. In my mind, I could see myself in that cozy little birthing room, surrounded by my

---

The Lord Is My Pace Setter

The Lord is my pace setter...I shall not rush

He makes me stop for quiet intervals

He provides me with images of stillness which restore my serenity

He leads me in the way of efficiency through calmness of mind and his
    guidance is peace

Even though I have a great many things to accomplish each day, I will not
    fret, for his presence is here

His timelessness, his all importance will keep me in balance

He prepares refreshment and renewal in the midst of my activity by
    anointing my mind with his oils of tranquillity

My cup of joyous energy overflows

Truly harmony and effectiveness shall be the fruits of my hours for I shall
    walk in the Pace of my Lord and dwell in his house for ever.

A VERSION OF THE TWENTY-THIRD PSALM FROM JAPAN[4]

husband's tender arms, singing praise songs. "Hallelujah…Halle—ooo!—jah. Wow, that was a big one!" I'd say with a smile as John gently stroked my brow. The nurse would come in, amazed at my speedy progress. "You'll have that baby any minute now, Mrs. Weaver. I've never seen anyone handle labor as well as you."

Suffice it to say, once again: It didn't happen. Instead of triumphing through glorious labor, I was rushed to an emergency C-Section. My baby was breech. "Either this is your baby's bottom," my doctor told me matter-of-factly, "or your baby's head has a crack in it."

Nothing about the birthing process came easily for me. When I finally surfaced from the anesthetic and held my baby boy, my eyes refused to focus. "I wish I could see him," I mumbled as I held the little bundle five inches from my face. Two and a half years later, Jessica was born after fourteen hours of hard, decidedly untriumphant labor.

"Oh yeah?" I can hear you say. "Let me tell you about pain…"

I know, I know. My point is not to exchange birthing horror stories, but to remind you that good things rarely come easy. A few weeks following the birth of my children, after the incision healed and the searing, ripping, excruciating pain was just a not-so-distant memory, I could honestly say, as I held my babies in my arms, "It was worth it all."

And it was.

IT WILL BE WORTH IT ALL

That's exactly what James was trying to say in his letter to the churches scattered abroad. That's exactly the point of his amazing statement about the painful process of partnering with God in our Christian growth:

> Consider it pure joy, my brothers, whenever you face trials of many kinds, because you know that the testing of your faith develops perseverance. Perseverance must finish its work so that you may be mature and complete, not lacking anything. (James 1:2-4)

Pure joy? What was this guy talking about? The churches he addressed were undergoing tremendous persecution. After the death of one of the first deacons,

Stephen, many Christians had fled Jerusalem and spread throughout Judea and Samaria (Acts 8:1), many of them joining Jewish communities around the Mediterranean (Acts 11:19-20). But instead of being welcomed by their Jewish kinsmen, they were rejected and persecuted—denied protection by the Jews, exploited by the Gentiles, robbed of possessions, hauled into court, treated worse than slaves.[5] And it was to these lonely, hurting outcasts that James directed those unbelievable words: "Consider it pure joy"—or, according to the *New English Bible,* "Count yourselves supremely happy."

How nice—as Kent Hughes puts it, "a letter of encouragement from Pastor Whacko!"[6]

But what was James really saying to those hurting Christians? He was telling them to look *beyond* the painful surface of what was happening to what God was doing in the midst of it all. He wanted them to see that the trials—the *peirasmos*—they were undergoing weren't haphazard. The testing of their faith had a purpose. Their trials were directed toward a glorious end. It would all be worth it if they would only persevere.

THE GLORIOUS RESULT

The trouble, of course, is that most of the time we'd rather not persevere. We all want a *test*imony, but we'd rather skip the *test* that gives us one. We all want a product. But we'd rather skip the process.

As Charles Swindoll writes,

> I fear our generation has come dangerously near the "I'm-getting-tired-so-let's-just-quit" mentality. And not just in the spiritual realm. Dieting is a discipline, so we stay fat. Finishing school is a hassle, so we bail out. Cultivating a close relationship is painful, so we back off. Getting a book written is demanding, so we stop short. Working through conflicts in a marriage is a tiring struggle, so we walk away. Sticking with an occupation is tough, so we start looking elsewhere....
>
> And about the time we are ready to give it up, along comes the Master, who leans over and whispers: "Now keep going; don't quit. Keep on."[7]

When it comes to our spiritual lives, a lot of us are all-or-nothing people. If we aren't automatically perfect, we just give up. When Christlike virtues like patience and kindness seem hard to come by, we abandon our character development and decide holiness is for those better equipped. But when we give up, we're giving up on our part of the partnership. Perseverance is one of our responsibilities in this process of being changed.

And what a change it will be! The rewards of perseverance James outlines for us are so much more than mere words. He tells us that the glorious result of perseverance will make us "mature and complete, not lacking in anything." The word he uses for *mature* is *telios,* which describes a dynamic maturity, a personality that has reached its full development. And when James says we'll be complete, the word *holokleros* means we'll be "entire, perfect in every part." It was the word used to describe the condition of the high priest and the animal sacrifice given every year. It meant they were free of any disqualifying or disfiguring blemish.[8] Perseverance makes us ready to be the living sacrifices Paul describes in Romans 12:1 as "holy and pleasing to God."

God uses the pressure of trials to perfect our lives. He fashions facets in humble stone to reflect his glory. The last phrase in James 1:4 echoes through my heart with incredible hope. When we persevere, we become mature and complete, "not lacking anything." *Leipos medeis.* We suffer no deficiency. We have everything we need.

Of course, there will still be areas in our lives where we struggle. There will still be battles, and we'll lose a few now and then. But if we're willing to persevere in the process, one day—with Christ beside us—we'll win the war.

That's why I can tell you: Persevere, my friend! Persevere. Do you want more of God? Then don't settle for anything less. Do you want to be more like Jesus? Then persevere—press in, press on, press through!

And as you do, I promise you, you will be changed. Changed as Mary and Martha were changed.

MARY HEART—MARTHA WORLD

I love the last picture we see of Mary and Martha in the Bible. John 12:1-3 sketches a portrait of two women at rest. At rest with their Savior. At rest with themselves.

Martha is still serving, but she does it with an attentive heart. Rather than barricading herself in the Kitchen, she serves in the Living Room, within the presence of her Lord. The busy servant has become a focused student as Martha drinks in his every word.

Mary may have started the evening sitting at the feet of Jesus, but rather than passively listening, she gives all that she has. She breaks open her treasure, spilling it out in prophetic ministry to Christ. With loving service, she prepares the Master for burial and the end of his sojourn on earth. The contemplative student has become an effective servant as Mary shows her love through extravagant deed.

And I, too, have been changed, in ways I never anticipated. I, too, have learned surprising lessons about what it means to have a Mary heart in a Martha world.

It hasn't been a comfortable process. To be truthful, I would have preferred a trip to a heavenly day spa. A twenty-four-hour makeover complete with body wrap, face-lift, and a new spiritual wardrobe. But God decided to do it the old-fashioned way. He decided to use life to teach me. He decided to use the process of writing this book.

"I'm bankrupt, God!" I cried one lonely, empty night. My words had dried up and, though my heart still echoed with the message, I couldn't seem to get past an invisible wall. I'd lived each chapter individually—the awful paranoia of "Lord, don't you care?"; the fearful anxiety of "you are worried about many things"; the wrenching grief of "if you had been here."

That night in the darkness, I felt completely alone.

But somewhere in all the wrestling, God met me there.

He spoke peace and direction, though I can't explain how he did it. Somehow his grace helped me live one day at a time—not in fear of the future or in regret of the past. More wondrous, more incredible, God began to heal the dichotomy of my life. He began to unite the two-sided spiritual schizophrenia that had plagued me for years.

Instead of trying in my own strength to mesh Living Room Intimacy with Kitchen Service, I started focusing on Christ alone. Instead of fretting about what was and was not getting done, I began to surrender my days to the Lord, asking him to direct my paths. "You know what needs to be done today, Lord. Show me the 'one thing' and I'll do it."

With the surrender came a newfound peace. I was able to leave the tunnel vision of all-or-nothing thinking and just enjoy each day. Opportunities began to open all over the place. I had the privilege of leading a woman to the Lord when I took time to drop off a book. I bumped into an acquaintance at Jessica's basketball game who really needed prayer. Even my writing began to flow better.

Then, several weeks later, as I drove toward the hospital to visit one of our ailing church members, I found myself wondering, *Is this visit a Martha thing or a Mary thing?* I'd been asking the same question about this book. "All the work I'm putting in, all the writing and rewriting—is this Martha duty or Mary devotion?" I wasn't certain.

Suddenly as I drove along, in the midst of my mental eenie-meenie-miney-mo, I realized it was both! Visiting the hospital was doing the Martha Mary-ly. Writing about intimacy with God was Mary doing the Martha faithfully. In my once-divided heart, the two had become one. I no longer had to worry about my motives, whether I was acting out of duty or devotion. God had knocked down the wall and made the Living Room and Kitchen all one.

"It's both!" I cried, thumping the steering wheel, a huge smile on my face. "It's both."

I SURRENDER ALL

I can't tell you the freedom I felt that day. It was as if a giant puzzle I'd been working on for years suddenly solved itself. Joining the two parts of my heart seemed so natural, so simple. Almost embarrassingly easy.

But perhaps you've already discovered that God delights in an undivided heart. Perhaps you're already living in that place of perpetual ease before the Lord, simply serving him and loving him one day at a time. But if you aren't, if you are a struggler like me, take heart! God has a better way.

Ken Gire, in his book *Intense Moments with the Savior*, writes: "I've learned my strength is not found in how intensely I struggle...but in how completely I surrender."[9] When we come to the end of ourselves and our abilities, when we relinquish our lives, Jesus promises to use them. Little is much when God is in it. Especially if that little something is you and me.

"Give yourself fully to God," writes Mother Teresa in *Life in the Spirit*. "He will use you to accomplish great things on the condition that you believe much more in his love than in your own weakness."[10]

When we surrender our lives to Jesus Christ, we release the Lord of the Process to do his work. For it is in our weakness that Christ is strong. It is in our inadequacy that we find him more than sufficient. And it is in our willingness to be broken that he brings wholeness—more wholeness and completeness than we ever dreamed possible.

This is a lifetime journey, the fruit of which we will enjoy for eternity. The fruit of which will remain long after we're gone.

Henrietta Mears is known for all she did in God's kingdom (developing a huge Sunday school, discipling leaders). "Yet amid all her doing," Jan Johnson writes in *Living a Purpose-Full Life*, "she positioned herself frequently at the feet of God—studying, listening, enjoying him."

In spite of her busy schedule, Henrietta "opened her Bible in the sacred silence of personal fellowship with God with much the same attention as a starving man approaches a banquet." And when she died, Henrietta Mears was depicted as having "slipped through the veil between the present and the hereafter, which she had described over the years as being so very, very thin. Someone remarked, 'It was nothing new to meet her Lord alone, for she had often done so. This time she just went with him.'"[11]

Do you want that kind of Mary heart in a Martha world? I know I do.

I want to live so intimately with Jesus that when it's time to leave this world, I, too, slip through that very thin veil Henrietta Mears spoke about. From one glory-filled lifetime to another. From sitting "in his presence" to standing "face to face"!

But in order for that to happen, I need to persevere and be patient—because it takes a process to produce a product, and a process takes time. But never forget, Christ's beloved, this process is divine. God is right beside you! He is the one who's in charge. All he asks is that you partner with him and surrender to what he is doing in your life.

"Therefore we do not lose heart," Paul writes in 2 Corinthians 4:16-17. "Though outwardly we are wasting away, yet inwardly we are being renewed day by day. For our light and momentary troubles are achieving for us an eternal glory that far outweighs them all."

From glory to glory, he's changing us.

So don't worry that you haven't arrived, my dear sister. Just don't give up on the process. Don't miss the journey.

For it will be glorious! It will be worth it all.

A Prayer for the Journey

O Christ, do not give me tasks equal to my powers,

but give me powers equal to my tasks,

for I want to be stretched by things too great for me.

I want to grow through the greatness of my tasks,

but I shall need your help for the growing.[12]

E. STANLEY JONES

Resources for a Mary Heart in a Martha World

Appendix A

Study Guide

Nothing has transformed my life like the study of God's Word. Something powerful happens when we go beyond other people's opinions and revelations and discover for ourselves what God has to say. I designed this twelve-week Bible study to help you do just that.

I recommend using a translation of the Bible that you enjoy and understand, as well as a notebook and a pen to record your answers. Before each lesson, ask the Holy Spirit to increase your understanding as you examine God's Word and then help you apply the truths you discover.

Each lesson starts with questions for individual reflection or group discussion, then moves into a study of scriptural principles. At the end of the lesson, you'll have an opportunity to write about what spoke most to you in that chapter. The stories, quotes, and sidebars within the chapters may provide further opportunities for discussion or reflection.

My prayer is that each of you will begin to experience the blessing God promises to those who look "intently into the perfect law that gives freedom…not forgetting what he has heard, but doing it" (James 1:25). There is a holy makeover waiting for each one of us. It is found in God's presence and within the pages of his Word. Dig in, ladies! You'll be glad you did.

CHAPTER ONE: A TALE OF TWO SISTERS

Questions for Discussion or Reflection

1. What preconceived ideas did you have about Mary and Martha before reading this book? Which woman do you relate to most—Mary or Martha? Explain your answer.

2. One woman told me, "My life is like a blender—and it's stuck on frappé!" What inanimate object best describes how your life currently feels?

Going Deeper

3. Read Luke 10:38-42. List at least two things you learn about Martha in this passage and at least two things you learn about Mary. How would you sum up Martha in one word? How would you sum up Mary?

4. A woman told me, "I guess I'm just a Martha and that I'll always be a Martha." Is it possible for our basic character to change, or are we destined to live our lives stuck in a predetermined nature? Explain your answer.

5. What does the Bible say in the following verses about our potential for change?
   Ezekiel 36:26-27 _____
   2 Corinthians 5:17 _____
   Philippians 1:6 _____

6. Have you seen God's work of transformation in your own life or someone else's? How did you know it was a "holy makeover" and not just a temporary "facelift"?

7. Read Matthew 11:28-30. Circle key words and meditate on these verses—really think about what Jesus is saying. Then memorize this passage phrase by phrase. Write it on an index card, and refer to it frequently, repeating it until it becomes a part of you.

8. What spoke most to you in this chapter?

CHAPTER TWO: "LORD, DON'T YOU CARE?"

Questions for Discussion or Reflection

1. The story of Mary and Martha stirs up memories of sibling rivalry for many of us. What battles with your siblings do you remember the most? What did you do to get your parents to notice you?

2. Read Luke 10:38-42. Have you ever asked Martha's question, "Lord, don't you care?" What was the situation? How did God answer your question?

Going Deeper

3. All of us have felt alone—even great heroes of the faith felt this way. Read 1 Kings 19:1-18. How did the "Deadly Ds" of distraction, discouragement, and doubt attack Elijah after the great victory over the prophets of Baal in 1 Kings 18? I've completed the first one as an example:

   DISTRACTION: *Jezebel's anger made him run for his life.*
   DISCOURAGEMENT: _____
   DOUBT: _____

4. In this passage how did God minister to Elijah in the midst of his discouragement? How has God ministered to you when you felt alone and were hurting?

5. In Mark 4:35-41 the disciples echoed Martha's question: "Don't you care?" What does this portion of Scripture teach us about the difficult times in our lives? (Consider Isaiah 43:1-2.)

6. Read Psalm 103. List at least five of the many ways God shows his love for us. (If you are struggling to know the Father's love, consider memorizing this chapter so you won't forget "all his benefits.")

7. Write Jesus a letter beginning with "Lord, I know you love me because...," and list the ways he has shown his great love for you.

8. What spoke most to you in this chapter?

CHAPTER THREE: THE DIAGNOSIS

Questions for Discussion or Reflection

1. Martha wanted Jesus to tell Mary to help out in the kitchen, but instead of giving her what she wanted, Dr. Jesus made a diagnosis: "Martha, Martha…you are worried and upset about many things." If you had been Martha, how would Jesus' words have made you feel?

2. According to Dr. Edward Hallowell, over half of us are chronic worriers. Which of the ten signs of a big worrier on page 33 do you struggle with? How do worry and anxiety spill over into your daily life and affect your behavior? your physical health?

Going Deeper

3. Fear not only affects us physically but spiritually. Read Luke 8:14. List three things that may choke the Word of God out of our lives. Which one do you struggle with most, and how does it choke you spiritually?

4. Look at the "Concern and Worry" diagram on page 38, and read the quote from Gary E. Gilley. What concerns are you currently facing? What worries?

5. What do the following passages tell us to do with our worries and concerns, and what will be the result?

   Proverbs 3:5-6   COMMAND: _____
        RESULT: _____

   Philippians 4:6-7   COMMAND: _____
        RESULT: _____

6. a. Rewrite Matthew 6:25-30 as if God were speaking directly to you and your current situation.
   Therefore, I tell you, __(your name)__, *do not worry about…*

   b. Read Matthew 6:31-34. Respond to this passage in a prayer to the Lord.
   Lord, I don't want to worry as the world does. Help me to…

7. According to 1 John 4:16-18, how can we respond to God's love, and what will happen to fear when we do?

8. What spoke most to you in this chapter?

CHAPTER FOUR: THE CURE

Questions for Discussion or Reflection

1. Read the wagon and the rocks story on pages 48-51. Take a look in your wagon. Which rocks has God asked you to carry? Which rocks have you unwisely and sometimes unconsciously volunteered to carry for someone else?

2. Do you ever feel the driven, perfectionistic, spiritual Martha Stewart coming out in you? What does she look like at home? What does she look like at church?

Going Deeper

3. What do you think Jesus meant in Luke 10:38-42 when he told Martha that only one thing was needed?

4. a. Turn a few pages, to Luke 18:18-25, to another exchange Jesus had. What qualification did the rich young ruler give for entering the kingdom of God?

   b. What was the one thing Jesus said he lacked?

   c. Why do you think Christ focused on his wealth?

   d. Why may the one thing God asks us to do be different from what he requires of someone else? (Consider 1 Corinthians 13:3 and Philippians 3:4-7.)

5. Perhaps like the rich young ruler you find yourself trying to perform for God, carrying more rocks in hopes of earning God's love and favor. What do the following verses say about works-based Christianity?

   Galatians 3:3 _____

   Titus 3:5 _____

6. What did Paul say in Philippians 3:13-14 was his "one thing"? Why was forgetting what was behind him so important for Paul? (Consider Acts 26:9-15.) What things in your past hold you back from experiencing all God has for you? Take a moment to ask the Lord to help you let go of anything that holds you back.

7. Using the guidelines on page 55, sit down this week and begin

"dumping rocks." But before you start, ask the Lord for wisdom (James 1:5). He loves to give it, and he wants to set us free!

8. What spoke most to you in this chapter?

CHAPTER FIVE: LIVING ROOM INTIMACY

Questions for Discussion or Reflection

1. Someone has said that each of us is created "with a God-shaped hole" and that we will never be truly satisfied until we fill that space with him. Unfortunately many of us, as Teri described on page 69, fill up on spiritual Snicker Bars. What do you turn to instead of God when you're feeling empty?

2. I've written that intimacy with God comes through Prayer + the Word + Time. Which of these three disciplines is most difficult for you? Which comes easiest?

Going Deeper

3. We all face barriers to intimacy with God. Put a check by the one or two you struggle with most, then look up the verses next to that barrier. Circle the verse that is most meaningful to you.

    _____ Unworthiness   (Isaiah 41:9-10; Ephesians 2:13-14)

    _____ Busyness   (Psalm 90:12; Isaiah 40:29-31)

    _____ Guilt / Shame   (Psalm 32:5; 1 John 1:9)

    _____ Pride   (Psalm 10:4; James 4:6-7)

    _____ Depression   (Psalm 42:11; John 14:1)

    _____ Trials / Hard-   (Hebrews 13:6; 2 Corinthians 4:7-10)
    ships

4. Meditate on the verse you circled, then personalize it in the form of a prayer to God. Here is an example based on 1 John 1:9.

    God, thank you for the forgiveness that comes when I admit my sin rather than deny it. I'm so glad I don't have to clean up my act before I come to you. All I have to do is come. You promise to do the cleaning.

5. I've written that before we become Christians, Satan tells us we don't

need a Savior. After we become Christians, he tells us we don't deserve a Savior. How have these lies affected your walk with God?

6. God longs to have fellowship with us. Read the following verses, and describe the metaphor Scripture uses to describe the intimate relationship we can have with God.

    John 15:5 _____

    Romans 8:15-16 _____

    2 Corinthians 11:2 _____

7. Read the excerpt from "My Heart Christ's Home" (pages 72-73). How does it make you feel to think that Jesus longs to have time alone with you—to be at home in you? How could this realization turn your devotional life from a duty to a delight?

8. What spoke most to you in this chapter?

CHAPTER SIX: KITCHEN SERVICE

Questions for Discussion or Reflection

1. Dwight L. Moody said, "Of one hundred men, one will read the Bible; the ninety-nine will read the Christian."[1] Who was the first Christian in your life to live in such a way that you could clearly see Christ? How did this person affect your life?

2. Read the story of the little boy and the evangelist on page 97. How would you like Jesus to "stick out all over" your life—that is, what attitudes and characteristics of the Savior would you like God to develop in your life?

Going Deeper

3. Read John 13:1-17. Jesus' washing of the disciples' feet was a totally unexpected example of what true Christian love should look like. According to page 82, why was it so shocking?

4. J. Oswald Sanders said, "It is noteworthy that only once did Jesus say that he was leaving his disciples an example, and that was when he washed their feet."[2] In what unexpected ways could we wash the feet of those around us?

5. Place one (or more) of the following letters beside each verse that follows. In this passage Jesus ministered (a) as he went *on his way;* (b) as he went *out of his way;* (c) in *all kinds of ways.*

_____ Mark 1:29-34

_____ Mark 6:30-34

_____ Mark 7:31-35

6. How could you practically administer Christ's love in each of these ways? I've completed the first one as an example.

As I go on my way: *I thank the school crossing guard for keeping my kids safe.*

As I go out of my way: _____

In all kinds of ways: _____

7. Read Acts 3:1-10. What can we learn from this passage about how to actively show God's love to those around us?

8. What spoke most to you in this chapter?

CHAPTER SEVEN: THE BETTER PART

Questions for Discussion or Reflection

1. Read the "hoopy birthday" story on pages 99–100. Name the Hula-Hoop responsibilities you have in your life. Which one is the most difficult to keep in motion?

2. Consider Wilbur Rees's thought-provoking words:

> I would like to buy $3 worth of God, please, not enough to explode my soul or disturb my sleep, but just enough to equal a cup of warm milk or a snooze in the sunshine. I don't want enough of Him to make me love a black man or pick beets with a migrant. I want ecstasy, not transformation; I want the warmth of the womb, not a new birth. I want a pound of the Eternal in a paper sack. I would like to buy $3 worth of God, please.[3]

In all honesty, how much of God do you want? What keeps you from wanting more?

Going Deeper

3. We live with so much less than God intended us to have. Ask God to illuminate your understanding as you read Paul's prayer for believers in Ephesians 3:16-19. Then list three truths from this passage you'd like God to make real in your life.

4. How does Matthew 6:33 relate to Stephen Covey's "First Things First" principle (page 103)—that is, putting in the big rocks first? Give an example of a time you found this principle true in your life.

5. Read on pages 107-108 about Sidlow Baxter's personal struggle to develop a devotional time. How important is our will in this process of seeking God? How important are our emotions?

6. Explain how the following Bible characters chose to put God first despite overwhelming emotions or circumstances.
   David (2 Samuel 12:13-23) _____
   Daniel (Daniel 6:3-10) _____
   Jesus (Matthew 26:36-39) _____

7. Use the "Journal the Journey" outline in Appendix D and the instructions on page 114 to meditate on and write about one of the following passages.

   Psalm 139   Romans 8   Ephesians 4
   Isaiah 55   1 Corinthians 13   James 1

8. What spoke most to you in this chapter?

CHAPTER EIGHT: LESSONS FROM LAZARUS

Questions for Discussion or Reflection

1. What is your favorite kind of story and why?

   Romance   Mystery   Biography
   Adventure   Sci-Fi   Fantasy

2. Which of the following lessons from Lazarus have you found most true in your life? Explain the circumstances involved and what you learned.

   • God's will does not always proceed in a straight line.
   • God's love sometimes tarries for our good and his glory.

- God's ways are not our ways, but his character is still dependable.
- God's plan is released when we believe and obey.
- The "end" is never the end; it is only the beginning.

Going Deeper

3. Read John 11:1-6. Circle key words, and think about this family's situation and Jesus' response. When you face difficulties, which of these verses might comfort you most and why?

4. Because time and space confine us, we can't always see what is really happening. What do the following verses say about this in-between time in which we find ourselves?

John 16:33 _____

Hebrews 11:13-16 _____

James 1:2-4 _____

5. Martha Tennison says, "We only trust people we know. If you're struggling to trust God, it may be because you don't really know God."[4] We come to know God better through his Word. What do the following verses reveal about our heavenly Father?

Psalm 27:1   "The Lord is _____."

Psalm 34:18   "The Lord is _____."

Psalm 100:5   "The Lord is _____."

Psalm 145:8   "The Lord is _____."

6. Look up the word *trust* in a concordance. Find two phrases that speak to you, and write out the corresponding verses.

7. Laura Barker Snow writes about the difficult times we all face and how we need to view such times through the sovereignty and goodness of God, to live as if God is saying:

My child, I have a message for you today; let me whisper it in your ear, that it may gild with glory any storm clouds which may arise, and smooth the rough places upon which you may have to tread. It is short, only five words, but let them sink into your inmost soul; use them as a pillow upon which to rest your weary head…. This thing is from ME.[5]

How would your life be different if you could receive these words as truth and not only truth but as evidence of God's love in your life?

8. What spoke most to you in this chapter?

CHAPTER NINE: MARTHA'S TEACHABLE HEART

Questions for Discussion or Reflection

1. Which of the following best describes the kind of student you were in school?

    Intellectual   Absent-Though-Present   Teacher's Pet

    Procrastinator   Party Animal   High Achiever

    What did you like most about school? What did you like least? How have you carried these likes and dislikes into adulthood?

2. Think of someone you consider teachable. What character qualities make you view him or her that way?

Going Deeper

3. Fill out the "Are You Teachable?" questionnaire on page 139. What did you discover about yourself?

4. We have to accept the diagnosis if we're ever going to experience the cure. I believe Martha did just that. Read Luke 10:38-42. Now read John 11:17-28. What differences do you see in Martha in these two stories?

5. Read Hebrews 12:5-11, and then list four reasons why God disciplines us and four results of that discipline.

REASONS	RESULTS
_____	_____
_____	_____
_____	_____
_____	_____

6. The Bible is filled with if-then propositions. *If* we will…, *then* God will… What do the following verses promise us if we obey? I've filled out the first verse for you.

    Joshua 1:8   If…   *I meditate on God's Word and do it,*
                   then… *I will be prosperous and successful.*

John 8:31-32   If... _____

              then... _____

James 1:25   If... _____

              then... _____

7. God is willing to forgive and change us—even at our very worst. Consider the prayer David prayed in Psalm 51:10-12 after his murderous, adulterous affair with Bathsheba. Rewrite this cry for transformation in your own words. Then read it aloud to the Lord.

8. What spoke most to you in this chapter?

CHAPTER TEN: MARY'S EXTRAVAGANT LOVE

Questions for Discussion or Reflection

1. Describe a time you expressed love and concern for others and were misunderstood. How did it make you feel? Did you pull back or press in closer?

2. Consider the differences between Mary's and Judas's love for Christ:

MARY...	JUDAS...
• had a heart of gratitude	• had a heart of greed
• came with abandon	• came with an agenda
• heard what Jesus said and responded	• heard but did not understand
• held nothing back	• gave nothing up

Which aspect of Mary's love comes easiest to you? Which aspect is the most difficult for you?

Going Deeper

3. Read John 12:1-11. What was Judas's response to Mary's extravagant love? What did John say was the motivation behind his response?

4. Read Matthew 16:21-23. What was Peter's response to Jesus' explanation that he must die? What did Jesus say was the motivation behind his response?

5. Read another account of Mary's anointing Jesus in Mark 14:6-9.

Finish the following four statements Jesus made about her extravagant love.

"She has done a _____ thing to me."

"She did what she _____."

"She poured perfume…to prepare for my _____."

"Wherever the gospel is preached…what she has _____ will also be told."

Meditate on one of these statements. Ask the Lord to show you practical ways you could love him more beautifully and sacrificially.

6. Matthew and Mark both place Judas's dark change of heart as happening immediately after Mary's extravagant act of love. According to the following verses, why are greed and the love of money so dangerous?

Matthew 6:24 _____

1 Timothy 6:9-10 _____

James 4:1-4 _____

7. Mary loved extravagantly because she had experienced firsthand the extravagant love of God. Read 1 John 3:1 and Romans 8:31-39. Write a love letter back to God, expressing your gratitude for his lavish love and extravagant grace.

8. What spoke most to you in this chapter?

CHAPTER ELEVEN: BALANCING WORK AND WORSHIP

Questions for Discussion or Reflection

1. What does your teetertotter look like when it comes to balancing work and worship? Draw a line to show which way it tends to tilt (if it does).

| WORK   WORSHIP |

Pivot Point

2. Read the "Listening to Your Soul" checklist on pages 182-183. According to the checklist, do you need to spend more time in the

Living Room or the Kitchen? What are some practical ways you could lean into your weak side to bring balance to your Christian life?

Going Deeper

3. On one side of the teetertotter we find the importance of loving people. Read the story of the Good Samaritan in Luke 10:25-37. Describe how the Samaritan fulfilled the following statements:

    He took NOTICE _____

    He took ACTION _____

    He took RESPONSIBILITY_____

    Which of these three qualities comes easiest to you? Which is the hardest for you?

4. On the other side of Mary and Martha's story we find Christ's teaching on prayer. What does Luke 11:1-13 show about our part in prayer and God's promised response?

    OUR PART   GOD'S RESPONSE

    _____   _____

    _____   _____

    _____   _____

    _____   _____

5. According to the following verses, why is it dangerous to spend all our time on one end of the teetertotter?

    Matthew 7:21-23 _____

    James 2:14-17 _____

    1 John 3:16-18 _____

6. We all need time to let our souls catch up. From Isaiah 58:13-14, list three ways we can "keep the Sabbath" and also three blessings we will receive from honoring the "Lord's holy day."

7. According to the following verses, what blessings do we receive from hospitality?

    Isaiah 58:6-8 _____

    Matthew 25:34-36 _____

    Hebrews 13:2 _____

8. What spoke most to you from this chapter?

CHAPTER TWELVE: HAVING A MARY HEART IN A MARTHA WORLD

Questions for Discussion or Reflection

1. Have you ever heard a great Christian testimony and wished you could have the faith of that person or live as he or she has lived? What was the process that gave them the product?

2. When you face difficulties in life, which approach do you usually take? Explain.

    The All-Star Wrestling Approach: "God! I'm doing this for you—howsaboutta little help here?"

    The Job Approach: "Where are you—and why don't you care?"

    The Jonah Approach: "Forget Nineveh—I'm headed for the Bahamas."

Going Deeper

3. Read John 12:1-3. Knowing what you now know about these sisters, what two things could you surmise about Martha and about Mary from this passage? How would you sum up Martha in one word? How would you sum up Mary? How does this differ from the way you described them in the study for chapter 1 (question 3)?

4. Read the following verses. Describe the process God uses and the purpose he intends.

    Deuteronomy 8:2   PROCESS _____

                                     PURPOSE _____

    Romans 8:28-29   PROCESS _____

                                       PURPOSE _____

    2 Corinthians 4:17   PROCESS _____

                                       PURPOSE _____

5. How do we partner in this process, according to Philippians 2:12-13?

    We do...

    God does...

6. Read Philippians 1:6 and Hebrews 10:35-36, then look up the following words in the dictionary, and write their definitions.

  Confident:

  Persevere:

  Complete:

  Which of these words mean the most to you right now and why?

7. Read Philippians 3:12-14. Circle key words, and then rewrite this passage in your own words. Read it aloud as a prayer, a declaration of faith, and/or a personal mission statement. Ask God to keep it ever before you as you run the race for the prize.

8. What spoke most to you from this chapter?

Resources for Living Room Intimacy

Devotions

Everyday Light by Selwyn Hughes. Nashville: Broadman & Holman, 1998.

Experiencing God (workbook) by Henry T. Blackaby and Claude V. King. Nashville: LifeWay Press, 1995.

My Utmost for His Highest by Oswald Chambers. 1935. Reprint, Uhrichsville, Ohio: Barbour & Co., *n.d.* Updated version: Grand Rapids, Mich.: Discovery House, 1992.

OverJoyed by Women of Faith (various authors). Grand Rapids, Mich.: Zondervan, 1999.

Shaping a Woman's Soul by Judith Couchman. Grand Rapids, Mich.: Zondervan, 1996.

Springs in the Valley by L. B. Cowman. Grand Rapids, Mich.: Zondervan, 1996.

Streams in the Desert by L. B. Cowman. Grand Rapids, Mich.: Zondervan, 1996.

We Brake for Joy by Women of Faith (various authors). Grand Rapids, Mich.: Zondervan, 1999.

Windows of the Soul by Ken Gire. Grand Rapids, Mich.: Zondervan, 1996.

Christian Classics

Adventures in Prayer by Catherine Marshall. Grand Rapids, Mich.: Chosen Books, 1996.

Beyond Ourselves by Catherine Marshall. Grand Rapids, Mich.: Revell, 1994.

The Christian's Secret of a Happy Life by Hannah Whitall Smith. Nashville: Thomas Nelson, 1999.

Hinds' Feet on High Places by Hannah Hurnard. Uhrichsville, Ohio: Barbour & Co., 1998.

In His Steps by Charles M. Sheldon. Tulsa, Okla.: Honor Books, 1998.

Mere Christianity by C. S. Lewis. New York: Simon & Schuster, 1996.

The Practice of the Presence of God by Brother Lawrence. Nashville: Thomas Nelson, 1999.

The Screwtape Letters by C. S. Lewis. New York: Simon & Schuster, 1996.

With Christ in the School of Prayer by Andrew Murray. North Brunswick, N.J.: Bridge-Logos, 1999.

Quiet Time Music

Instrumental Praise series produced by Don Marsh. Brentwood, Tenn.: Brentwood Music, 1999.

Instruments of Praise series produced by Tom Brooks. Mobile, Ala.: Fairhope Records (a division of Integrity Music), 1998.

My Utmost for His Highest series by various artists. Nashville: Word Music, 1993.

Simplicity series produced by Trammell Starks. Portland, Oreg.: Pamplin Music, 1997.

Resources for Kitchen Service

Service

Designing a Woman's Life by Judith Couchman. Sisters, Oreg.: Multnomah, 1995. A separate Bible study and workbook are also available.

Improving Your Serve by Charles Swindoll. Dallas: Word, 1997.

Living a Purpose-Full Life by Jan Johnson. Colorado Springs, Colo.: WaterBrook Press, 1999.

Roaring Lambs by Bob Briner. Grand Rapids, Mich.: Zondervan, 1995.

Women of a Generous Spirit by Lois Mowday Rabey. Colorado Springs, Colo.: WaterBrook Press, 1998.

Hospitality

Creative Counterpart by Linda Dillow. Nashville: Nelson, 1992.

The Joy of Hospitality by Barbara Ball and Vonette Bright. Orlando: New Life Publications, 1996.

Open Heart—Open Home by Karen Burton Mains. Wheaton, Ill.: Mainstay Church Resources, 1998.

The Personal Touch by Rachael Crabb. Colorado Springs, Colo.: NavPress, 1991.

Things Happen When Women Care: Hospitality and Friendship in Today's Busy World by Emilie Barnes. Eugene, Oreg.: Harvest House, 1990.

Home-Keeping

Decorating on a Shoestring by Gwen Ellis and JoAnn Jannsen. Nashville: Broadman & Holman, 1999.

The Hidden Art of Homemaking by Edith Shaeffer. Wheaton, Ill.: Tyndale House, 1985.

Living a Beautiful Life: 500 Ways by Alexandria Stoddard. New York: Random House, 1996.

Once-a-Month Cooking by Mimi Wilson and Mary Beth Lagerborg. Nashville: Broadman & Holman, 1999.

Welcome Home by Emilie Barnes. Eugene, Oreg.: Harvest House, 1997.

Organization

Confessions of an Organized Homemaker by Deniece Schofield. Cincinnati, Ohio: S & W Publications, 1994.

Disciplines of a Beautiful Woman by Anne Ortlund. Nashville: Word, 1984.

Emilie's Creative Home Organizer by Emilie Barnes. Eugene, Oreg.: Harvest House, 1995.

The Messie's Manual by Sandra Felton. Grand Rapids, Mich.: Revell, 1983.

When You Live with a Messie by Sandra Felton. Grand Rapids, Mich.: Revell, 1994.

Journal the Journey

While many people keep journals of daily events and feelings, a Bible reading highlights journal records what God is saying to us through his Word and our response to him. Here is the format that I've found works well for me.

Date _____ What I read today _____

Best thing I marked today: *Reference:* _____

Thought: _____

_____

_____

_____

How it impressed me: _____

_____

_____

_____

_____

_____

_____

_____

_____

This Bible reading highlights format is used in the Navigator's 2:7 Discipleship Course, with seven days on one page.[6] But I've also used spiral notebooks and bound lined journals (available at stationery stores) when I've wanted more space to write. You can even draw up your own form and have it photocopied.

A Simple Plan for a Half-Day of Prayer

"God's acquaintance is not made hurriedly," says E. M. Bounds. "He does not bestow His gifts on the casual or hasty comer and goer. To be much alone with God is the secret of knowing Him and of influence with Him."[7]

Something powerful happens when we set apart a block of time to seek God's face intensively. Here are a few guidelines for a half-day of prayer that I've adapted from the Navigators:

1. *Find a place free from distractions.* I've found it helpful to go away for my extended prayer times. A friend's vacant house, a church or Christian conference center, or even a motel room will do.

2. *Take along your Bible, a notebook, a pen or pencil.* You may also want a devotional, hymnal, a prayer list, memory verses, and your weekly schedule. Wear comfortable clothes and bring a sack lunch.

3. *Stay awake and alert.* Get adequate rest the night before. Change positions frequently. Sit awhile, walk around—vary your position to keep from growing dull or sleepy.

4. *Try a variety of approaches.* Read the Scriptures awhile, pray awhile, plan or organize awhile, and so on. You might divide the time into three parts: (a) wait on the Lord, (b) pray for others, and (c) pray for yourself.

5. *Pray aloud* in a whisper or soft voice. Sometimes thinking aloud also helps.

6. *Make a worry list.* Things often come to mind during prayer. Instead of trying to ignore them, write them down. Prayerfully prioritize them into a to-do list. Ask God to show you how to accomplish what needs to be done.[8]

Christian Rights in the Workplace

Religious discrimination—including requiring Christians to work on the Sabbath—has long been forbidden under Title VII of the 1964 Civil Rights Act. The following information is taken from *Christian Rights in the Workplace: What the Law Says About Religion at Work*, a booklet published by the American Center for Law and Justice.

Employers must accommodate requests by employees for absence on their Sabbath or other religious holidays. An affirmative duty arises under Title VII for the employer to make a good faith effort to arrange the employee's schedule to allow the employee to have Sabbaths off. The employer will be in violation of Title VII if they have "made no real effort" or have taken a "don't care" attitude.... (p. 9)

The employer's affirmative duty to attempt to accommodate the employee's request for time off is not limited if the employee asks for more than one accommodation...[i.e.,] time off in view of two sincerely held religious beliefs.... (p. 9)

The same rule applies where an employee's religious beliefs prevent him from working on Sundays, *and* prevent him from asking someone else to engage in this prohibited activity for him. Merely allowing the employee to swap shifts with someone does not constitute reasonable accommodation in this instance.... (p. 9)

There are very few times when employers can require employees to violate their religious beliefs, or refuse to allow the employee to practice his religious beliefs at work.... In order to successfully assert this defense, courts require that the employer demonstrate attempted accommodation before claiming undue hardship.

Employers must also be able to show evidence of undue hardship that is more than mere speculation. (p. 13)[9]

For a more thorough discussion of "undue hardship" and our rights as Christians in the workplace, you can request the ACLJ booklet by writing:

The American Center for Law and Justice
P.O. Box 64429
Virginia Beach, VA 23467-4429

NOTES

Chapter One

1. Vera Lee, *Something Old, Something New* (Naperville: Ill.: Sourcebooks, Inc., 1994), 102-3.

2. Excerpted in *Growing Strong in God's Family,* The 2:7 Series (Colorado Springs, Colo.: NavPress, 1987), 20.

3. Miriam Neff and Debra Klingsporn, *Shattering Our Assumptions* (Minneapolis: Bethany, 1996), 194.

4. Taken from *A New Beginning,* copyright 1995 by Stonecroft, Inc. Used by permission. To read more, go to www.stonecroft.org and click on "A New Beginning."

Chapter Two

1. Dutch Sheets, *The River of God* (Ventura, Calif.: Gospel Light, 1998), 195.

2. A version of this story first appeared as Joanna Weaver, "Out in the Cold," *HomeLife* 54, no. 6 (March 2000): 20-2.

Chapter Three

1. Joel Gregory, *Growing Pains of the Soul* (Dallas: Word, 1987), 31.

2. Edward Hallowell, *Worry: Controlling It and Using It Wisely* (New York: Pantheon, 1997), xi.

3. Adapted from Hallowell, *Worry,* 79-83.

4. "An Average Person's Anxiety Is Focused on..." quoted in John Underhill and Jack Lewis, comp., Bible Study Foundation Illustration Database, Bible Study Foundation Web site (*www.Bible.org*).

5. See Archibald D. Hart, *Overcoming Anxiety* (Dallas: Word, 1989).

6. Tony Evans, *No More Excuses* (Wheaton, Ill.: Crossway Books, 1996), 223.

7. Sheila Walsh, *Bring Back the Joy* (Grand Rapids, Mich.: Zondervan, 1998), 53.

8. Hallowell, *Worry,* 70.

9. Anne Driscoll interview with Dr. Edward Hallowell, "What, Me Worry?" *On Air Dateline NBC,* 4 November 1999, at the Website: http://MSNBC.MSN.com/news/210941.asp, 3.

10. Gary E. Gilley, "Think on These Things" newsletter 4, no. 2 (February 1998).

11. Oswald Chambers, *My Utmost for His Highest* (1935; reprint, Uhrichsville, Ohio: Barbour, *n.d.*), 135.

12. Corrie Ten Boom, quoted in *Moments—Someone Special* (Minneapolis: Heartland Samplers, 1997), n.p.

13. Selwyn Hughes, *Every Day Light* (Nashville: Broadman & Holman, 1998), day 1.

14. Bill and Kathy Peel, *Discover Your Destiny* (Colorado Springs, Colo.: NavPress, 1997), 202.

15. Quoted in Chambers, *My Utmost for His Highest,* 30.

16. Joseph M. Scriven, "What a Friend We Have in Jesus," *The Hymnal for Worship & Celebration* (Waco, Tex.: Word Music, 1986), 435.

Chapter Four

1. Adapted from a story by Rosemarie Kowalski. Used by permission.

2. Bernard R. Youngman, *The Lands and Peoples of the Living Bible* (New York: Hawthorn, 1959), 213.

3. Youngman, *Lands and Peoples,* 213-4.

4. G. Ernest Wright, ed., *Great People of the Bible and How They Lived* (Pleasantville, N.Y.: Reader's Digest Association, 1974), 324-5.

5. William Barclay, *The Gospel of John,* vol. 1, rev. ed., *The Daily Study Bible* series (Philadelphia: Westminster, 1975), 248.

6. Charles H. Spurgeon, *Morning and Evening* (Nashville: Nelson, 1994), January 24, Evening.

Chapter Five

1. Robert J. Morgan, *On This Day* (Nashville: Nelson, 1997), January 5.

2. Philip Yancey, *What's So Amazing About Grace?* (Grand Rapids, Mich.: Zondervan, 1997), 97.

3. Anne Wilson Schaef, *LAUGH! I Thought I'd Die If I Didn't* (New York: Ballantine Books, 1990), May 27.

4. Kent Hughes, *Liberating Ministry from the Success Syndrome* (Wheaton, Ill.: Tyndale, 1988), 139.

5. Excerpted in *The Growing Disciple,* The 2:7 Series, Course 1 (Colorado Springs, Colo.: NavPress, 1987), 69-73.

6. Adapted from Emilie Barnes, *The Spirit of Loveliness* (Eugene, Oreg.: Harvest House, 1992), 109-10.

7. From an e-mail interview with Robin Jones Gunn, 30 January 2000.

8. Excerpt from Gwen Shamblin, "Love the Lord with All Your Mind," Week 2 of *Weigh Down Workshop: Exodus Out of Egypt* video series, Weigh Down Workshop, Inc., 1997. For more information call 1-800-844-5208.

9. Max Lucado, *The Great House of God* (Dallas: Word, 1997), 4.

10. Matthew Henry, *Matthew Henry's Commentary on the Whole Bible,* vol. 4 (New York: Revell, n.d.), 153.

11. Confirmed in a telephone conversation with Eugene Peterson, 29 January 2000.

12. Adapted from quotation in Henry Blackaby, *Experiencing God* (Nashville: LifeWay Press, 1990), 34.

13. Hughes, *Liberating Your Ministry,* 72-3.

Chapter Six

1. Taped sermon and interview with Dr. Donald Argue, Billings, Montana, March 1999.

2. William Barclay, *The Gospel of John,* rev. ed., vol. 2 (Philadelphia: Westminster, 1975), 138-9.

3. J. Oswald Sanders, *Discipleship Journal* 76 (July-August 1993): 39.

4. Quoted in Mother Teresa, *In My Own Words* (New York: Random House, 1996), 100.

5. Quoted in Philip Yancey, *What's So Amazing About Grace?* (Grand Rapids, Mich.: Zondervan, 1997), 262.

6. Brother Lawrence, *The Practice of the Presence of God* (Virginia Beach, Va.: CBN University Press, 1978), 10.

7. Charles Grierson, "Martha," *Dictionary of the Bible*, ed. James Hastings (New York: Scribner, 1909), 588.

8. Brother Lawrence, *The Practice of the Presence,* 22.

9. C. S. Lewis, "The Efficacy of Prayer," *The World's Last Night* (New York: Harcourt Brace Jovanovich, 1960), 9.

10. Henry Blackaby, *Experiencing God* (Nashville: LifeWay Press, 1990), 13-5.

11. Blackaby, *Experiencing God,*, 13-5.

12. Linda Andersen, "Love Adds a Little Chocolate," in Medard Laz, *Love Adds a Little Chocolate: One Hundred Stories to Brighten Your Day* (New York: Warner, 1998), 15. Reissued as *Love Adds the Chocolate* (Colorado Springs, Colo.: WaterBrook, 2000).

13. First quotation from Daphne Kingsma, *Weddings from the Heart* (New York: MJF Books, 1995), 111. Second quotation from Mother Teresa, *In My Own Words,* 33.

14. Kenneth C. Kinghorn, *Discovering Your Spiritual Gifts* (Grand Rapids, Mich.: Zondervan, 1984); C. Peter Wagner, *Finding Your Spiritual Gifts: Wagner-Modified Houts Spiritual Gifts Questionnaire* (Ventura, Calif.: Regal, 1995).

15. Jack B. Hocy Jr., "Breaking the Unplowed Ground," *Discipleship Journal* 39 (May-June 1987): 4.

16. John Milton, "When I Consider How My Light Is Spent," *Norton Anthology of English Literature*, vol. 1, rev. ed. (New York: W. W. Norton, 1968), 1015.

17. Jan Johnson, *Living a Purpose-Full Life* (Colorado Springs, Colo.: WaterBrook, 1999), 151-3.

18. John Ortberg, *Love Beyond Reason* (Grand Rapids, Mich.: Zondervan, 1998), 11-14,18.

19. Yancey, *What's So Amazing About Grace?* 258-9.

Chapter Seven

1. See Janet Holm McHenry, *PrayerWalk: Becoming a Woman of Prayer, Strength, and Discipline* (Colorado Springs, Colo.: WaterBrook, 2001).

2. Quoted in Dennis Rainey, *Planting Seeds, Pulling Weeds* (San Bernardino, Calif.: Here's Life, 1989), 114.

3. Selwyn Hughes, *Everyday Light* (Nashville: Broadman & Holman, 1998), day 1.

4. Robert Robinson, "Come Thou Fount of Every Blessing," *The Hymnal for Worship & Celebration* (Waco, Tex.: Word Music, 1986), 2.

5. Adapted from Stephen R. Covey, *First Things First* (New York: Simon & Schuster, 1994), 88-9.

6. Wilbur Rees, "$3.00 Worth of God," quoted in Tim Hansel, *When I Relax I Feel Guilty* (Elgin, Ill.: David C. Cook, 1979), 49.

7. Cynthia Heald, "Becoming a Friend of God," *Discipleship Journal* 54 (November-December 1989): 22.

8. From J. Sidlow Baxter's personal correspondence, 8 September 1987, as quoted in Kent Hughes, *Liberating Ministry from the Success Syndrome* (Wheaton, Ill.: Tyndale, 1987), 78-81.

9. Howard E. Butt Jr., *Renewing America's Soul: A Spiritual Psychology for Home, Work, and Nation* (New York: Continuum, 1996), 232-3.

Chapter Eight

1. Max Lucado, *God Came Near* (Portland, Oreg.: Multnomah, 1987), 79.

2. Ray C. Stedman, "God's Strange Ways," sermon given 9 September 1984 at Peninsula Bible Church, Palo Alto, California.

3. Martha Tennison in a sermon given 25 September 1999 in Billings, Montana.

4. Stedman, "God's Strange Ways."

5. CeCe Winans, *On a Positive Note* (New York: Pocket Books, 1999), 207.

6. Quoted in L. B. Cowman, *Streams in the Desert* (Grand Rapids, Mich.: Zondervan, 1996), 35.

7. *NIV Study Bible: New International Version* (Grand Rapids, Mich.: Zondervan, 1985), text note on John 12.

8. My editor wants you to know she disavows all responsibility for this extremely corny (but very effective) memory device.

9. Tennison, a sermon given 25 September 1999.

10. Philip Yancey, *Disappointment with God* (Grand Rapids, Mich.: Zondervan, 1988), 211.

11. Yancey, *Disappointment with God*, 211.

12. Adapted from Harry Pritchett Jr., *Leadership* (Summer 1985), quoted in Charles Swindoll, *Tales of a Tardy Oxcart* (Nashville: Word, 1998), 491-2.

Chapter Nine

1. Quoted in *Daybreak Quotes* (Wheaton, Ill.: Tyndale, 1991), n.p.

2. Carol Mayhall, "Listening to God," in Judith Couchman, ed., *One Holy Passion* (Colorado Springs, Colo.: WaterBrook, 1998), 109-11.

3. Oswald Chambers, *My Utmost for His Highest* (1935; reprint, Uhrichsville, Ohio: Barbour, *n.d.*), 210.

4. Kathleen Norris, *Amazing Grace: A Vocabulary of Faith* (New York: Riverhead Books, 1998), 14-5.

5. Adapted with permission from author Joanie Burnside.

Chapter Ten

1. Josephus said that Sadducees "in their [conversation] with their peers are as rude as to aliens." *NIV Study Bible: New International Version* (Grand Rapids, Mich.: Zondervan, 1985), text note on John 11:49.

2. James B. Pritchard, ed., *Everyday Life in Bible Times* (Washington, D.C.: National Geographic Society, 1977), 305.

3. Charles Panati, *Sacred Origins of the Profound* (New York: Penguin, 1996), 323.

4. *NIV Study Bible*, text note on Mark 14:3.

5. Ruth V. Wright and Robert L. Chadbourne, *Gems and Minerals of the Bible* (New York: Harper & Row, 1970), 6.

6. William Barclay, *The Gospel of John,* rev. ed., vol. 2 (Philadelphia: Westminster, 1975), 111.

7. Theodore Parker, quoted in Cora Lee Pless, "How Do We Return?" *God's Abundance: 365 Days to a Simpler Life* (Lancaster, Pa.: Starburst, 1997), Dec. 27.

8. Quoted in Barclay, *The Gospel of John,* 2:111.

9. Barclay, *The Gospel of John*, 2:112.

10. Tom Fennell Timmins, "Homecoming for a Hero," *Maclean's,* 25 January 1999, 26.

11. Hannah Whitall Smith, *The Christian's Secret of a Happy Life* (Nashville: Nelson, 1999), 45-6.

12. Peter Kreeft, *Three Philosophies of Life* (San Francisco: Ignatius Press, 1989), 94-5.

Chapter Eleven

1. Tim Hansel, *Holy Sweat* (Waco, Tex.: Word, 1987), 12.

2. Jill Briscoe, *Renewal on the Run* (Wheaton, Ill.: Harold Shaw, 1992), 109.

3. Note that some of these symptoms could indicate a physical or emotional imbalance as well as a spiritual one. If they are persistent or severe, you might consider seeing a doctor as well as praying for God's direction in balancing your life.

4. Elizabeth Moll Stalcup, "Seizing the Sabbath," *Virtue,* August-September 1998, 26-7.

5. Stalcup, "Seizing the Sabbath," 26-7.

6. Interview with Jane Johnson Struck, "Hospitality on the Run," *Today's Christian Woman,* January-February 1992, 58-9.

7. Kathleen Norris, *Amazing Grace: A Vocabulary of Faith* (New York: Riverhead Books, 1998), 265-6.

8. Adapted from Karen Mains, *Open Heart—Open Home* (Elgin, Ill.: David C. Cook, 1976), 171-6.

9. William Plummer, "Taken by the Sea," *People,* 14 December 1992, 59-61.

Chapter Twelve

1. Quoted in Howard L. Rice, *Reformed Spirituality* (Louisville, Ky.: Westminster/John Knox, 1991), 179.

2. Claire Cloninger, *When God Shines Through* (Dallas, Tex.: Word, 1994), 132.

3. Henrietta Mears, *What the Bible's All About* (Ventura, Calif.: Regal, 1983), 84.

4. Quoted in Mother Teresa, *Life in the Spirit* (San Francisco: Harper & Row, 1983), 76-7.

5. Kent Hughes, *James: Faith That Works* (Wheaton, Ill.: Crossway Books, 1991), 17.

6. Hughes, *James,* 17.

7. Charles Swindoll, *Growing Strong in the Seasons of Life* (Portland, Oreg.: Multnomah, 1983), 47-9.

8. William Barclay, *The Letters of James and Peter,* rev. ed. (Louisville, Ky.: Westminster/John Knox Press, 1976), 44.

9. Ken Gire, *Intense Moments with the Savior* (Grand Rapids, Mich.: Zondervan, 1985), 86.

10. Mother Teresa, *Life in the Spirit,* 24.

11. Jan Johnson, *Living a Purpose-Full Life* (Colorado Springs, Colo.: WaterBrook, 1999), 95.

12. Quoted in *Daybreak Quotes* (Wheaton, Ill.: Inspirations, Tyndale House, 1991), n.p.

Appendices

1. Quoted in Philip Yancey, *What's So Amazing About Grace?* (Grand Rapids, Mich.: Zondervan, 1997), 262.

2. J. Oswald Sanders, *Discipleship Journal* 76 (July-August 1993): 39.

3. Wilbur Rees, "$3.00 Worth of God," quoted in Tim Hansel, *When I Relax I Feel Guilty* (Elgin, Ill.: David C. Cook, 1979), 49.

4. Martha Tennison in a sermon given 25 September 1999 in Billings, Montana.

5. Quoted in L. B. Cowman, *Streams in the Desert* (Grand Rapids, Mich.: Zondervan, 1996), 35.

6. Format adapted from *The Growing Disciple,* The 2:7 Series, Course 1 (Colorado Springs, Colo.: NavPress, 1987), n.p.

7. Quoted in *The Growing Disciple,* 77.

8. Adapted from *The Growing Disciple,* 84-5.

9. *Christian Rights in the Workplace: What the Law Says About Religion at Work* (Virginia Beach, Va.: The American Center for Law and Justice, 1997), 9,13.

Dear Reader,

After writing this book, I have a new appreciation for the disciple John's final statement in his gospel: "Jesus did many other things as well. If every one of them were written down, I suppose that even the whole world would not have room for the books that would be written" (John 21:25). If John could walk away from his gospel knowing he hadn't said it all, then I must be willing to let the Holy Spirit take over where I've left off. After all, only he can lead you into all truth. My words are but an empty shadow of the glorious things God desires to do in you.

May the Lord take this simple story of two sisters and use this ink and paper, these words, as a doorway to bring you into a deeper relationship with him than you've ever known. Remember, it is a lifetime process and a work of the Holy Spirit—not something we have to conjure up on our own. Isn't that good news!

God, himself, desires to write a love letter upon your heart, a letter "known and read by everybody" (2 Corinthians 3:2). I'd love to hear about the story God is writing in you. While I may not be able to answer every letter, I'd consider it a privilege to pray for you. You can reach me at:

Joanna Weaver

P.O. Box 755

Whitefish, Montana 59937

joannaweaver@hotmail.com

God's richest blessings to you, my dear sister and friend!

Joanna

I thank my God every time I remember you. In all my prayers for all of you,
I always pray with joy…being confident of this, that he who began a good work
in you will carry it on to completion until the day of Christ Jesus.

Philippians 1:3-6